What people are saying

"I met Jessie Boone on March 16, 2009, in the Trauma Room at St. Mary's Hospital in Grand Junction, CO, when she presented with a devastating head injury from an accident while on a church youth vacation at a local ski resort. As her pediatric trauma surgeon and surgical critical care specialist, I cared for Jessie for the next 40 days as she journeyed through the wilderness of her acute injury and care in Grand Junction before being transferred to a hospital back home in Oklahoma City, Oklahoma.

Soon after I met Jessie, I met Lisa and Bill Boone. I came to know Lisa as a fierce vocal advocate for her daughter and Bill as a quiet pillar of strength. With the magnitude of her injury, the odds were against Jessie surviving at all or with any meaningful brain function. Yet she did, with God's love and grace, along with many appointed helpers along the way—her Christian village.

In *Severed Sacredness,* Lisa chronicles Jessie's long and difficult journey to the miracle she is today, noting the many times God made His presence known when most needed. This book would be especially helpful for those with a family member undergoing a health crisis—there is hope, even in the most dire circumstances. 'With God, all things are possible.' (Matthew 19:26)"

Charles W. Breaux, Jr., MD, FACS

"*Severed Sacredness* is a deeply heart-rending story, beautifully told by a mother, about the devastating skiing accident which shattered her young daughter's dreams. But far beyond that, it is an experience of love and miracle and grit and faith. Jessie Boone is an exquisite young woman who has far exceeded the overwhelming circumstances life handed her. What emerges through Jessie's gentle, glowing presence is a powerful encounter with love itself. Extremely moving."

Paula D'Arcy
Author of *Gift of the Red Bird* and *Stars at Night*

"For many years, I have thought and said, 'If we really knew how much we were loved by God, we would fall to our knees in tears.' This book will bring anyone who reads it to their knees in tears. It is beautiful. Lisa's way with words has a way of bringing the reader (me) to that place. I was there with her with the anxiety, the fears, the gratitude, the love through the overwhelming signs that God provided at every turn."

Julane Borth
Spiritual Director and Author of
The Shadow Cast and *Living in the Layers*

"*Severed Sacredness* is a wonderful book telling the story of Jessie Boone and her family as they traverse the very rugged landscape of recovery from a severe, life-threatening, head injury. Lisa Boone does an excellent job describing the significant emotional turmoil of loving parents trying to be certain their child receives the very best care and works toward recovery. It is a very stormy and long journey but faith, love, hope, and Lisa's steely determination to advocate for her daughter overcomes the adversity. It is a hopeful book for families facing similar circumstances, especially when it comes to traversing a very opaque and complicated medical system. It is a good read for those in the medical profession (doctors, nurses, therapists, aides, administrators, etc.) to get a cogent, outside take on what our patients and families encounter and why listening is such an important aspect of care. Finally, it is a beautiful testimony as to how many people (some who never knew or met Jessie) came together, going well beyond what one would expect over the years, to help Jessie and her family rejoin their community."

Timothy B Mapstone, MD
Professor Emeritus
Department of Neurological Surgery
University of Oklahoma Health Sciences Center

"There are moments when we know for certain that the book we're reading is changing us. This is one of those books. Boone takes the reader on a journey through a powerful true story of tragedy, trauma, grief, pain, faith, inspiration, hope, healing, and new life. For those who have gone through (or are going through) something traumatic, it points to the places where hope peeks through, providing a pathway toward courage to face tomorrow. For those who are part of a support system, it provides guidance on how to be fully present to people in their pain. Regardless of where you are in your spiritual journey, it heralds those precious messages of hope and love that God provides. Every tree needs nutrients and water, whether it's a sapling just getting started or a mature tree that's already a towering source of shade. In the pages of *Severed Sacredness,* there are nutrients and water that will help the reader grow."

Rev. Tim Travers
United Methodist Pastor since 1993
Author of *Driven*

"What an incredible story. It is truly amazing and so beautifully written. I highly recommend it for anyone suffering loss. I cried, shook my head in disbelief of all the things that occurred during the years, laughed at special moments, and saw God's hand throughout the story. This story will help many and provide the encouragement they need to continue moving forward and to stay present in each moment."

Yvonne M Morgan
Award-winning Author and Blogger

"It's a moving narrative of deep strength, resilience, fidelity, commitment, courage, and so much more. And I love that she owned her part in that along with so many supportive people around her. Imagining what this ongoing adventure has been for Jessie is beyond mind-boggling."

Anne M Luther
Adult Spiritual Renewal & Empowerment

"This story captures your heart from the beginning and transforms it by the end. It is both riveting and heartbreaking at the same time. You will be transported through a harrowing journey of grief, loss, redemption and above all Love. *Severed Sacredness* is for anyone searching for hope and faith during life's most difficult trials."

Kara McDaniel, OTR

"This is a story of hope. When the unimaginable happened to young Jessie Boone, the foundation of her family's faith held firm. Every miraculous step of their horrific journey was held together by our compassionate God. Lisa's beautiful writing and truthful telling offers encouragement to everyone."

Jane Jayroe Gamble
Writer, Founder of Esther Women
Former Miss America

"Lisa has written a powerful story. It speaks to everyone who has experienced this type of horrific tragedy with a loved one, but especially one's child. Those of us who are traveling this lifelong journey will nod our head throughout this read and say, 'Yes, yes. I know how this feels.' We are all connected through Christ within her path. This book will be a recommendation to every TBI caregiver Brainxcite serves. Our stories are hard to read and even harder to write. To Lisa Boone ... 'Well done, my sister.'"

Linda Tracy
Mom of TBI
Founder of Brainxcite.com

The Miraculous Journey of Jessie Boone

by

Lisa Boone

Severed Sacredness
The Miraculous Journey of Jessie Boone

Published by
Saved By Story Publishing, LLC
Prescott, AZ

www.SavedByStory.house

Copyright © 2024 by Lisa Boone

Cover Art by Kristi Self

Cover Design by Alyssa Noelle Coelho

Interior Design by Dawn Teagarden

Paintings/Photos/Illustrations by Kristi Self, Dawn Normali, Barbara Bonham, Erin Beth Lawrence, Jim Keffer, JM Larson, Bethany Pigott, Susan Gainen, Amy Elise Havern, Julie Acosta, Marshall Hawkins

All rights reserved. No part of this book may be reproduced or transmitted in any form or by any means, electronic or mechanical, including photocopying, recording, or by an information storage and retrieval system without written permission of the publisher, except for the inclusions of brief quotations in review.

Disclaimer: The Publisher and the Author does not guarantee that anyone following the techniques, suggestions, tips, ideas or strategies will become successful. The advice and strategies contained herein may not be suitable for every situation. The Publisher and Author shall have neither liability nor responsibility to anyone with respect to any loss or damage caused, or alleged to be caused, directly or indirectly by the information in this book. Written permission has been obtained to share the identity of each real individual named in this book.

Any citations or a potential source of information from other organizations or websites given herein does not mean that the Author or Publisher endorses the information/content the website or organization provides or recommendations it may make. It is the readers' responsibility to do their own due diligence when researching information. Also, websites listed or referenced herein may have changed or disappeared from the time that this work was created and the time that it is read.

ISBN: 978-1-961336-09-4

Printed in Canada

www.SavedByStory.house

To God

I kept my promise to You ...

Contents

1

FOREWORD
by Bobbie Roe, PhD

5

INTRODUCTION
The Sacred Tree

21

PART 1: SEVERED AT THE ROOT
40 Days in Acute Crisis

97

PART 2: THE REMNANT
18 Months of Intensive Rehabilitation

279

PART 3: RESEEDING THE FOREST
7 Years of Reclaiming Capacities

405

PART 4: EMERGING SAPLINGS
5 Years of Growth, Grief, and Grace

461

CONCLUSION
From Severed to Sacred

469

A Special Invitation to Share the Hope

471

About Lisa Boone

473

Acknowledgments

Foreword

by Bobbie Roe, PhD

The voice of one crying in the wilderness:
"Prepare the way of the LORD ... "
~Isaiah 40:3 (NKJV)~

Within seconds of reading Lisa's opening story, you will hear the voice of one crying out in the wilderness and feel the swift undertow of chaos as she and her husband, Bill, are plunged into the terrifying unknown of their daughter's life-eclipsing brain injury. Despair is paralyzing. Who can "prepare the way of the Lord" in such darkness? Where is the light that will pierce it with hope?

For many years, Lisa has been *professionally* prepared for medical trauma and crises. Especially as a hospice and palliative care night nurse, she has often driven into dark, isolated Oklahoma locales to tend the failing bodies of the dying and to comfort their fearful hearts with her own calming peace. But when Jessie's body was thrust so close to death, *nurse* Lisa was not prepared. Not at all.

As you will soon read, she and Bill would suffer excruciating trauma themselves as they fought for their teenaged daughter's life after Jessie careened into a tree on a ski slope. But even more so, Lisa proclaims how the *Lord* is the One who prepared the way—the One who was

Foreword

the Light that came into their darkness and the One who ultimately empowered Lisa to write this book with a sure voice of unbridled faith to ignite hope in others.

For more than two decades, I have known the sacred rhythms of Lisa's faith. We have shared spiritual talks, sabbath walks, and monastic retreats, as well as holy play in joyous fellowship with many others. But I was also with her in the Grand Junction hospital as she fell prostrate beneath the chapel altar and cried out to God with wordless groans. In both the best and most horrific of times, she has believed from the unshakable center of her being that the God of the fathomless universe is also the God who loves and holds each of us in the palms of his hands.

As Lisa chronicles the hours, days, and years of Jessie's miraculous journey, she also reveals the love language with which God reassures her of his constant Presence. First, through every season, nature often seems in communion with Lisa's interior life. As contrasted with the forests of darkness, for instance, diverse trees are sentinels of hope that mark the written landscape of the unfolding story. Secondly, God sends his servants with dispatch. Friends, of course, but also complete strangers—doctors, nurses, therapists, pastors, small children, food-bearers, artists, tree experts, nuns, runners, prayer warriors—all repeatedly show up with what is most needed in any moment. They arrive in timely, miraculous fashion, as surely as the gift-bearing magi landed in Bethlehem at the appointed hour, ostensibly with only their inner compass, a few good camels, and a wise, bright star to guide them.

All this time, life was teeming around Jessie, but Jessie remained mostly *hidden* before her speech and other responses to the world were slowly restored. Still, Lisa was adamant that everyone who tended Jessie *see* her, *speak* to her, with the faith that Jessie was indeed very, very present and visible. Having walked alongside the Boones, I also am confident that the One who would prepare Jessie's way out of the wilderness was very, very present, if seemingly invisible. When Jessie was still a young child, I used to joke that she was the Boones' "household priestess" because her beatific expressions, Jesus words, and praise songs reflected an old soul in a little girl's coltish body. So when Jessie was hidden in her own dark forest, I trust that she was nevertheless in sanctuary with Jesus. What that sanctuary was like, however, I can only wonder. Was Jesus whispering, "'*Talitha koum* ... Little girl, get up!'" (Mark 5:41 NLT)? Was Jessie, like Lisa, remembering, believing, following the Way Maker back into the teeming world?

Severed Sacredness: The Miraculous Journey of Jessie Boone impels us all to ponder the sometimes hidden but always faithful Presence of God in every detail of our daily lives—to dive deeply to the ceaselessly replenishing wellspring of Hope and to resurface, quenched moment to moment, by the gift of living water. "Come, drink, all who are thirsty," God invites. May Jessie's story replenish you in both dark wilderness and blazing Light.

INTRODUCTION

The Sacred Tree

Oklahoma City, Oklahoma
March 16, 2009

I was enjoying lunch on the sunbaked patio with a friend, sharing how it was my last day of freedom before Jessie arrived home. At fifteen, she was challenging my momma heart with a continual stretching and pushing for more independence, so I was not surprised when she begged me to not come on her youth group's spring break ski trip as the chaperone nurse. Part of me had wanted to go to protect her and the other part had been eager for a parental break from the constant pushing for more freedom.

But missing her was harder than the boundary pushing, so I was excited for her to come home and share what she was willing to share about her adventures.

I could feel the vibrations in my back pocket and answered the call from my son.

"Hey Justin—"

But before I could get another word spoken, his voice broke through with a barrage of words, "Mom, there's been an accident. It's Jessie. She's hurt. She's hurt real bad."

I knew my son and his prankish ways, always going the distance to get a reaction.

"Justin, this isn't funny. Stop," I said in my stern mom voice.

Introduction

His voice changed to a different rhythm. "Mom, I promise I'm not kidding. She's hurt and the helicopter is here taking her to a hospital."

Is that a helicopter in the background?

Unconsciously picking up my purse, I found my car keys, hearing the proof needed to know it was real and that I needed to get to her as fast as I could.

"Son, what happened?"

Words I knew from my nursing career were striking my ears in a different, disbelieving sort of way. "Skiing accident, head hit tree trunk, ski patrol, intubation, head injury, vomiting, not responding ... It's bad, Momma." Sobs broke through his words.

Shock and disbelief overtook my mind as I sorted out how I would traverse the distance of 700 miles in the shortest possible time.

Will I ever see her alive again? Oh Jessie, Oh God, Oh God, Oh God! Please help my baby!

Within two hours, my husband, Bill, and I were quickly fastening our seatbelts, awaiting takeoff to Denver with a connection to Grand Junction, Colorado. After several attempts to get an update on her condition, I was finally speaking to the ER physician when the flight attendant's announcement intruded and interfered with my ability to hear and understand clearly. My body was bent over, one hand over one ear, pressing the phone against my head with the other. Closing my eyes helped me concentrate on what was being said.

"She needs surgery immediately. She's suffered an open depressed skull fracture with part of the ski goggles penetrating her right frontal lobe from impact. Do we have your consent for surgery for a debridement to remove the goggle pieces?"

My terror escalated as I began to "hear" what was being said.

"Yes, do whatever it takes to save her life."

Save her life? Oh God!

My ears were roaring with confusion, or was that the plane preparing for takeoff?

There was another voice escalating, but I couldn't make out the words. My eyes lifted from the floor to see her coming at me making gestures.

"You have to get off the phone now. The plane is taking off!"

Being cut off abruptly, like a limb being chain-sawed from its life source, resulted in a painful lash of rage on this poor stewardess, who had no idea that my only connection to my critically-injured daughter was in my hand.

I need more information. I need someone to tell me she'll be there when I arrive.

I'll Be Your One

If you have picked up this book, it's likely because you are dealing with an unimaginable tragedy and wondering if your loved one (and you) will survive it … if someone else has survived it.

I remember the night I sat frightened and desperate for hope, with my computer open, the screen light breaking through the darkness of the rehab unit in search of a story or book of anyone who had similar injuries to Jessie's. Was there a story of someone who'd had both sides of their skull removed, a right frontal lobe debrided, with diffuse axonal injury throughout their brain? Was there one person in the world who had such extensive injuries and was able to recover? Could I dare believe there was one person who could help guide and fuel my faith in the foreign land of this devastating traumatic brain injury?

Introduction

Show me one. Just one, God, I prayed as I searched.

But I could find no one. Not one story. After several unsuccessful hours of searching, I began to speak quietly to God, *If You choose to let Jessie be the one, to be the hope and light for the someone who is desperately searching for the possibility of a recovery, I will write the story. I will write that story for the one person whose loved one's future doesn't seem possible. Let my fingers scribe Your story of Hope to be a LIGHT unto those places that feel hopeless.*

This is that story. Experiencing the depths of anguish, I have walked through the paralyzing fear and inability to take another step. I have held the crushing pain of grief when a beloved is suddenly tragically injured and given little or no hope of survival. And I have witnessed thousands of answers to hundreds of thousands of prayers.

Answers Before I Needed Them

As with most stories, the one you are about to read started long before that dreaded call on March 16, 2009. In fact, I can look back and know for certain that I had been more prepared for this moment than most.

This wasn't my first encounter with brain injuries or navigating traumatic experiences in a healthcare system. As I entered my sophomore year of nursing school, my older brother's head went through the windshield of his truck, launching me into the depths of family trauma and researching traumatic brain injuries (TBI's) as we struggled and searched to find the resources to help him recover from his devastating injuries.

Then early in my nursing career, I worked in a small community hospital ER, which provided me with widespread opportunities to care for the trauma of others, including the one tragic night when the ambulance brought a small child into the ER with a massive head injury. After hours of heroic measures, the child didn't survive. Witnessing and attempting to comfort these young parents in the loss of their beloved little one seared into my heart—a horror I would never forget.

Spending the next several years as an ONC (orthopedic nurse certified) nurse manager in an orthopedic hospital, my focus was providing exceptional health care by implementing the highest standards of orthopedic nursing to assure people would have the best possible outcomes for the quality of their life.

With the newly built rehabilitation unit within the hospital, I transitioned into a unique opportunity for the position of rehab nurse manager, developing policies and procedures and hiring professionals while supervising the nursing care of this twenty-four-bed unit.

Surrounded by expert physiatrists and therapists, my experience and knowledge grew each day as I witnessed the brutal pain and life-changing struggles of injured people, and the tiny miracles of recovery and regaining the quality and independence of one's life.

After twenty years in orthopedics and rehabilitation, God orchestrated an unexpected job change and altered the course of my life. Becoming a CHPN (Certified Hospice and Palliative Nurse) helped me master evidence-based practices in the education and management of end of life symptoms, with a heavy focus on bringing comfort and peace to the patient and their families.

I remember the day I walked in to see one of our patients, a momma who had been in a tragic accident and sustained a TBI. She was lying immobile in the electric bed, her body and limbs twisted, unable to speak or move. Above her head, a wall of pictures told her story. Picture after picture of her smile and the love radiating

Introduction

out of her soul to her children and husband brought me to tears for her and her beloved family, knowing they'd all lost the fullness of life they had before "the day they will never forget." I could not fathom the hell this family had endured.

My eyes fell upon a handwritten letter taped by her bed. I could only assume her husband had written it. "Hi, my name is Joan. I am a mom of three incredible children and a wife to a wonderful husband. Please treat me as the person I am and not the person you see. Thank you."

I took a few steps back, halting in the moment as I beheld such sacred love demanding to infiltrate the darkness of her injury, asking for her to be seen from a much deeper vision found within the folds of one's heart.

Prayers began to spontaneously arise from within me to the God of all comfort and peace, beseeching for this beautiful suffering lady and her brokenhearted family. I remember thinking, *Lord, how is it possible for anyone to survive and get through this type of pain and tragedy?*

Being a mom of three incredible children and a wife to a wonderful husband myself, I begged, *Oh Lord, never this. I just don't think it would be possible for me to survive or endure this type of unimaginable suffering.*

We Can Survive and Endure

What I thought would be impossible to survive, I found myself suddenly hurled into—the dark, hell-like abyss of my fiercely independent, wildly active, and love-filled daughter's massive brain injury. Freefalling out of control, I began to fiercely claw to find some way to regain the orientation of *who* I was and *whose* I was.

It began in the moment.

Finding each moment helped me to defiantly refuse the zero visibility of the grief of the past and the immobilizing fear of the future. In the moment, I could find God. I could find breath. I could find me.

In the moment, I found the first Scripture that I hammered the stake into the wall to help anchor me. In the moment, I found the first song that announced hope: "Savior, You can move this mountain." In the moment, I found the first Carepage entry to share the cries of our desperate hearts, engaging the strength and faith of the hearts of our family, friends, and our living faith community. In the moment, I found the first good, which meant I could find God.

All of these moments began to breathe into the next moment, slowly weaving a type of netting to help hold me, and us, above the abyss that threatened to swallow us up.

Writing her story within the hallowed Carepages became a foundational ritual, helping me to see the deeper connections of God within His people, whom I believe He created and blessed to be blessings of healing and help to others.

The breadth and width of the Carepages became the church we were no longer able to attend. The prayers and hopes of the communities of love communicating within the Carepages were the yeast, slowly expanding our hope and strength into the courage to take the next right step.

I discovered, in the midst of overwhelming fear, a way to "Be at Peace"—to survive the impossible by living within the moment and never underestimating the power of prayer and the unspeakable gifts of being within a community that helped carry the load of our horrendous grief with their presence and generous support.

With my eyes focused on the moment, I witnessed a greater Power that is always present, bringing forth provision even before we know we need it or ask for it.

Introduction

My prayer is that this book assures you that you are never alone, and help is on the way. That you may have the grace to see beneath the surfaces of your circumstances and find the hidden seeds that are just waiting to burst forward in the moments of your deepest needs.

Life experiences hold infinite possibilities of survival and recovery.

As I listened to a speaker, many years before Jessie's accident, sharing how she had survived the loss of three of her boys within a few years, I could feel the obvious question rising: *How is that even possible for one human to absorb the depths of so much pain?* I couldn't take my eyes off this woman who had found the strength to not only survive but to stand and share her story of faith in the hopes of helping others who find themselves in the midst of overwhelming grief and loss. This woman's experience changed the landscape of my soul, and I not only never forgot the treasures and truths she discovered in the midst of her "dark nights of her soul," but I clung to the hope and truth that there were treasures within mine.

Why the Trees?

As I learned of the details of Jessie's accident, I felt a glimmer of hope rising when I discovered that one of her friends had carved her name, the date of her accident (3/16/09), and a cross in the bark of the very tree of her *death as we knew her*. A promise from those crevices within the bark quietly seeped into the crevices of my own shattered heart, whispering John 3:16 (New International Version), mystically intermingling Jessie within those ancient words, "For God so loved (Jessie) that He gave his only begotten Son (whose life changed on a tree) that whosoever believes in Him, shall not die but have everlasting life."

The Sacred Tree

It was as if someone had cut her life off at the root, leaving only a remnant. Within the chambers of my heart, I could hear the promises of the Old Testament in Isaiah 11:1 (NIV) vibrating, "A shoot would come up from the stump of Jesse, from the roots, a Branch will bear fruit." My heart began massaging those words into the hope that Jessie's stump would have a shoot, and that from her roots, a branch would appear and bear fruit.

We nourished her stump with everything we had, tending to her hidden roots left below, in great hopes that after the harsh winter of rest and stillness, a shoot would appear. As we tended to hers, others showed up to care and tend to ours, for our own trees were fully exposed to the harsh and bitter elements of her winter.

Throughout this journey, God used one of my childhood loves—trees—to speak hope into some of my darkest moments. Sometimes they were live trees that nourished me as I nourished them or fought to save their lives from harsh weather and tragedies. Sometimes they were on canvases found at the exact moment I needed their unspeakable beauty and messages of hope. Sometimes they were dead, using their old branches to say goodbye to the past and prepare me for a rebirth. Wherever they appeared, the gentle presence of the powerful tree would provide an imagery to my heart of how God was working in the hidden unseen places of her recovery and mine. Of how God has always been using trees to guide, comfort, and restore me.

From the first several months of not knowing if she would survive the brain injury, surgeries, and infections, through the long recovery of the beautiful remnant of that fiercely-independent and sweet-souled fifteen-year-old, through the phase of rebuilding and reclaiming the parts of life that she could, through the hell of life- and

Introduction

limb-threatening attacks, and even through the process of rediscovering ourselves, our marriage, and our lives, God has used trees to comfort and guide me, and I hope the trees will help to guide your journey through this story (and your own) as well.

No Two Trees or Forests are the Same
My heart of grief wrote these stories in hopes to connect with the heart of grief of others, no matter how different the details of our injuries, stories, or spiritual beliefs. My hope is that you will find connection within the commonalities of our journeys of tragedy and healing and grasp the opportunity to think outside the confines of the survival mode you find yourself in while navigating this journey.

    Knowing that every injury, recovery, and outcome is as unique as the human experiencing it, I want to encourage you to not focus on the outcomes as much as how God can journey alongside those of us faced with a tragedy that devastates our entire family system and changes our lives forever. My hope is that you'll see how the power of faith and the compassionate support of others is critical in the survival of hope while traveling the road.

    The truth is that every single brain injury is different. Many in the community of brain injuries have had astounding recoveries with return to a normal life. Many have had heartbreaking outcomes of their loved ones being declared "brain dead" and becoming organ donors. Many have had sufficient recovery where they can function with great support within their families and communities. Many have had minimal recovery with the need of total care in their homes or in long-term care facilities. Whatever your loved one's prognosis or outcome, I believe there is something in these pages to comfort and guide you through the dark forest you find yourself in.

Being a nurse and mom of a daughter with a TBI doesn't qualify me as an expert on brain injuries, but through the witness of this book, you will find I have experienced the depths of grief and fear that comes with a tragic injury of a child, the mountains and valleys of complications arising from her traumatic injuries, and the vast amount of varied encounters with multiple health care systems and staff on the receiving end of health care.

Please always consult with your team of physicians and experts, as some of what worked for us may or may not benefit your loved one's particular recovery process.

Before You Get Started
I believe God is present to all people suffering and He will send help in all different ways. The question is: Do you have the eyes to see beyond the circumstances to find how He is sending help through love and support in the darkest of times? This life-changing journey has transformed me into a wounded healer who hopes to come alongside you, side by side, to help you find the help and hope that is always present.

I'm also committed to helping you ask for help. I know when one is so overwhelmed with the circumstances, it is impossible to know what to ask for, or how to ask for help. As you read through this book you will see many of the ways people around us showed up without us asking and literally became God's saving grace for our hearts, minds, marriage, finances, and so much more.

So, in addition to sharing my story, I have put together a resource to help those around you—the people who know you're in pain and in great need, but don't have a clue what to do to help you. This will give them a variety

Introduction

of practical ways to help you stay healthy and hopeful in every possible way.

Before you continue reading, scan this QR code and share the link with at least five people you know who love you and want to help. Include a little note explaining that a woman who has walked a similar journey before suggested you do it. If they are who you think they are, they will be grateful for this resource and will take action to rally the troops around you for the long journey ahead.

Come Walk with Me in the Trees
Within these pages are recollections of real stories in the midst of real tragedy, revealing a terrified, desperate mom navigating her devastated heart with her faith and determination to never give up hope even when little hope was given.

An invitation lies before you to find hope, healing, and powerful strength within the trees of your own dark forest by journeying alongside me in mine, gathering truths and experiences that will reveal a Presence that will never leave you, finding the determination to never, never give up, and witnessing the promise of hope that suddenly shows up when you feel you have none. It's an invitation to discover how, after a long and dark night, the sun always rises and how after the long winter of cold and darkness, spring will always appear and bring resurrection. When the torrential flooding rains destroy your life's landscape, the rains will always cease and the sun will appear once again, bringing light and warmth, and maybe even an unexpected rainbow will display its magnificent beauty, renewing and bringing forth the promises of new life from within the tomb of tragedy.

> The QR codes I've included throughout the book will take you on an audiovisual journey of this emergence.

I believe that with God, suffering, isolation, and chaos will never have the last word—that we are able to suffer because our stories are written within a greater Story, promising it will not end in pain but in joy, not in isolation but in communion.

A Note about Trees and Time in Dark Forests

By now, you know that trees are not only sacred to me, they are one of the primary ways God has spoken to me throughout my life and especially throughout Jessie's journey.

As you read, you'll find that each chapter begins with a short excerpt about a particular tree (or set of them) that somehow captures or illustrates the theme of the chapter and the stories in it. Some of these trees made their mark in my heart very early in my life, and some of them appeared along this journey with Jessie.

You might also notice that as you move through my story, your sense of the flow of time will change. For instance, in Part 1, as I share the experiences of those first forty days, you'll feel like I'm giving you the daily and sometimes hourly play-by-play. Through Parts 2 and 3, you'll find that there are bigger stretches of time between events, sometimes weeks or months separating them. And by Part 4, I'll be catching you up with the big life events that have occurred across bigger spans of months or years.

The hard truth that I had to digest while writing this book is that I couldn't tell our entire story. Fifteen years of fears, doubts, challenges, and miracles had to be sifted and distilled into the phases, scenes, and moments that

Introduction

would communicate the deeper message that I received across time.

God is with us ... in every dark forest ... and the present moment is all we have.

When we walk through a dark forest of tragedy, our sense of time becomes strangely distorted. It's hard to remember what day we're on, how long it's been since we ate or slept, and so on. It's easy to lose ourselves in reflections or regrets of the past, and it's even easier to lose ourselves in the unknown uncertainties and anxieties of the future.

But God is here ... right where you are in your dark forest.

So, take your time and don't worry about your sense of it. Be present for what's here for you in each moment. And trust that you will be guided through and out in His good time.

JESSIE B
4/1/03

3/16/09 †

PART 1

Severed at the Root

—

40 Days in Acute Crisis

CHAPTER 1

The Wisteria Tree

Abundance

The truth of abundance dances in my mind when I think of the large panicles of the wisteria tree's vigorously blooming blue flowers. Aggressively growing, these vines reach up to thirty feet, working their way into any nook or cranny and living over one hundred years. It is not unusual to see me pause in the middle of a neighborhood street to witness the magnificent "fontality" of grace flowing from a wisteria's branches. These sacred blooms command a reverence overwhelming the senses to stop, creating an experience of the holy in the ordinary moments of the day. Their fragrance and colorful displays have painted memories throughout the pages of my life.

One of my spiritual mothers, Sister Benedicta, once shared her story of the wisteria within the monastery grounds. For the first couple of years she lived there, it looked dead, yet she would never abandon the hope for its "life with us yet." One spring, it began to grow, to slowly expand and upon returning from her own sister's funeral with such a heavy heart, she was greeted with these cascading waterfalls of purple blooms. She called it the "fontality" of the wisteria and said it reminded her of the Fount of Baptism, the wellspring of Christ's living water, and the gift of eternal life. This backyard fontality resurrection signified the ceaseless overflow of God's love in every season, even the ones that feel and look barren and dead.

Part 1: Severed at the Root

Descent and Determination
St. Mary's Medical Center | Grand Junction, CO
March 16, 2009

Nothing prepares you for the moment you step into a Neuro ICU and see your loved one lying there.

She was unrecognizable. Motionless. Head wrapped with bandages. Tubes coming out. Attached to machines making sounds that weren't comforting. Both eyes swollen shut. An endotracheal tube, protruding out of her mouth, connecting her to the machine's breath of life.

And then I saw her hand.

It's Jessie's hand.

I reached down and took her pale, lifeless hand to my cheek and closed my eyes. I would recognize her nail-bitten hand anywhere.

Darlin' little girl, Momma is here.

Not moving from her side, I watched every breath the ventilator pushed into her lungs. Rhythmic and forceful, ordering oxygen to take its place in her body.

I couldn't help but think about the last time I'd seen her. She was lugging her big bags to the charter bus, refusing help. It felt like she was leaving for college. When I'd reached for a hug, she'd rolled her eyes and laughed. "Gosh, it's not like I am going to die!" Then she'd disappeared into a sea of screaming, giggling youth. I'd paused, taking a long deep breath to center my heart to God, and patted the bus like I used to pat her tiny bottom while putting her to sleep.

God, keep my baby safe and bring her home.

Little did I know the depth and height of that simple breath prayer.

The only communication between us during the week had been one text checking in to see how she was doing. Her long fingers had hit the keys quickly: "We just finished taco night and it was amazing. See you in two days!" Silence again. Yet I knew no better place for her to be immersed than in her loving community of youth ministers and best friends.

I'm so sorry I wasn't there.

I shook my head, thinking about the moment I'd discovered that my brother, whom I hadn't talked to for months, had been there at the hospital hours before I arrived.

I can't believe he passed the ski patrol that was triaging his niece.

He and his family were enjoying their spring break on the same mountain ski resort and, within hours of the accident, had discovered it was Jessie he had seen being airlifted away from the mountain. He'd driven hours to the hospital and comforted Justin and Erin while they waited for us.

God was already at work, putting them on the same mountain before the accident.

I sat next to her, a mess of fear, confusion, and wonder.

Several hours had passed when a nurse entered the dark room with a Ziploc bag.

"We kept this for you."

Confused, I leaned closer to examine it.

"What is this?"

Nonchalantly, she offered, "This is her hair. We shaved it off before surgery."

Waves of nausea immediately hit me as I stood to my feet.

"WHAT?"

Her beautiful blonde hair?

All I saw was a chaotic mass of darkness—a dried and blackened, blood-matted mess—a glaring prophetic glimpse into the reality of her devastating condition.

Earth gave way as I fell to my knees, not knowing what to do with "this."

It only took a moment for this momma heart to shriek, *OH HELL NO! I refuse to accept any part of this unthinkable offering of death and darkness! Nope! Not today. Not now. Not EVER! RISE UP!* my deep within demanded.

I rose up with my heart and soul set in stone that I would fight for her. I would not accept what the world was offering. My God was so much bigger than any of this. My heart, soul, and mind attuned to God, knowing He would fight this battle with me. Refusing any further thoughts of death, the bag filled with her death and darkness became a tangible declaration as I threw it into the trash to never be seen again.

> *"All new life labors out of the
> very bowels of darkness."*
>
> ~Julian of Norwich~

Echoes in Darkness

St. Mary's Medical Center | Grand Junction, CO
March 18, 2009

Sitting at her bedside, I felt the echoes of a dark tomb with no signs of life—just a somber melody of unfamiliar rhythmic beeps, hissing, and alarms. She was motionless and surrendered to the assault upon her brain. I too found myself motionless with absolutely no idea what to do.

"Jessie, can you hear me? Baby, I am so sorry this has happened. Are you hurting? Can you hear me? Mom is right here and I will not leave you."

The grief was suffocating. Breathing hurt. Seeing hurt. Hearing hurt.

No words came. I wanted to ask God for help. I wanted to pray for Jessie as I had so many other times for others. But nothing came. This dark tomb had overtaken me, continuing to disorient and confuse. My silence screamed to a depth I hadn't known before. I recalled a scripture promising that when we are unable to pray, the Spirit Himself intercedes for us through wordless groans.

The dark hollow of my bowels vibrated the wordless groans of the chaotic agony, slowly transforming them into a familiar song that began rising ever so quietly up to my heart. Jessie had been singing this song for months. A humming spontaneously appeared until the memorized words began to form on my lips. Tears falling down my cheeks, her hand in mine, my heart holding hers, I closed my eyes and lifted my quivering voice, "Savior, You can move this mountain. My God is mighty to save. He is mighty to save. Forever, Author of salvation. He rose and conquered the grave. Jesus conquered the grave." Comfort appeared as if to witness the humble prayers of a broken mommy. It was all I could offer.

God, You can move this mountain if You want to.

Even if she couldn't hear me in her physical being, I believed her spirit could hear and joined me in this song of her heart. Each time the words spontaneously arose, I would find the strength to sing a little louder as I desperately reminded myself and God of His strength and ability to move this huge mountain and save her life if He wanted to.

As I sat and sang, God began to move mountains through her relentless nurse. She had been in and out of Jessie's room several times over a few hours, voicing concerns about the increasing pressure in Jessie's brain to the older, experienced neurosurgeon. He answered with the same response every time, "Continue to monitor."

Suddenly a different, much younger neurosurgeon appeared at her bedside. He introduced himself as Dr. Witwer and explained that he had taken over for the weekend. Speaking swiftly and confidently, he relayed the conversation he'd just had with our nurse about the increasing intracranial pressure of her brain. His recommendation was to do a craniectomy immediately to attempt to preserve any remaining brain function.

Any remaining brain function!? What? Oh God, what's happening?

Within minutes, we were faced with the unthinkable decision of removing part of her skull. After being assured her pressures were being closely monitored by the much older, wiser-appearing neurosurgeon who had just left for the weekend, this young "hotshot" neurosurgeon insisted on a horrifying solution.

Unable to make the decision, we turned to our nurse. Her wise and experienced grandmother eyes said it all: "Hurry!"

The plan was to remove a small window of her left skull to give her brain the room it needed to swell.

My groaning returned and deepened as I waited with Bill.

Is this the small window of hope we were told about? What does a small window in her skull look like? What does hope look like in this place? What do we hope for? If we hope for her life and there is no brain function, then there is no life. If there is no brain function, then God giving her eternal life would be the hope. So many unknowns. His ways and thoughts are higher than the heavens to ours, so we will hope that God comes through that window and gives us His miracle. Whatever miracle that is. He knows her, all of her, and He is faithful in all the windows.

Dr. Witwer suddenly appeared again.

"Come quickly, so I can show you."

We followed him to a computer screen displaying her CT scan, and I couldn't believe what I was seeing. It was her brain, over-inflated like a balloon through the side of her skull that had just been removed to relieve the intracranial pressure that would have otherwise stamped out our beautiful daughter's life.

"It was much worse than we thought. I ended up removing her entire left side and now I need to remove the right or she won't survive."

She won't survive? I gasped for breath.

"We have no time. What do you want me to do?"

Without hesitation, we both said, "Do it."

He turned back to the OR, hesitated, and took one last look at us.

"I don't know if I am doing you any favors."

Then he was gone.

The magnitude of that statement was as cold and hard as the wall that held me. Horrified at the thought of both sides of her skull being taken off, I wondered if it was even possible.

Oh God, what is happening? Never in my years of nursing had I seen or heard of anyone having a skull removed to that extent. *I can't breathe.*

Fear and anguish erupted through tears and groaning as we gravely trudged our way to the only place we knew to go—the chapel.

Over 700 miles away from our Oklahoma home, family, and friends, Bill and I found ourselves alone, face down on the floor at the foot of the altar, crying and pleading with

God to help our daughter. Our salty tears mingled with the tears of others who had gone before us in their own crushing catastrophes, as the sacred walls absorbed and held the anguished groans with ancient strength. After what seemed like hours of pouring out grief and pain like a roaring river, it finally quieted, pooling on the plains of the chapel floor.

A momma's prayer found its way through my disoriented soul, *Oh God, help her. Help our little girl. She is Yours. You created her and You know all things. Help us, God.*

My face rested on the fibers of the musty carpet as the awareness of the stark silence struck me. I lifted my head to see Bill lying motionless with his back turned to me and said, "We should go back to the waiting room."

Neither one of us moved, unable to comprehend the next moment. Yet at some point, we were lifted up and carried into the waiting room. We didn't know what we were waiting for, but we both knew Who was with us holding the next moment. We just couldn't have imagined all the ways, or people, through which He was about to show up.

Glimmers in the Dark
St. Mary's Medical Center | Grand Junction, CO
March 18, 2009

Groping in the darkness of unknowing, far from our home and community of support, God brought a village.

A local pastor came to us in the waiting room during her skull removal surgery and placed food in our hands. He sat with us in the ash heap of our lives, providing provisional prayer and presence. Other pastors would just

The Wisteria Tree

appear throughout the days, being present with prayers and offers of provisional care.

Unbeknownst to me, Erin, my daughter-in-law of three months, created a lifeline in an attempt to bridge the distance between us and home. She accessed Carepages, an online journal used for posting updates about a loved one, and used the first email I had sent out to family to make the first entry into Jessie's Journal. A communication major in college who was wise beyond her years, she knew I would need a means of communication to update our church, family, and friends. She placed her own laptop into my trembling hands and said, "I want you to keep this and use this online journal to keep us updated every day." Then she showed me how to use it.

One evening, a quiet earthly angel suddenly appeared with a basket of sustenance. She introduced herself as Diane. Part of the local faith community, she had received a call from her brother-in-law who lived in Oklahoma City and heard about Jessie's accident. Her kind brown eyes and gentle spirit were breaths of life to me as I felt the sisterhood of our spirits connect.

Another stranger showed up in our doorway and introduced himself as Dave Bowles. His mom lived in Tennessee and called him after she learned of Jessie's accident. She told him to find us and help, so he had come bearing a bag full of personal necessities and snacks, insisting he was available to pick up anything we needed.

We quickly discovered how very uncomfortable and difficult it was to step away from her bedside to "meet" these unknown helpers, as we were in no frame of mind for "visits," finding no energy or desire to engage with anything outside of the time we had and felt was limited at her bedside. But God knew what our basic needs were and sent the exact help we needed before we even asked.

As the reality of a massive brain injury and her critical condition began to settle in, it was evident the time had come to fly her other brother, Joe, in from Florida. When he arrived, we circled her bed as a family and prayed with the deepest parts of our hearts, opening our hands of hope to wait upon God's merciful decision. The night was quiet and dark as we waited together for the arrival of a miracle, which took me back to the night Jessie was born and how we had also waited with incredible love for the arrival of our miracle and were so thankful for the gift of our girl. She had completed our family.

The week before she left on spring break, she had shared with me how much she loved her life, her friends, her church, and her family. As I sat with her in the darkness, I was so thankful her last memories were being surrounded in incredible love.

Garments of Protection and Praise

St. Mary's Medical Center | Grand Junction, CO
March 19, 2009

Three days into this unimaginable horrific game of "Is she going to survive?" Jessie developed a MRSA infection in her lungs. Being placed in full isolation required isolation gowns and gloves for anyone entering or staying in her room. This enforced precaution protected others from acquiring the infection but it added another layer to the unbearable weight we were already carrying. Continuously wearing the oversized bulky yellow paper gowns with the nitrile blue exam gloves was not only smothering, but time consuming. Each time we left the room for a bathroom break or to get a drink meant a ritual of removing the garb and redonning each time we went back in. I was reeling in the overwhelming question of how I was going to be able to function under such strict restraints.

A timely answer appeared in the response of a friend in the Carepages, bringing new light to the impossible circumstances we were facing:

> **Carepage Posting**
>
> Wear those required gowns as garments of praise and hope, not of despair.

My heart leapt at this timely shift in my despairing attitude, as it helped me to find the good in the midst of awfulness. With this new perspective, I eagerly donned that yellow garment of praise, as if wrapping myself up totally with the hope we had in Jesus. It was GOOD to be completely enveloped and reminded of His protection from the harsh storms threatening to destroy all we loved.

Carvings of Hope

St. Mary's Medical Center | Grand Junction, CO
March 20, 2009

"Sis, I am just checking in on how things are going." My brother's voice comforted my heart when I picked up the phone and quietly crouched behind the monitors as phones weren't allowed in the ICU.

"Oh, Mark, I still can't believe you were on the same mountain she was and none of us knew. I am just so

Part 1: Severed at the Root

thankful you were there and able to come to the hospital to be with our kids. *Only God. Only God.* Jessie is still with us. That's all we know."

"Do you need me to come back to the hospital? Do you need me to bring you anything? What can I do?" he asked.

"Ugh, who knows? I think you should stay with your family, and I will let you know. Right now, I can only get through this moment."

"Well, I wanted to tell you what happened when I got back to the ski resort after leaving the hospital. I overheard a man having a conversation about the skiing accident and decided to introduce myself. He told me his wife, Jenise, a nurse from Texas, had been one of the first to come upon Jessie after her accident. She provided supportive care for her until the ski patrol arrived. I actually got to meet her, and she told me exactly what happened. I also got her phone number in case you would want to connect with her later."

I could feel my heart tremble upon hearing and knowing that God had placed a nurse in that exact location in that exact moment to help my daughter.

"How unbelievable is that? *Jenise, an angel of God* ... My gosh, the perfect timing of it all ... and certainly another reason she is still with us."

"Sis, there is something else."

I held my breath as I wasn't sure I wanted to know.

"I can't explain it but I felt drawn to find where her accident occurred. I wanted to try and get a better understanding of what had happened and how exactly she hit the tree. I heard reports that the slopes were slippery that day, causing her to fall and skid down the slope head first, crashing into the trunk of a tree." He paused and continued with great tenderness, his voice breaking, "Sis, did you know that someone carved her name with the date 3/16/09 and a cross on that very tree?"

"What? They did what?" My knees were trembling as I lowered myself to the floor.

"Sis, I just have to tell you this. I felt this deep message of God being spoken as I looked upon that tree with that date etched above where she hit. I heard the promise of Life in John 3:16 (NIV), 'For God so loved the world, He gave His only begotten Son, that whosoever believes in Him will have everlasting LIFE.'"

I closed my eyes and held tightly to his words of life, hoping they would settle deep within the marrow of my dry bones, as I feebly fumbled to grasp the depth of Light that had just pierced the darkness of this moment.

Jessie's beloved name, hand-carved in love on a tree, echoed the one that held Christ many years ago, giving her the promise of Eternal Life. Finding footing on that forever promise created a small influx of fresh wind and fresh fire, bringing breath and life to my rattled bones, strengthening me to believe, hope, praise, and to give thanks for the breadth, width, depth, and height of God's love, far-reaching and knowing no boundaries.

"Brother, I don't know what to say. I still can't wrap my head or my heart around the fact you were on the same mountain on the same day. I mean, you can't make this up. Who could have ever imagined? Only God could have orchestrated such timing. Just knowing you were with her until I could get there was such a gift. I love you so much."

*"We must use any signposts that exist
to help us through the wilderness."
~Anne Morrow Lindbergh~*

Part 1: Severed at the Root

Battle Wounds and Beacons
St. Mary's Medical Center | Grand Junction, CO
March 21, 2009

Being a nurse in the midst of this horrific battle was an incredible advantage in many aspects but torturous in others. Hearing the extent of her brain surgery with facial and skull repairs and the complications she was battling, my experience was invaluable in understanding and communicating with physicians but came at the great cost of knowing "too much," which increased the overwhelming weight of fear, grief, and despair. In moments like these, watching the ICU nurses provide such extraordinary intensive care to Jessie was comforting, yet gripped me with anguish.

One such warrior was Sarah from Brazil. Her name, I later learned, meant "woman of high rank" or "woman minister," and she lived right into it. This beacon of hope moved with immovable expectation and belief. Every move, word, or task—everything she did—intentionally spoke the name of Jesus. She didn't plead or beg for healing. She commanded it. I unknowingly witnessed a transfiguration the morning she stepped across a dimension and reached across the bed with her anointed hands for Jessie's bandaged head, lifting it off the pillow ever so gently and speaking directly to Jesus about her brain functioning, healing, protection, and ultimate recovery. Heaven bent low, listening to this woman of high rank speak with such authority as she interceded for Jessie, and I stood in silent awe of the powerful words spoken boldly for her life. Some might say she was just a nurse, but I believed she was appointed by God to help fight this battle at this moment for this little girl on earth. Her kind eyes and words of support were spoken to me with every encounter, "I am so proud of you" or "You are doing such a good job, Mom," giving me unexpected comfort and hope within the shattered spaces we inhabited.

Early one morning, she stepped across yet another dimension. This time, it felt like hell itself spoke, "We need to change the bandages on her head."

WE? We need to do what? Oh God no, I can't and won't do that unthinkable thing.

Waves of nausea and shortness of breath immediately joined forces with fear and anxiety. Until this moment, the bulky white bandages had shielded me from the full reality of what was unseen. Envisioning her head with no skull, no hair, her scalp held together with roadmaps of suture lines, was inconceivable and seemed unsurvivable.

"Lisa, you can do this." She reached for my hand and I turned away. She stepped closer into my shattered space and embraced my whole body as the sobbing crumbled the wall that I had been fighting desperately to hold up. Her gentle, loving eyes reached within me, saying, "You can do this because we will do it together."

"I can't, Sarah. Please don't. I just can't do this."

No, no! I can't bear this!

With no walls left standing, my reality was brutally naked.

But Love was stronger. Love knew this was the reveal I needed to destroy the fear that held me captive. Seeing Jessie's head was indeed worse than I could have ever imagined.

How can someone so precious be so ravaged by life?

But through God's mighty hand and Sarah's immovable faith, this huge mountain of fear fell into the ocean with great tidal waves of relief, helping me begin to see a new vision and move in the direction of embracing the gift of this extreme surgery—the ravaging of her beautiful head was the very reason she was alive that day. She had to go through all of it so her brain could survive and not be further damaged.

The relief slowly shifted to gratitude, enabling me to lift my voice in praise to God, our Abba, Sustainer, Strength, Healer, Comforter, Peace-giver, Assurance, Truth, and Light in this darkened world. Only God could bring this momma through such fear and grief to the raising of praise in the midst of such traumatic destruction in the life of such a precious child.

Goodness

St. Mary's Medical Center | Grand Junction, CO
March 21, 2009

Every day that she survived was a miracle, and we knew it. Morning rounds at her bedside were dreadful and unyielding as the doctors spoke the reality of the physical realm. Little hope was offered.

My eyes would close as my ears and brain tried to grapple with the enormity of words being spoken about my petite little girl. Critically injured. A diffused axonal brain injury, debridement of nonviable brain tissue, orbital fractures, and issues with blood clotting causing increased risks of hemorrhage. Albumin level critically low, resulting in fluid shifts within her body, causing her blood pressure to plummet. Critical sodium imbalances threatening more brain swelling. Her lack of spontaneous breathing. MRSA pneumonia threatening her already compromised lung functioning. Non-reactive pupils. Lack of response to painful stimuli.

The neurosurgeon had informed us her latest CT scan showed her brain still significantly swollen, and the possibility of her requiring a shunt to help manage the fluids in the brain. The thought of a shunt in her brain brought massive waves of nausea, leading me to rise up and fervently demand NO SHUNTS as I cried out to God.

The list went on and on.

The immensity of the knowns swam in synchrony with the depth of the unknown extent of her brain injury. There was no way of knowing if she would even wake up. And if she did wake up, would she have any cognition or movement?

Will she even know me?

All of this should have destroyed me, but hidden within the mystery of God's grace, another way was offered unexpectedly—a much more narrow road to travel.

"Look for the GOOD, Lisa," was the instruction I heard.

His grace led me to begin to look for the GOOD. I discovered if I could find the GOOD, I could find God. Being able to find God in the midst of the awful helped me to find the strength and hope I needed to survive.

Every breath she was given by the ventilator was GOOD. Her CT scan remaining unchanged was GOOD. Her brain pressure being stable was GOOD. Attempting to decrease her sedation to see if she could tolerate it was GOOD because it would help improve her low blood pressure, helping her body to work better. Starting nutrition in her IV line was GOOD because she needed nutrition to heal. Her blood gasses were stable and this was GOOD because her body was getting the needed oxygen. Every issue she had, I was able to find something GOOD in it, enabling me to see beyond the circumstances, to look beneath the obvious, to find gratitude in the smallest improvement or stability. There was a whole lot of GOOD going on in Jessie, and we were giving praise for His mercy and compassion upon her in every moment of every circumstance. For every breath we were taking. For the ways we could see and not see God carrying us through each step.

CHAPTER 2

The Tree of Life

The Tapestry of Signs

God planted a life-giving tree in the Garden of Eden to enhance and sustain the physical life of humanity. It reappears in Revelations 22:1-3 where John described, "Then the angel showed me the river of the water of life, as clear as crystal, flowing from the throne of God and of the Lamb down the middle of the great street of the city. On each side of the river stood the tree of life, bearing twelve crops of fruit, yielding its fruit every month. And the leaves of the tree are for the healing of the nations."

A tapestry of this Tree of Life has been threaded through my spiritual journey, uplifting my home with its powerful symbolism. It envelopes my dining room wall, declaring its purpose of supporting the physical and spiritual life of mankind.

For years, every month, sitting in the presence of my spiritual director, a "tree of life" rug has been at my feet where my eyes rest, helping me to mine the depths of my experiences in hopes of deepening my awareness of God's presence within the leaves of my life. These "leaves," I believe, God also uses to bring healing to others.

Healing has been a powerful cry in my heart since becoming a nurse. A Presence overshadows me each time I enter into a patient's pain, bringing a slower, gentler way of listening and speaking. Compassion and kindness lead the way with empathy, appearing without thought as the river of life flows from the throne for the healing of another.

I have never met a soul who wasn't in need of some kind of healing.

> *"Each of us does sit next to a pool of tears."*
> ~Trevor Hudson, *Befriending Our Tears*~

Streams of Loss and Life
St. Mary's Medical Center | Grand Junction, CO
March 20, 2009

My pool of tears had become a floodplain.

My own "beloved tree" had been severed at the root, leaving a chasm where her branches of life had once danced on the wind while serenading all of creation.

Isaiah 11:1 (New Living Translation) declares, "Out of the stump of David's family will grow a shoot. Yes, a new Branch bearing fruit from the old root."

Could a shoot grow out of her stump? Could she have new branches? Is it possible, God?

Though our forest was devastated, other trees began to offer their own leaves for her healing. What magnitude was being bestowed, intersecting the sacred Tree of Life with hidden hopes of her sprouting new branches.

And the river of life flowed.

Care packages from home began appearing, bringing great comfort, support, and provision in the forms of ChapSticks, lotions, soaps, shampoo, toothbrushes and toothpaste, deodorant, blankets, snacks and candy, books, cards filled with words of love and hope, stamps, and money.

Boxes and envelopes became leaves of medicine, slowly uniting and banding together to form a canopy of healing light and hope that covered our darkened room. Never had we been recipients of such overwhelming abundance.

Unceasing prayers for Jessie were surging into this river of love, nourishing the Tree of Life to bring streams of healing throughout the desert we had been driven into.

In the midst of this river, powerful heart medicine would rise to the top, within my reach, though I was often unaware of the intentional unreleased strength it contained within.

As I held the "Clinging Cross" (a hand-carved, olive wood cross designed to fit perfectly into the palm of one's hand to provide comfort and be a tangible reminder of God's presence), I would read the prayer "Be At Peace" by St. Francis de Sales.

"BE AT PEACE"
St. Francis de Sales | 1567-1622

Be at peace. Do not look forward in fear to the changes of life; rather look to them with full hope as they arise. God, whose very own you are, will deliver you from out of them. He has kept you hitherto, and He will lead you safely through all things; and when you cannot stand it, God will bury you in His arms. Do not fear what may happen tomorrow; the same everlasting Father who cares for you today will take care of you then and every day. He will either shield you from suffering, or give you unfailing strength to bear it. Be at peace, and put aside all anxious thoughts and imaginations.

Part 1: Severed at the Root

Unspeakable strength was found within these words, sent through the mail by the "mother" of our church. Her powerful gift of love became a tangible infusion to my heart as I read the prayer several times a day, imprinting the power of peace within my spirit.

More powerful heart medicine arrived in the form of the devotional book called *Streams in the Desert* by L.B. Cowman.

Sitting by Jessie's bed, I opened the book to glance at the introduction written by Jim Reiman and found deep resonance with his words, "October 25, 1995 is a date I will never forget. I was called out of a business meeting with the terrifying news that my son, Aaron, had just had a massive brain hemorrhage while away at college for only six weeks."

I was stunned motionless by what I'd just read. Tracing the words with my finger, "my son, Aaron, massive brain hemorrhage," my mom heart yearned to know more.

Did he survive? Is he okay now? What happened?

I searched to find the answers within the pages of this offertory hope.

My heart was pierced with an immediate knowing God would use this book as a daily guide through this unspeakable desert, providing streams of sacred words and scriptures to reach into those deep unreachable death valley places, leaving hope, comfort, and strength along the way.

More leaves, in the form of a large packet of information on traumatic brain injuries surrounded by miscellaneous comfort gifts, came from Evansville, Indiana. Her letter introduced herself as Becky Smith, a stroke/neuro RN coordinator who had been doing some online research on the actress Natasha Richardson's accident and death when she came across the news of Jessie's accident.

Two days after Jessie's accident, Natasha was taking ski lessons on the bunny slopes at a Montreal resort when she took a tumble and hit the back of her head. She had returned to her hotel unaware of injury, but medics were called after she developed an excruciating headache. She was airlifted to a hospital with a subdural hemorrhage that tragically ended in death, which they suspect was due to the delay of receiving medical attention. It was unthinkable that this beautiful actress had died after seeing the stark differences between the level of their injuries.

Becky closed by sharing she had never seen such extensive injuries as Jessie's and would be following her progress, offering any support that could be helpful in her recovery.

Supported Steps

St. Mary's Medical Center | Grand Junction, CO
March 20, 2009

Each moment was haunted by the same question, "Will she survive?"

The unknowing held us vulnerably suspended between hope and grief.

In a moment of clarity, unable to grasp the enormity of her condition, we knew we needed some serious emotional and physical support. One phone call to dear friends, Bobbie and Tommy, was all that was needed.

That day in the chapel, Bobbie's foundation of love and strength was immovable against the immense roaring of my pain. My spiritual mom cradled me in holy silence. Her strength and faith held firm as I emptied from my shattered heart. The small hospital chapel transformed into my wailing wall—a place to release pain and grief to God, rolling it up and tucking it within the deep crevices of love.

Hoping, just hoping.

When my sobs subsided, she gently encouraged a moment of fresh air and warm sunshine. As the distance increased from the sanctuary that held my daughter's life, my struggle to breathe intensified. My legs, wrapped in heaviness and terror, refused. She pointed at gentle noticings of the bird's song, a tiny pink flower coming out of the crevice, the white pillows fluffed and shadowing the desert mountains in the distance.

Every time I hesitated, her voice compelled me to take another deep breath and one more step. Being in the midst of such beauty was a stark contrast of the horrific, ugly, and sterile just inside the walls that were towering behind me and within me.

How can one be in two places at once?

Step by step, she guided me to breathe and see, to remember and experience the familiar life-giving power of God's creation, hoping for an infusion to my diminished and darkened soul.

Desperate to return, I abruptly refused another step.

"Let's go back."

The tunnel vision intensified as my heart raced in anxious overdrive with the horror of her not being there when I returned.

Back at her bedside, I gripped the rails attached to her bed, refusing to let go of the closeness that helped to keep my fears caged within the moment.

As Bobbie and Tommy were preparing to leave for the evening, my appearance must have prompted her inquiry, "What might we do to help you get what you need for your stay?"

I only NEED one thing.

"I don't even know." My thoughts refused to leave her bedside. "Maybe some shampoo?"

The Tree of Life

Bobbie gently encouraged a trip to a mall close to the hospital to gather a few necessary items, and my heart seized.

The next day, I sat frozen in the passenger seat, thinking about how this trip would have thrilled Jessie Boone, but seemed an impossible feat to me, given the lingering pain of yesterday's outdoor plod.

Bobbie opened the car door, and my body followed her verbal cues. The gravitational pull of overwhelming fear crushed my posture, making it impossible to lift my head. My heart pain pounded my chest. My trembling hand on Bobbie's shoulder, I let her guide me to the door, catching a glimpse of the large red ball, invoking the memory of my last Target run with Jess.

Will I ever shop with her again? I wondered as Grace silently accompanied me to one of the clothing stores and found three outfits, and then moved quietly next door to find shampoo and lotion and panties. She navigated my inability to see or hear through the crowded mall full of young people and life.

After what seemed endless hours but was only several minutes, the harsh reality forced its way in.

You must go back now, my aching soul insisted. The separation demanded attention.

Back in the car, I had just begun my search for the tower of the hospital when a brown-bricked funeral home came into view. My thoughts spiraled to the reality of seeing her pale, still body lying quietly in white velvet. I squeezed my eyes shut, trying to not see any more, as tears magnified an imaginary meeting with the funeral director and discussing transporting her body back home.

Are you showing me the way this is going to end, God?

Part 1: Severed at the Root

After what seemed like eternity, the car turned into the hospital parking garage. My heart pounded, unsure of what would happen next.

When I stepped into her room, I was overcome.

OH God, I see her. She's so pale and still.

Her hands were folded across her chest, holding three beautiful white carnations, her bed neatly made around her.

OH GOD! Could all this mean … ?

I felt my knees crumbling next to her bed as my worst nightmare was staring me in the face, and Bobbie reached out to ground my runaway heart of fear.

"No, don't go there. Don't go any further."

Her voice snatched me back to the present moment and the monitors showing what her body wasn't—signs of life.

Rest Amid Daffodils

St. Mary's Medical Center | Grand Junction, CO
March 22, 2009

After several days of being right by her side, breathing in every single moment of her essence, exhaustion and lack of personal care overwhelmed me. I could feel the sludge of her critical injuries suffocating my body and breath. The heaviness engulfed me. Hospitality had been offered since the first day, but I was unable to hear or see anything except her.

My precious, perfect little girl.

Gazing at her lifeless body, I remembered the very day we brought her home as a newborn from the hospital with such joy. She'd mesmerized my heart and others'. Our family expanded that day with such great love. So many had spoken the words "old soul full of wisdom" in her fifteen short years.

Once again, I was mesmerized with my heart so full of love, but then sheer panic and apprehension quickly overtook me. What would all of this mean going forward?

Bill gently encouraged me to go rest and shower and assured me he would call me with any change.

I can't leave her. I'll never see her again.

Stepping away from her presence meant she might not be there when I got back. The time I would take for myself would rob me of the time I had left with her. I didn't want to choose.

Why do I have to choose between me and her?

He held me as I wept. Slowly, he made our way to the door and hugged me tighter. He knew I wouldn't be able to make the choice, so he made it for me.

Each step I took away from her, I felt a flood rising up within me, insisting I scream, "STOP! Just STOP! Doesn't anyone know what has happened? Just a few feet away is one of the most precious gifts I have ever known in the most horrendous state anyone could ever imagine! What is happening?"

I was so disoriented that I was having a hard time remembering the directions to the hospitality inn and was forcefully putting one foot in front of the other. While attempting to cross the street, I was overcome by people talking and laughing and walking dogs. Cars zipped by, stoplights clicked, music played, and birds chirped. Life was everywhere, everywhere but where I stood. How could I be in such a foreign far-off place within the same dimension of time?

Overwhelmed with the distance, I finally found my way to the inn across the street from the hospital. I stumbled through the threshold into this oasis of grace as my eyes fell upon yellow daffodils.

Yellow daffodils??? My gosh, they are everywhere! What is happening? Where did they come from?

On the front desk, by the chairs, on each side table, the coffee table, wherever there was an available space, yellow breaths of life were raising their faces upward, reaching for the unseen hope within the atmosphere of faith.

My eyes were wide as I reoriented with my first big deep breath of this fragrance of hope, taken back to a memory of a beloved friend who had always sent me yellow daffodils in March to support the American Cancer Society in honor of her mom. I remembered reading her note, telling me yellow daffodils were the beginning signs of spring and the tangible sign of hope for healing.

Feeling a reconnection to the moment, Hope was being ushered in with the simple yet abundant gift of the daffodil. Falling into the chair, I reached out to touch the sunny petals to see if they were real. They were soft and cool to touch. Tears began to fall, quickly transforming into audible sobs of a deep release as I was being engulfed with the love and presence of hope revealed in living color within that moment. The strength to take the next right step, shower, and rest filled me and pulled me out of the chair. With the daffodil fragrance still upon me, I walked down the hallway and, remembering Bill's words of direction, turned right and found the last room on the left.

When I reached into my pocket, there was a key waiting for me, which I slipped into the slot. Unlocking the door, my eyes lifted and found the room number: 111. Gently gasping, my tears had a different, much quieter, rhythm. It was the number God had used to reveal His constant presence since a spiritual retreat I'd experienced decades before. As I stepped inside, I heard myself whisper, "Thank You, God." His signature had been engraved on the door of my room and on my heart, waiting for me to take this most treacherous journey across the street.

"I AM WITH YOU. YOU ARE NEVER ALONE. 'I AM' right here by your side."

Waiting for me were more daffodils sitting in a simple vase on the bathroom counter as I stepped into the shower where I washed off the grime and sludge of the past week, and even more on the bedside table. Before I crawled into the white crisp sheets that had been turned down for me, my eye caught another yellow offering waiting for me—a beautiful, soft yellow blanket sent by a beloved friend with a note of love inviting me to rest. Cocooning in the yellow blanket of comfort, with yellow daffodils at my bedside, I felt eased and held and finally surrendered to sleep.

Symbols and Signs

St. Mary's Medical Center | Grand Junction, CO
March 24, 2009

When a large, sturdy, crated box was wheeled into our room, we had no idea what could possibly be in it. Inside we found the masterpiece of our hearts—another life-giving leaf. My heart was overwhelmed with the intimacy and intention of this priceless portrayal of the fun-loving, crazy personality girl we missed so much.

JM Lawson, a father of one of Jessie's school friends, had found a recent picture of her on social media and painted this perfect canvas, capturing her beauty and spirit in living color.

Part 1: Severed at the Root

Enclosed were his words,

> Bill and Lisa, I want to let you know how many people are thinking of you. Hope you like this portrait. Also hope that it provides healing energy for you and Jessie. My daughter Bethany and Jessie have known each other since kindergarten. My prayer for Jessie to the Divine is 'Please open her eyes!!!' Very Sincerely, J. Mark Lawson (and Bethany too)

All I could focus on were her beautiful blue eyes.

There you are, baby girl. Please open your eyes, Jessie.

I hadn't seen her eyes for days and now here they were, wide open, looking back at me from this creation of compassion and love. This moving gift of hope for healing became my heart's icon, perched over her bed for all to see. This momma's heart was given the priceless gift of simply seeing her blue eyes open every day in the hopes of the one day when she would "OPEN HER EYES" and see this incredible painting. Until then, we SAW it in faith for her.

Physical therapy's daily arrival was comforting to this old rehab nurse's heart. Watching therapists who were trained to help Jessie's body move was welcomed anytime in our room. It felt forward-moving and preventative for immobility complications I knew were on the horizon without it.

They would position the hospital bed like a chair, fully supporting her with pillows, and I would watch in amazement. They resembled puppeteers taking over her body, manipulating and creating movements from this inanimate object, creating an illusion of her moving. Tears flowed as my breath was taken away, seeing her lifeless body move with such intention by the experienced hands of others.

Will it be possible? I see her muscles remembering movement, but her mind?

This experience whispered the power of the Hand of God and how we live and move and have our very being within Him. I had never witnessed such expertise as they commanded her muscles to gently follow their directions by touch: to squeeze a hand, raise her leg, push her leg down, hold her head up, touch her face.

I watched as a dance of resurrection was performed, calling her up and out of the grave clothes that bound her so tightly. I joined in the dance with my rising whispers of "Talitha Koum, my little girl, I say to you, ARISE."

Part 1: Severed at the Root

When the dance was over, Jill, her physical therapist, came over to me and knelt down with a gentle compassion inviting me to dance even more.

"I had this CD in my car and thought you might like to listen to it."

I smiled through my tears of grief with such gratitude at the overwhelming kindness of her offering. I wondered how she knew the power of music soothed my soul. As I held this gift and gazed at Jessie, I thanked God for these special people He had sent to help.

I opened up the inside cover to find she'd handwritten the words:

> John 11:11 (NIV)
> "Our friend Lazarus has fallen asleep;
> but I am going to wake him up."
> ~Jesus~

And then the most powerful words startled my heart with a deeper hope:

> And I will help.
> ~Jill Wanous, PT, St. Mary's Hospital~

The Tree of Life

She is going to help Jesus wake her up!

I could hardly contain all these glistening shimmers that began to awaken seeds of hope that laid dormant in the deep recesses of my darkened soul. This moment of promise and life sent my hope reeling in the faithfulness of God.

I cannot explain this powerful movement within, but I do know it became another touchstone where my feet were once again grounded deeply on His solid foundation. Knowing my house was not going to be washed away, I could feel the breath of hope ebbing and flowing once again. Tears were my outward sign of gratitude for this holy moment of grace.

Talitha Koum, my little girl, I say to you, ARISE.

As I was reflecting on that special moment with Jill, I remembered our appointed conversation from the day before. We had talked about the number 11 and 111 during Jessie's therapy session as Jessie's heart rate had stayed at 111 during most of the session with her and her BP at 111/60. She had intimately shared how the number 11 was very special to her as she recanted stories of how it had been a very important part of her and her family's faith journey, being a reminder of how God was always with her.

She couldn't have known that I also had a special relationship to the number 11—that it was also one of the ways God illuminates his presence to me. Or that just a few days earlier God had deeply comforted me with the number 111 etched into the door of the place He had prepared for me in a moment of needing to surrender in the midst of great grief.

Jill stuck her head in the door a little later to check on Jessie.

Part 1: Severed at the Root

"How's it going in here? I just looked at my watch and it's 11:11!"

We both smiled at the mystery of God's grace and His gift of this divine appointment of our spirits calling attention to His faithful presence with us through the simple way of numbers.

My head bowed and shook in disbelief. As the music she had shared with me played over Jessie and soothed my aching heart, I looked at my daughter and thought of the enormous challenges she had to face every moment. Yet with tears of gratitude, I had been deeply reminded that God was fully aware of each and every one, and He was holding her closely, pouring forth His strength through His loving children whom He had strategically placed throughout our day to help us with the unbearable moments.

With comfort overflowing, my heart whispered, "Thank you, Father, and bless Jill for her tender understanding of human frailty and for sending her to me at this moment."

I smiled as I looked at the monitor above her bed. Jessie's blood pressure reading at that moment: 111/68.

"The tree builds its strength in unseen places beneath the surface where its roots reach to conquer darkness and fill that space with life."
~Deep Roots by Craig Cunningham,
Feel Free Magazine by Leanne Ford Interiors~

CHAPTER 3

The Miracle Tree

Grace and Miracles

One late night during the early part of my hospice career, I was called out for the death of a momma. The family was encircled around her bed as I placed my stethoscope on her pink ruffled nightgown, closing my eyes in both prayer and concentration to confirm the heartbeat was no longer there.

Silence. Pure silence.

The family wept as I spoke the words of finality and sat with their broken hearts. After several moments, my invitation, "Tell me about your momma," was all that was needed to hear the stories of her life, her hopes, her faith, and her family. Stories became bridges that opened hearts and provided a way of crossing from one place to another.

The story of her mystical tree became a bridge, leading us outside to the backyard where her son shared how his mom would sit for hours at night underneath her mystical tree, watching the leaves shimmer with light and movement.

"She believed miracles were happening with each movement of the shimmering leaves," he said.

When my eyes lifted to her life-giving tree, the wind answered and the leaves glistened with yellow tones of light.

I stood still, eyes wide, while the earth shifted, time held its breath, and something mystically deep within me opened up a deeper seeing and knowing that something extraordinary had just happened within a different realm.

The miracles I had experienced as a small child were different, as each were physically witnessed, like the time I was on a 4x4 piece of Styrofoam with my little brother in the middle of the lake without life jackets when a storm hit, threatening to swallow us up whole, or the traumatic day when I watched my dad save the life of a fisherman whose arm had been shredded by a boat propeller.

In high school, I had learned the importance of perseverance in miracles while playing the role of the teacher, Anne Sullivan, in *The Miracle Worker,* the story of the young educator who never gave up on the young deaf and blind girl named Helen Keller.

As my life progressed, I had begun to find words were not able to grasp the dimensional display of miracles. I believed in miracles and grew to experience them happening within each moment of each life in each day. Extraordinary moments of miracles in a sunrise ... a sunset ... a rainbow ... a breath ... a birth ... a death ... children ... family ... life ... love ... all being infinite miracles of God's creation.

Shimmers of Hope

St. Mary's Medical Center | Grand Junction, CO
March – April 2009

Jessie was attended by breathing miracles throughout her hospital stay. A nurse in ICU, a breast cancer survivor who lives life big and loves fiercely. A respiratory therapist, also a breast cancer survivor, living life out loud on her motorcycle, loving God and people immensely. An ICU night shift nurse, the survivor of a horrific car accident at the age of nineteen who had spent many days in this very ICU. Another ICU nurse who had been stabbed in the carotid at the age of twenty-two and life-flighted to this very ICU in this hospital. Another ICU nurse who spent thirty-one days in ICU with esophageal cancer and was not expected to live. Not only was she still living, she was commanding others to live through her nursing skills and presence on earth.

How is this possible? So many miracles! Miracles caring for my miracle.

Then came the unexpected moment when the twenty-two-year-old marine walked into our room and shared his miraculous survival of an explosion in Iraq. He had suffered a traumatic brain injury with other severe injuries and was not expected to survive. But there he was, standing before us. He was beautiful, alive, and retelling his story of hope of recovery after a three-month coma, more than fifty surgeries, and a year in a military rehabilitation center.

These sightings of hope made real were incomprehensible to me.

What does this mean? Could I be seeing shimmering hope poured into the landscape of our journey by "seeing" and "hearing" the living miracles, transplanting the air within their healed souls into our broken ones? Do I dare believe these possibilities that have been paraded in front of us, or is this just some cruel joke as we wait for the dreaded punch line?

Closing my eyes, I could feel my heart trembling, whispering so no one could hear my doubt, especially me.

Is it possible, God? For her to have a recovery journey like his?

Something shifted deep inside, creating a bridge perhaps, helping me to take another step toward hope—to the possibility of the ultimate Miracle Worker persevering and triumphing over such devastation in her life.

Yellow Ribbons of Prayer
Oklahoma City, OK
March 28, 2009

When the news of yellow ribbons tied around trees in our hometown, wrapped with prayers and petitions, began to reach my ears in Colorado, my heart quickened to this united HOPE being actively displayed in proclamation.

Our home on Clayton Park Road was silent and dark. A shell remained with no life evident within its walls. Everything had stopped at the moment of impact with the fallen tree, except a small quiet vibration in the hearts of two women. This vibration within their hearts began rising up in their quiet spaces. These prayer warriors, trained to listen within, began to discern that those vibrations were awakening, organizing, and intentionally moving them toward a battle cry of hope: JESSIE BOONE WILL COME HOME.

Many may remember the song "Tie a Yellow Ribbon 'Round the Ole Oak Tree" from the 70s written about a soldier's homecoming from war. As a teenager, with a guitar and self-taught method, I would belt out this passionate song of homecoming as if I were the one wanting and waiting to come home.

The Yellow Ribbon Rally materialized to an awakening movement to call Jessie Boone home. Gina Rowsam, one of the women, wrote, "Some have asked if the rain and cold will impact the Ribbon Rally for Jessie. The answer is YES! It gives us an even better backdrop from which to position ourselves and petition God on behalf of Jessie and her family. As I see it, we are all in a 'gray' zone, so to speak, as nothing 'seems' clear in the natural world right now. And if Jessie is living in a colder environment to support her brain's needs, then we can put up with a little cold and dampness. Let's use this to lean into our faith and trust in things unseen in the spiritual realm more than ever. With these overcast skies and mists of rain coming down, I am more energized for this than ever. So get out that rain gear you hardly ever get to use, put on some waterproof shoes, get your ribbons ready, and let's Rally for Jessie!!"

The blowing of the shofar emanated from a thick cloud of grief, declaring God as King, and prepared hearts for battle against the enemy not wanting her to come home. This calling brought forth a large gathering of family and friends to drive to Clayton Park Road, open the doors of our home and enter in to bring breath and life back within the walls of our empty tomb. Hundreds of yellow ribbons held handwritten petitions of powerful prayers believing in Jessie's recovery and homecoming. Young and old carefully tied them around every tree, branch, and structure, scattering the color of hope over the two acres embracing the cold dampness of the day.

One prayer warrior spoke fervently, "We surround the Boone's home with our physical presence and literally stake a claim for Jessie's return home with the adornment of ribbons around the property signifying our belief. I think it's a God inspired 'TP' party—Total Prayer, Total Praise."

That evening, we were able to watch from hundreds of miles away the visual recording holding all the moments with their voices and prayers, their faces and tears, their hopes and cries for our family. This sacred yellow hope was cascading LIGHT and LIFE all over our home in a unified cry of COME HOME, JESSIE BOONE!

As I was preparing to re-enter Jessie's room, I looked down to tie the yellow gown around my own waist once again. Only then did I realize God had found His own unique way to include us in joining their petitions to bring her home.

Holy Week and Sacred Support
St. Mary's Medical Center | Grand Junction, CO
April 9, 2009

Three weeks within the walls of St. Mary's hospital evolved into a rhythm of receiving nourishment and tender care as we intently watched for signs of emergence. My eyes searched endlessly for any movement or connection with the world outside of her. My heart was fragile yet feeling a soft remembrance of Holy Week echoing our own journey, knowing resurrection comes after the brutal beating and death of Jesus on a tree and three days in the grave. Each prayer being laid down like branches, we invited Jesus to make a triumphal entry into her very body to raise her up and bring her new life.

Closing my eyes, I could see sweet Jessie at three years old in her car seat as we drove to church early one Palm Sunday. She raised her angelic face to the sky revealing the exclamation of the sunrise, clearly saying, "Hosanna! Blessed is the one who comes in the name of the Lord!" only as a beloved child can, revealing a mystical moment of knowing her own "old soul."

The rhythm of Holy week quickly moved as I felt my heart rate and breathing rising in synchronization with her high fevers, rapid shallow breathing, rapid heart rate, and relentless vomiting. Her deafening silence and non-movement spoke even louder to the assaults being inflicted upon her. The scenario that kept playing in my nurse brain was her diagnosis of MRSA pneumonia, which placed her

The Miracle Tree

at high risk of it traveling to the most fragile place in her body—her brain. I closed my eyes as my thoughts began to spiral out of control. The suffocation of the reality of what this could mean closed in on me again.

Dr. Charles Breaux, Jr., her pediatric surgeon, entered our room bearing small palm branches folded into crosses. He had finished a choir performance of a special Palm Sunday service and wanted to share a part of his experience with us. His outstretched offering of love and remembrance calmed my anxious heart as he began the exhaustive search of what was happening within the hiddenness of her body.

Who is this man?

Every day, at least twice daily, he rounded on her and commanded her chaos into order with great medical expertise and love for our family. He was unsure of what was happening to generate these new symptoms but said he would find the source, using words like infections or abscesses. A methodical search of every part of her body with blood and urine workups and body scans finally revealed the truth.

"I found it," as he triumphantly entered our room announcing, "You are not going to believe this but thankfully it isn't her brain!"

I burst into tears recognizing God had said no once again. Relief came pouring in as I laughed out loud. "Her gallbladder? Really? Her gallbladder?"

His gentle eyes and small smile confirmed my disbelief.

"I thought it might be overkill to scan her abdomen but something told me it was necessary. And there it was. She has a very sick gallbladder that needs to come out."

I felt my knees give all the way to the floor as my heart gave way to the heavens in praise and thanksgiving that

Part 1: Severed at the Root

it wasn't an abscess in her already fragile and severely injured brain, and for the immaculate health care she was receiving from her care team, all saturated in compassion and love.

As we moved forward, antibiotics were given in an attempt to shrink the size of the inflamed gallbladder in hopes of making it easier to remove.

But can she survive another surgery in her condition?

Dr. Breaux explained he would attempt to do a laparoscopy, hoping the gallbladder had decreased in size because of the antibiotics, but it was more likely he would "have to open her up." He discussed the risks and benefits of the surgery, the anesthesiologist he had chosen to watch over her fragile state as she slept, and of course all other kinds of details a mommy nurse needed to know. He was a steady, hope-filled reassurance to my anxious heart.

Her surgery was scheduled for Holy Thursday, bringing an unexpected comfort in the familiar rhythms of the day, remembering it was a time of Jesus preparing his disciples for the time he would enter into his time of great suffering.

The day before her surgery, Dr. Duane Hartshorn, the ENT surgeon who had worked with neurosurgeon Dr. Robert Fox on Jessie's initial brain surgery and facial/skull repairs and later performed her percutaneous tracheostomy and placed a PEG tube in her tummy, came bearing a basket filled with brightness, joy, and hope that seemed to radiate light into our darkened room. His voice trembled a bit as he gently pushed out the words, "My girls were decorating their eggs for Easter last night."

I smiled at him as the thought of little girls coloring eggs pushed out a bit of the dread and darkness that had already taken up residence without invitation.

"They wanted Jessie to have some eggs too!" I felt this gentle surge of deep love move within me. This towering tree with his branches bending down bearing such simple yet extravagant fruits of love and kindness from children. This moment shifted my focus to the power another has to bring forth great comfort in the most difficult times.

As I sat beside her the evening before the surgery, looking at this sweet offering of intentional love, I thought back to some of my favorite Easter moments. Closing my eyes, I could see and smell the coloring of eggs with dye stains on the fingers and floor with the vinegar fragrance wafting in the air. The laughter of our kids running freely, hunting and seeking, sometimes knocking the other one down to secure the most or the best of the eggs. The family gatherings, church services, and meals that shouted Easter just by their presentation and taste. The annual Easter cake served after lunch was the sweet tradition sure to make one want seconds if the first piece wasn't big enough. The licking of fingers and bowls during and after the preparation time was always one of my most favorite parts. But then how could one forget the delicious shavings of the chocolate layers and the process of using toothpicks that could become secret swords waiting to stab you if you weren't watching for them!

When I opened my eyes, tears were rolling with my questions.

Will she ever? Could she ever color an egg? Go Easter egg hunting? Make the Easter cake with Grandma?

My gaze was falling lower and lower as I was ushered back into the reality of the moment with the sounds of the monitors amplifying her life forces one beat at a time.

How does one face such defining and difficult moments in life? This isn't what Easter is supposed to look like.

Part 1: Severed at the Root

We would be going to a Maundy Thursday service to celebrate The Last Supper by receiving holy communion and remembering Jesus washing His disciples' feet to remind them to serve others as He has served them. Jessie would have been in an actual foot washing service with her friends.

As I was praying for her to have a restful night after days of sickness to help prepare her for yet another surgical assault on her already-ravaged body, a young nurse named Heidi entered into our pain with the utmost kindness and gentleness. Experiencing her presence in the midst of the brewing storm was simply heaven "scent." The fragrance of comfort and hope permeated the room, helping me to breathe a little easier that night. Around 2 a.m., it was time for her pre-op bath. As I helped her bathe Jessie in the middle of the night, she quietly began to share some of her own personal story.

Did I know she was a living miracle and survived a devastating car wreck? Did I know she had overcome many impossible moments? Did I know she was here for the purpose of bringing hope and help to the ones in her care?

When she moved to wash Jessie's feet, the room shifted. My eyes didn't move from this visual icon as I witnessed this familiar holy act of love preparing her for what was to come the next day.

How is this even possible, God? You bring this angel of light into our night, and she quietly and unassumingly steps into the rhythm of Maundy Thursday, bridging the gap of the seen and the unseen.

Her procession of words continued as she shared her faith and belief in miracles through her own journey near death and how so many helpers showed up to usher in God's merciful miracle for her.

I reached out and touched her, whispering, "Are you real?"

She smiled at me, making a bold claim over Jessie's lifeless body, "I believe Jessie will also be a miraculous survivor of all she is enduring right now."

My heart melted into her words as I studied this love made flesh. Even though my eyes were seeing something different, I knew she was a messenger sent to proclaim a message of hope over this child and her momma's ravaged heart.

Communion and Answered Prayers
St. Mary's Medical Center | Grand Junction, CO
April 10, 2009

Her morning erupted into a flurry of activity of physical preparations for surgery, including blood transfusions, fresh frozen plasma, ultrasound of her abdomen, the continued battles with fever-fighting tactics, and pain medication.

As time drew near for her to be taken away, my breathing was as rhythmic as the clock ticking on the wall. However, the relief of the culprit being her gallbladder and not her brain seemed to fade as the reality of the risks of the surgery were coming into full view, as I recalled the conversation I had with the surgeon just hours earlier.

"Can she survive this?" I had asked, already knowing she wouldn't survive without the surgery. I was thankful we didn't have to make that decision. It had been made for us. Intentionally choosing to stay in the moment and breathing simple breath prayers (Be at peace) (Trust in the Lord) (He will never leave me) held me steady.

Part 1: Severed at the Root

Two hours quickly turned into three, and still no word from surgery. The staying in the moment and breathing was replaced with bullet-like questions piercing my brain, *What is happening? Is she okay? Didn't he say it would take about an hour?*

The separation, the not knowing, began to spiral my heart into that familiar fear of never seeing her again. My pounding heart caused tightness in my chest, changing my intentional rhythmic breathing moment by moment into shallow rapid exchanges of fear and dread. It was late into the evening and the emptiness of the waiting room was a stark reflection of how my heart and arms were at that moment. Empty.

Oh God! What is happening? Where are You?

Bill and I had moved closer and closer to the surgery doors as the time passed, somehow hoping it would provide a connection or a bridge to what was on the other side of them. We were sitting on the floor, leaning up against the wall, knowing when someone finally came through those doors with our daughter's outcome, we would be the first to be encountered.

My eyes lifted as I heard the ding of elevator doors opening instead. A recognition of tender eyes brought us both to our feet.

"I brought you holy communion," he said. "Sweet communion in the name of the Great Physician on Jessie's behalf." His offering of a small brown paper bag turned our eyes away from those doors and upward to the face of God.

Doug disappeared as a mist in a matter of moments.

I couldn't speak.

How did he know? How did he know to bring this sustenance to the empty tables of our hearts?

Now fully aware of the nearness of God, with my heart pounding, my hands shaking, and tears flowing, I opened the bag to find a note tucked in beside the grape juice and wafers.

> Bill and Lisa,
>
> Just in case you cannot get to Passover, Passover has come to you. Enclosed is some unleavened bread and fruit of the vine. Perhaps in a quiet moment this evening you will invite Jesus to join you as you remember and rejoice, despite knowing the dark days ahead, that Sunday is coming. Come share the bread. Come share the cup. Come share the Lord. Holy is the Lamb and His loving kindness endures forever.
>
> Grace and peace,
> Doug Clayton

Passover has come to us. Would death "pass over" us again?

Right then, right there, in front of those OR doors, we accepted the invitation to come and share the bread and cup of life at the hardest moment. The very moment I asked, *Where are you, God!?* he came through an elevator, bringing Life to us, nourishing us with His living word. Telling us once again who He is and what He has done and what He will do. My heart found a quietness and was strengthened as He drew us in close, reminding me of Whose we are and how present He was in this very moment.

He sees and loves Jessie and has established her future in Him.

It wasn't long after that the doors opened and Dr. Breaux walked through. Our eyes met, and he wasn't smiling. His drained eyes told a different story of exhaustion and struggle.

"Is she still with us?" tumbled out of my mouth, still searching for some kind of assurance.

"She is still with us," he quietly said as he motioned us into the consultation room. I reached for Bill's hand, needing help to take the next few steps. I took a large breath in and remembered God is with us, the aroma of bread and juice still on my lips. I groped to find the chair in which to surrender to what was coming next.

Over the next several minutes, we listened as he reported the story of what had transpired behind the doors of the OR suite.

"Her gallbladder was extremely large, which required opening her abdomen in order to get it all out. It would have been impossible to remove it through the laparoscopic procedure. I was shocked when I saw it as I had never seen anything like it. It looked like a worn out football." Then his face changed, his words slowed, "There was a complication. Her common bile duct was cut."

"Okay," I said, "What does that mean?"

"The liver produces bile, and that bile flows through a series of small tubes (ducts) which drain into one large duct called the common bile duct which empties into the duodenum, the first part of the small bowel after the stomach. Without the bile duct, the bile will back up and could lead to life-threatening infections and a dangerous buildup of bilirubin. This could lead to liver disease and ultimately liver failure then death. But I reconstructed it."

"Can you do that? I mean, reconstruct a bile duct?"

He nodded his head as he continued with how he builds bile ducts for newborns that are born without them. My head was shaking in disbelief that this human in front of me was capable of building a bile duct in a newborn baby!

I could hear the words falling off my lips, "Who does that? How is that even possible?"

A whisper deep within answered first, *"With God, ALL things are possible."*

I sat back in my chair, tears flowing, thanking him for all that he was doing for our daughter and how he was a true gift from God for a time such as this.

In the truest humility, he smiled and reached out to take my hand, patting it gently, saying, "They will take her back to ICU and she will remain on the ventilator tonight. She has been through a long surgery and will need close monitoring and support for some time. It's been a very long day. You both go and try to get some rest and I am going to do the same."

Her pain during the night was evident, even though it was being communicated in a different way. Pain can be measured even in those who are nonverbal. Her pain was revealed through her elevated heart rate and blood pressure and what appeared to be a great tension within her body. The seven-inch incision on her right abdomen bore witness to her continued battle for life.

"How will we know if the reconstruction worked?" was my first question during his morning rounds.

"We will watch her grossly elevated bilirubin levels. They will need to start trending down over the next few days. And then we will know we are moving in the right direction."

Movements of Grace
St. Mary's Medical Center | Grand Junction, CO
April 11, 2009

Speaking of moving, we were notified her first postop morning that we were being moved seven doors down to another room in the ICU. My heart sank as I didn't know how I could handle one more change at that moment, especially an unnecessary room change. This room had become our safe familiar sanctuary for almost a month. I felt frustrated and angry, wanting to yell at someone. But then the pause came.

Movement is movement. Why is change so hard?

All I had been praying for was movement, any kind of movement, and here came a type of movement, and all I felt was resistance and found myself digging my heels in even deeper.

Tearfully, I resigned myself and began to remove the taped-up hope and mementos that covered the walls, packing up our fabricated nest of a home, shoving it in the unused trash bags I found in the bottom of the trashcan. Feeling defeated and rejected by the very ones who had been our biggest support and first to witness the hell we were traversing, my thoughts continued the revolt.

This makes no sense to me. What are they thinking? How can any of this be happening right now!? UGGHH! Why does everything have to be so damn hard?

And just like that, my angered thoughts and our newly post-op daughter were ushered out and moved into a different room, one that offered much-needed privacy with much more space. What an unexpected moment of transformation as our tiny tomb of survival expanded into a bigger womb of possibilities, as we were given the gift to see from a different perspective in the hopes to be able to see things anew. This unexpected movement of grace did just that.

Dr. Breaux's evening rounds were sprinkled with Good Friday hope. He was pleased with her latest lab work, her pain being well-managed, the pathological reports negative for infection, and her swift recovery from anesthesia.

The soft and gentle rain of the next morning seemed synced with the PT's movements of Jessie's joints speaking the unspoken words of awakening. Jessie's movements were unremarkable but, with a deeper look, one could see something was different.

During a deep suctioning session late into the night, I witnessed the profound moment where her hand suddenly reached up out of her grave and took hold of the nurse's arm and held on.

The next morning as his assistant was removing the remaining staples from her head incisions, Dr. Witwer suddenly appeared, wanting to witness this report of new movement in her arms. He was the one doctor who was always hesitant to speak of any hope for her recovery, but that all changed in his witnessed moment of movement as he proclaimed, "This gives me chills. Remarkable. Just remarkable. We should see more improvement in the next week," piercing our hearts with the hope for more.

Resurrection Day was here, and yes, we had an Easter Egg hunt with real eggs (compliments of Dr. Hartshorn's children), a real basket (compliments of the Kraver family), real hiding (compliments of Mom), with real finding (compliments of Dad)! But the most powerful play this Holy day was the scene we were witnessing, revealing there was more to come.

Of course this would have NEVER been what we would have chosen for Jessie and our family, but it was the path we found ourselves on. I was reminded of a silent personal retreat years earlier, when God had whispered a touchstone of guidance in my ear: "Your path will be one of unknowing, but I will guide you each and every step of the way." And God has been faithful to do just that.

Stirrings
St. Mary's Medical Center | Grand Junction, CO
April 13, 2009

This new path of unknowing had held us now for four weeks. Four weeks of survival in the ICU. Four weeks since we had been home. Four weeks since we had heard her voice. Four weeks since our lives were changed and four weeks we had been blessed to still have her. We had lived within each moment for the last four weeks unlike we ever had before. Four weeks revealed she no longer needed the ventilator, so the endotracheal tube was removed from her tracheostomy. As hard as it all had been, I somehow knew this time was also a sacred gift we had been given to fully embrace and be immersed in the depth of love we had for our daughter.

Jessie was exceptionally still after her extubation, and I wondered if she knew she was now breathing on her own. If she felt more comfortable with that tube finally out of her throat.

Darlin', I sure wished I knew what you were feeling and if you were able to think at all.

Her nurse, Deb, was giving her a bed bath with such gentleness, it made me pause. As I watched her slow kindness, I noticed Jessie slowly lifting her arm up off the bed.

We both waited to see what she would do next.

As she laid it back down on the bed, I wondered what it had meant. Was she trying to get our attention? Was she saying stop? Was it an attempt to touch Deb, as if to say, "Thank you for your kindness"? That would certainly have been something Jessie would have done.

Regardless of what it meant, witnessing this miraculous moment of movement continued to fuel this disorienting drive and determination toward recovery.

I know there is so much more to come. "Talitha Koum, little girl, I say, Arise!"

Bilirubin levels and liver enzymes continued to trend downward as our hopes for healing soared upward. PT re-entered this scene of recovery and, for the first time, attempted to position her sitting on the side of the bed, as she appeared to be having tiny beginning hints of head movement.

Feedings of nutrition and water were reintroduced as her gut reawakened. Skin care and oral care were impeccable, as the nurses were aggressive in minimizing skin breakdown and bacteria that wanted to harbor in her mouth.

Dr. Breaux's morning rounding revealed the next movements, "If she continues to improve, she could be transferred out of the ICU in the next few days."

My first thought? *WE ARE READY TO MOVE!*

I was quickly tested on those thoughts.

We were having to move again, but this time it wasn't the ICU. We had received notification later that evening it was time to vacate the hospitality inn we had been showering and resting in. This time, I was better able to embrace this forward move to a hotel, as it seemed as if God were saying things were better, which seemed to make it okay to not be as close to the hospital as we were. Our territory continued to be expanded little by little, preparing us toward the goal of our hearts—to the bigger move HOME.

I will never forget the moment of intoxication as I was sitting in a chair one afternoon facing Jessie Boone. PT had just transferred her out of bed into a reclining wheelchair. Her head was cradled with foam blocks with her body propped up with many pillows holding her in place.

Her eyes suddenly opened for the first time.

She just opened her eyes! Oh my goodness, her eyes are open! Disconnected, with a no-one-is-home look, but definitely open!

My eyes lifted to the prophetic painting above her bed that had been hanging in hope, speaking through the creative prayerful heart of another to open her eyes, and waiting for this miraculous moment to happen.

It wasn't long before I intentionally placed a large bouquet of colorful balloons a few feet in front of her face, swayed by the breeze of the fan in hopes she might reach for one.

We also attempted coloring (my hand taking her hand and making movements) in her new coloring book with crayons, trying to stimulate something familiar, hoping something would connect and she would spontaneously follow a command.

Her favorite Disney or worship soundtrack was always playing in the background, teasing her sleepy, injured brain to make a connection deep within her familiarity and love of music.

I continued to find myself swept up in these types of moments in such disbelief of what had happened to her and all she had suffered.

How did we get here, God? Will she ever awaken? Will she ever be able to speak? Do anything ever again?

As I was perched on the edge of my seat watching her, she began moving in the most unexpected ways.

Her hand moved right to her face and her finger found her nostril. It appeared she was trying to pick her nose. I burst out laughing, overcome with emotion at seeing her do any type of movement. She continued to mesmerize me as she reached up and scratched her ear and then wiped her eye. I will never forget the moment she had her first sneeze.

Bless you, sweet baby. Bless you.

These surreal and spontaneous random movements became the seeds of what we had been praying for—hope that the chaotic would eventually shift into organized and intentional movements of awakening, which soared as we watched her raise and lower her leg more than fifty times during that night alone.

Movements and Promises

St. Mary's Medical Center | Grand Junction, CO
April 15, 2009

With the witness of these moments of movement, the incredible medical care from this dedicated staff, her lab work stabilizing, and her antibiotic infusions being discontinued after weeks of fighting MRSA, this day had been overwhelming with answered prayers. I was a bucket of dripping joyful gratitude.

But the most delicious icing on the cake for this monumental day emerged during Dr. Witwer's evening rounds. He leaned toward us and whispered the words we could have never imagined him saying, "I promise you she will be walking and talking in six months."

Someone must have whispered to Jessie Boone that she was breaking free from the ICU to a stepdown unit because she wouldn't stop moving. She was reaching for everything, moving both of her legs, pulling at things, scratching her head, her ear, her eyes. She wouldn't lay still. It was almost as if her body had been turned on and was waking up to familiar movements, but her mind was disconnected and still in a deep sleep.

She was unable to follow any commands and even ended up having to have soft mittens on her hands to protect her from pulling tubes out or injuring her fragile scalp, especially at night. Even though I wasn't prepared for the excessive continuous random movements, I was deeply thankful for these signs of life that were breaking forth from the hard ground they had been trapped within.

Synchronicities and Faith

St. Mary's Medical Center | Grand Junction, CO
April 20, 2009

Doug, our minister in residence, made an early and unexpected appearance in our room one Sunday morning. He told us he was prompted to check on us before he headed to church to preach his Sunday sermon.

When we inquired about his sermon, he shared he was speaking about John 21, one of Jesus's post-resurrection appearances and included his uncertainty of why John was so specific to say in verse 11 that there were 153 large fish in the net. He continued on, "I really don't know the significance of the 153 and why it is mentioned in this text. It has been so on my mind this morning."

Bill and I looked at each other in stunned silence.

Doug asked, "What?"

"Well, we have a story that speaks to your very question and one you may want to hear before you preach your sermon."

He leaned in, "Let's hear it."

"Yesterday, Jessie had some very special visitors come to see her ... "

I told the story of how Jessie's gymnastic coaches, a special gym dad who called Jessie The Beam Queen, and two of her gymnast friends, had been in Denver for a high-level gymnastics competition. Before they headed back to Oklahoma, they decided to make the treacherous four-hour drive in the middle of a snowstorm to Grand Junction to come and show their love and support for Jessie. At one point, her coach even gave her one of the "old gymnastic pep talks" of pushing through the hard in order to make the comeback! Their visit was deeply comforting to us, as their love and devotion to our family had never wavered from the first moment we had stepped into their gym when Jessie was a tiny three-year-old.

Just before they left, her friend, Jaelyn, pulled out an envelope and quietly confessed, "This is the money that I raised, so I could go to this competition. Instead of spending it, I saved it. I want her to have it, so it can help her get whatever she needs to make her better."

Bill and I were speechless as we gazed upon this accomplished gymnast dripping with compassion and kindness. Neither one of us moved as she reached out to hand us the envelope with Jessie's name written in her own handwriting. Accepting her gift was a difficult thing to do, yet something deeper spoke, "Receive what is being offered."

It is through the pure intentional love gifted by others that healing is offered to all hearts. I knew her heart was hurting for Jessie, and it was her way of offering what she could to help her friend get better. Experiencing this powerful message of love through the heart of a child was powerfully humbling and hope-filled.

The sacred envelope lay untouched by Jessie's bedside for the next several hours, as neither one of us could bring ourselves to open this pure love and hope from a child whose heart was bigger than the mountains outside our window. Before Bill put the envelope in a safe place of keeping, he braved his tender heart and counted out her "hope" money.

His shoulders heaved as he tearfully shared the amount with Doug, "She gave us $153.00."

Doug looked at us in a stunned silence as we came face-to-face with the tangible awareness of the power and attentiveness of God, especially during the difficult and painful trials of life.

Some scholars have said the number 153 revealed something extraordinary had happened to the fisherman who had not been able to even catch one fish in their net until Jesus came along.

Bill and I knew something extraordinary happened when her gymnastic family made the trek across Colorado all in the name of love and support for their past fellow teammate, but the blessing was magnified by God Himself as he revealed His hidden presence within the 153 dollar bills, merging the envelope of great love with the great love of Jesus who had filled the fisherman's empty nets with 153 fish, once again revealing His great power to provide abundance in the areas of our lives where we have the greatest needs.

CHAPTER 4

The Survivor Tree

Stolen Life

The gift of the sapling brought forth a powerful moment of remembrance for me. The Survivor Tree is the symbol of strength and resilience for our city after the Alfred P. Murray bombing. Overlooking the South Reflection Pool as a living reminder of survival and hope, this sole, battered tree survived the 4,000-pound bomb blast that nearly leveled a nine-story building and took the lives of 168 people.

And now I was holding in my hands the very "child" of that tree—the tree that shouldn't have survived but it did. The tree that could have been destroyed when the shrapnel and evidence was removed from its trunk, but instead was nursed back to health by the New York City Department of Parks and Recreation and returned home in 2010 to the 9/11 Memorial site with the given name, The Survivor Tree. The inscription written around the 100-year-old American Elm reads, "The spirit of this city and this nation will not be defeated; our deeply rooted faith sustains us."

This living inscription imprinted its strength and resilience into my battered spirit. *We will not be defeated and our deeply-rooted faith sustains us.* This ancient survivor was nurtured back to health for fifteen years before it was ready to take its place as a symbol of hope and recovery. And now I was tending to one of its own as I tended to mine with the persistence and patience to never, never, never give up.

Tending included protection as the sapling settled into its new cultivated home. I carefully tied the wooden stake with red tape close to the tender trunk intended to help it stand firm against the high winds and my get-er-done lawn mowing efforts.

Looking out the kitchen window one morning, I was enjoying watching our fetch-loving lab "Tigger hopping," which meant he had found one of his favorite chew toys. It was only when I saw the red that I realized what "toy" he had discovered.

"STOP!" My screams while running toward him only fueled the full-on race of catch-me-if-you-can. He was thrilled while I was enraged. This unexpected snatching of the stake and stick with roots changed the future of our landscape forever.

Oh God, this echoes familiarity, I thought as I finally retrieved the broken sapling. *So much of my baby's life has been broken, severed, forever changed.*

1993 – 2009

The Beloved Daughter and Sister

Jessie has two older brothers, Justin and Joseph. Our family blended when the boys were eight years old, and one year later this perfect baby girl completed our family. She grew up in church, always in the midst of worship, small groups, and retreats while Bill and I volunteered as youth leaders.

We have so many sweet memories of her in church including singing "Happy Birthday, Jesus" to the entire church when she was four, and the evening when Michael

W. Smith was performing at our church and made the time to share a few words with our youth. In a sea of youth, three-year-old Jessie crawled up on his lap while he was talking. He held her the entire time. As he was leaving, he attempted to kiss her on the cheek, but she turned her face and was known as the girl who kissed Michael W. Smith on the lips from that moment on.

The Devoted Athlete
Her gymnastic journey began at the early age of three at a family-owned gym, Mattrotters, earning her the gym name Tater Tot. Her coaches, Jeff and Trish Carter, were instrumental in developing her fierce independence and self-confidence in tandem with her spirit of cooperation and teamwork.

After nine years, she began to have serious low back pain. X-rays and an orthopedic doctor confirmed stress fractures in her lower spine and recommended she stop gymnastics to prevent more serious injuries with possible long-term effects. She couldn't make that decision, so we, her parents, made it for her. Her anger was as fierce as her love for the sport and her team.

One afternoon, I found her upstairs packing her gymnastic paraphernalia in a big cardboard box.

"What are you doing, Jess?"

Her quiet posture with no eye contact answered me, "Mom, I just can't look at them anymore. It hurts too bad."

In her own handwriting with purple ink on the top of her cherished contents read, "My Tender Box."

I pondered those words for a moment as I watched her ceremonial movements of saying goodbye to a large part of her life. What she didn't know was she was *my* tender box as I grieved with her, hoping she would find her way through this young but real grief.

It took several months of healing and moving to a new school before track became her new passion. She loved running and started competing in the spring track meets of her ninth grade year.

One day, I picked her up after practice and was baffled yet amused at the sight before me. She was waddling like a duck, her legs wrapped with plastic bags filled with ice, as water dripped down her legs.

Trying to keep a straight face, I forced a serious, "Are you okay?"

Nodding with a grimaced smile, she said, "The trainer told me these would help with my shin splints."

She was changing before my eyes. Her chattering of details had shifted to her friends, leaving me in the silent zone. Her new choices of music were far beyond my grasp of experience which forced me into a heightened awareness of new genres. It was easy to see her struggling to find her place, settling into her new landscape, and she certainly made it known she didn't like being "staked" down.

The Thriving Teenager
The week before spring break in 2009, she made the unexpected announcement of her first boyfriend. Her excitement charged her with the inability to contain her words.

"He is so cute! He competes in pole vaulting. He is so different from the other boys, I like him so much. He even loves God a lot, Mom!"

It was a sweet moment of experiencing her chattiness returning, watching her filled with joy after such grief, as she gained momentum to the highly anticipated sweet sixteen.

Her demands of driving lessons were not as sweet, as her nerves and my impatience collided with untempered words and wildly demonstrative hands being thrown up, which meant they weren't on the steering wheel at all!

One of my most favorite memories of Jessie in her teens was the Friday before Spring Break 2009. I was waiting in the school parking lot, looking out the car window, enjoying watching her and her new boyfriend holding hands. They were laughing and talking as she waddled with her legs wrapped in ice, wrapping my heart at the same time with such a precious moment of sweet young love.

Within a few days of that precious moment, she was snatched from where she was taking root to a far off place, forever changing her landscape. Her first boyfriend would probably be her only boyfriend—lasting only one week. She would likely never finish driving lessons or be excited at the sight of her first car. She might never again choose her music or sing or dance interpretive moves that made me giggle. She would probably never finish ninth grade or compete in any more track meets.

She wouldn't move on to tenth grade or graduate high school with her friends. No more report cards. She would no longer go through the developmental phases of growing up at a similar pace as her friends. We might never have another fight. She probably wouldn't babysit or go on another youth retreat or even have a sleepover. There would likely be no more pushing of boundaries, or watching her go off to college to fulfill her dreams of becoming a pediatric physical therapist, a wife, and a mother. Life as we had all dreamed it was no more. It had been severed at the root, and all we could do was nurture what remained and pray that God would restore what had been ripped away.

CHAPTER 5

The Three Trees

Withering Life

Country living exchanged congested traffic and noise for quiet empty roads. Two acres backing up to farmland expanded our lives to open skies of blazing sunrises and sunsets, front row seats to storms rolling in, fields of daisies bouncing upward, and a milieu of animals and birds.

One step outside transported us into a kingdom of bountiful nature, seeing skunks, snakes, possums, deer, coyotes, rabbits, squirrels, owls, and more. In the pasture behind us, the bellowing cows, the gray gentle donkeys, and the bright stars at night would usher my heart to the stable of Love.

One morning sitting on the back porch, I was strangely moved by the unusual activity of birds wandering aimlessly on the ground, awakening me to the realization they needed trees. There was not one tree in our backyard.

Okay, sweet birds! Challenge accepted. I am going to plant you some trees!

Showing our goodwill and follow-through meant borrowing our neighbor's tractor and having three grown trees delivered into the deep holes waiting for roots, dirt, and water. The "trinity of trees" outside my kitchen window were planted in honor of our three children as they grew in grace and welcomed anyone who stopped by for a visit. Twenty seedlings soon followed surrounding the perimeter of our backyard, all planted to become perches and homes for the vagabond birds.

Decisions

St. Mary's Medical Center | Grand Junction, CO
April 20 – 24, 2009

Discussions of discharge planning were beginning to take place. There were more questions than answers: When would she be stable enough to transport back to Oklahoma City? What facility was equipped to manage her complex medical needs? What physician would accept her? How would we transport her back? What rehabilitation facility would be best equipped for her? What would happen to the pieces of her skull that were wrapped up, labeled, and stored in the lab freezer?

Our minds were as overloaded as our hearts with the many decisions that needed to be made. We didn't know how this was all going to work, having to enter a new healthcare system and reestablish care with many new doctors. Her fragile state without her skull deepened our concerns about her safety. Her inability to communicate or move with intention meant we could never leave her bedside.

Her eyes were open, but she didn't speak. Unable to sit or hold her head up, she required total assistance for any activities of daily living. She required low stimulation and remained in isolation for MRSA. Her doctors in Grand Junction documented her discharge diagnosis as a severe traumatic brain injury with bilateral craniectomies resulting in a mute, spastic, quadriplegia state as we continued to wrestle with the question of where she would go next.

One by one by one, with tremendous support from the hospital, each complicated decision was made. We knew home would never be the same. We knew our lives would never be the same.

The Gathering
St. Mary's Medical Center | Grand Junction, CO
April 24, 2009

A remarkable moment before we left was the impromptu gathering of all the people who had been our church, our family, and our sustainers of food and prayer who had never even seen or met Jessie. The gathering of this "sending forth" took place in the chapel of the hospital.

We placed Jessie in a wheelchair with her helmet on, all propped up and tucked in with pillows and a blanket, and traveled to "the church" where Bill pushed her down the aisle among the people who laid hands upon her as we worshiped, sang hymns, and received a blessing prayer over our family. We were given the opportunity to express our deep unending gratitude for all the "holding" and "giving" we had received from this family who had adopted us on the worst night of our lives. We knew these Good Samaritans had rendered the deepest aid possible to their brutalized neighbors they had encountered on the side of the road, offering their own denarius to help with our care.

Called Home
St. Mary's Medical Center | Grand Junction, CO
April 25, 2009

The night before we headed back to Oklahoma, I received an email with a video from Bobbie, my spiritual mother and now midwife. It was as if she knew what my heart was laboring within these very moments.

The words of her powerful prayer in the body of the email captured my attention as the anxiety of leaving this safe womb of care and being thrust into a new healthcare system in Oklahoma City was interlacing with the anticipation of being closer to home. I stood on the precipice of this moment, my heart unsure of which direction to choose.

I clicked on the attachment to find a video of Amy Grant playing the guitar and singing, "Softly and Tenderly Jesus is calling ... come home." Amy's iconic powerful voice, with the comforting chords of an instrument I love to play, and lyrics that were a timely witness sent my weary heart the affirming message: it was time to come home.

My heart shifted in a freefall toward home as my tears released with my grasp. All I knew at that moment was Jesus was calling us to come home. No longer did I cling to this sacred womb of life. Instead, I reached for the sacred womb of home that was waiting and watching for us to come home, no longer anxious about the unknowns. I knew it was time, and I knew God was with us.

Leaving the Wilderness

St. Mary's Medical Center | Grand Junction, CO
April 26, 2009

As we quietly waited for the ambulance to arrive to transport Jessie to the airport, in walked Dr. Breaux.

"I wanted to say one last goodbye and wait with you until transport comes."

His humble, quiet presence was deafening as my heart was shaking, looking for the right words to share our deepest gratitude for all he had done for Jessie and our family and how much he meant to us. As he sat down in a chair by the door, a deep silence filled the room. He would not leave until she was loaded onto the stretcher. Tears were our only communication until transport arrived. We all knew there were no words that could touch what we had all experienced together or what we were feeling.

His gentle forehead kiss to Jessie and his firm releasing hug was not a goodbye but something much deeper. It was an embrace of "Well done, Mom and Dad. Well done." My spirit, tuned to his spirit, could hear the undertones of his heart speaking, "I am so proud of you and all you have survived. Peace be with you, as it is now time to keep journeying to get our little girl back on her feet. Talitha Koum, little girl, I say arise." I felt his heart fully release us to the next chapter. This was the exact medicine we all needed to help close the door as she left the building of his heart and sacred institution of life-saving medicine forever.

As Jessie was loaded into the Eagle Med plane for transport back to Oklahoma City, I remained suspended in the fog of our goodbye. The fog quickly dissipated as I met the RN and paramedic who would be at Jessie's side the entire flight home.

Sitting in the "co-pilot" seat took me back to my days of personal private pilot experiences. Seeing the instruments and the latest GPS system, listening to the radio communication, and having "pilot conversations" was the best diversion therapy I could have been given.

Beholding the immensity of the mountain ranges flying out of Colorado from 19,000 feet after being in such a small, confined space, I found my senses overwhelmed with the vastness of space that was before me, hushed in reverence of how majestic His creation truly is.

After inquiring about Jessie's story and condition, the pilot began to share his own experience of recovering from a severe stroke and a tracheostomy several years earlier. I marveled at this pilot and his witness to God's power

Part 1: Severed at the Root

within his own life, knowing once again, God placed another miracle in our "flight" path who was now in charge of flying another one of His miracles home.

As the mountains faded, there was a slow and gentle transition into the plains. I felt a strong movement of being "ushered" home. The peace was palpable in the cabin's airspace as our precious Jessie slept the entire trip gifted with no medical issues.

When we landed in Oklahoma City, I physically felt my heart closing this chapter of the last forty days of battling for survival in the wilderness of the high deserts of Colorado, not knowing what was to come. As the door opened, I could see EMSA on the runway, waiting and watching for our arrival to transport us to Integris Baptist Pediatric ICU.

As the paramedics got her settled in the back of the ambulance, I took a big, deep breath of the Oklahoma air and gave thanks for this moment of coming home with Jessie.

Jessie, you are home. We are home. Thank You, God, for bringing us home.

As we drove away from the airport, my weary eyes were noticing the familiar landmarks of our city when two gray doves began flying alongside us, revealing the close presence of the Holy Spirit. I was awakened to the gift being given—our own personal escort. With this new chapter opening, my heart was being readied and assured, prepared to embrace what was to come next.

*"Be strong and courageous ...
for the Lord your God goes with you."*

~Joshua 1:9~

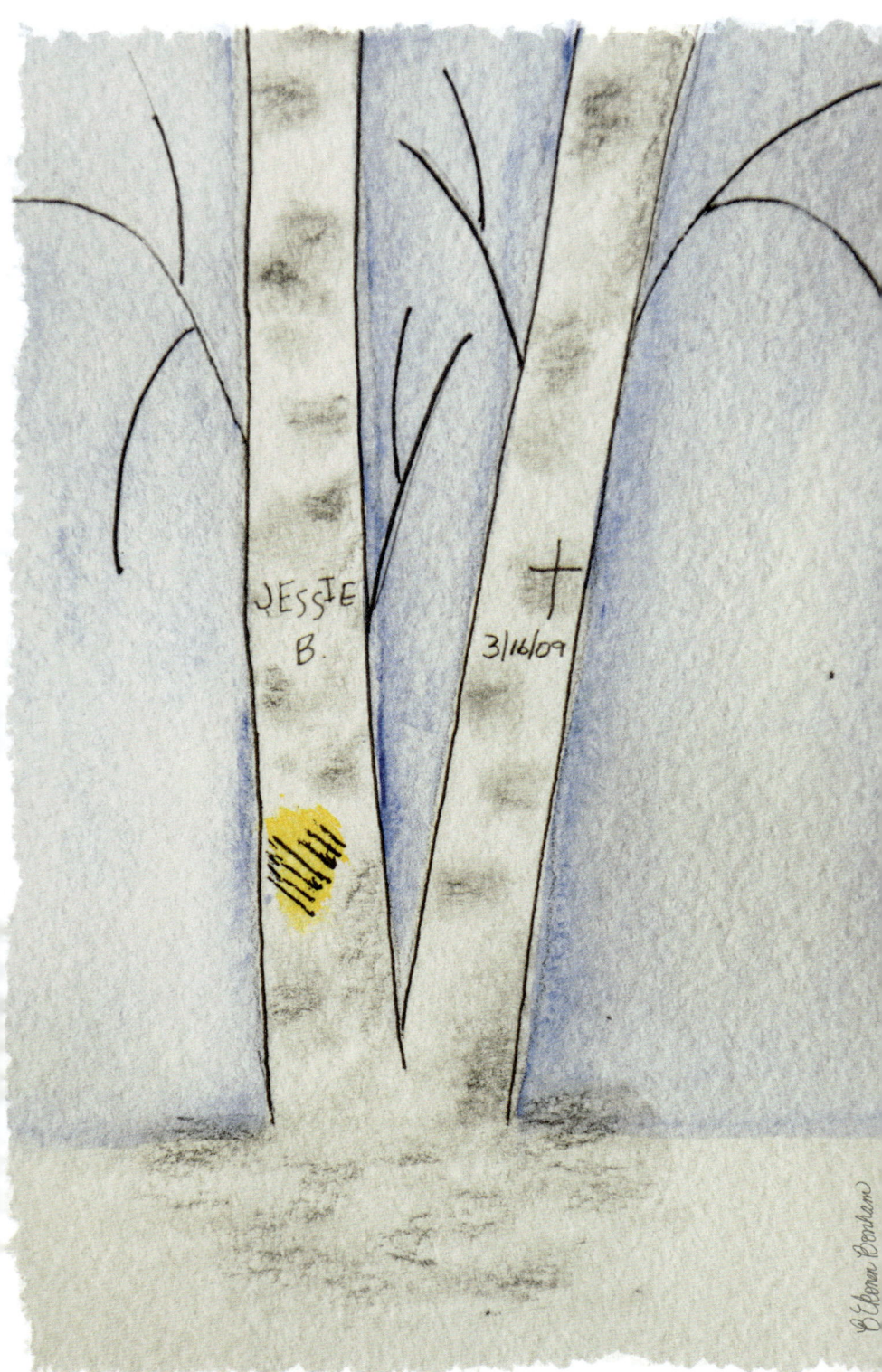

PART 2

The Remnant

—

18 Months of Intensive Rehabilitation

CHAPTER 6

The Majestic Cypress

Refrains

Tree after tree surrounds the sacred land that entombs the Benedictine sisters laid to rest. These ancient cypress trees, with their forty feet canopies, bow in reverence to the lives lived in dedication to God and others. Revered in ancient Greece as a symbol of eternal life, they are commonly seen in graveyards depicting the reverence of mourning.

These truly majestic displays of God's presence were arresting as I walked the hushed, enclosed path through the tombstone garden, my eyes transfixed, beholding their dignified postures gracefully leaning over, as if watching over His children. The power of their presence awakened me to the holy ground upon which I stood as the soft feathery evergreen foliage fragranced my soul with comfort.

Overlooking the pond on my parents' homestead, another ancient cypress tree reaches into the heavens with woody conical structures of various sizes popping up around the base. Each encounter I have with this tree surrounded by these distinctive figurine-looking "knees" invites a moment of silence to listen to these ancestral-appearing old souls that have gone before us, for the vibrations and echoes of the love being carried forward on the winds of time as they continue to keep watch over our lives upon this earth.

Stable and Seen
Integris Baptist Pediatric ICU | Oklahoma City, OK
April 2009

Arriving at Integris Baptist ER stirred strange familiarities as I stepped out of the back of the ambulance into the parking lot of my employer, not as an employee but as a shattered mom. As I inhaled a deep breath of home, I was flooded with emotions of the extensive support we had already received from Integris. My director had been with us every step of the way helping with the insurance paperwork, researching and coordinating air transport home, and completing paperwork for extended time off. Every detail was handled with such compassion and support.

As I supervised the ambulance crew unloading my precious cargo, the bright sunlight of the day immediately provoked distress about others peering at her grotesque disfiguredness. My face flushed with anxiety and grief as the raw truth was being revealed to my outside world. Any gratitude for being "home" was quickly buried under a mountain of ugly emotions.

Jessie was directly admitted for further stabilization until her rehab transfer could be safely coordinated. Enroute to the PICU, I saw an old friend whom I hadn't seen in years. Our eyes met in recognition as we passed, and I remembered the last time I saw her was when she had spoken at a women's conference. Reflecting on her powerful witness about waiting on the Lord in trying times, my heart began to pound with the hope that perhaps I could connect with her and ask for prayer for Jessie.

It wasn't long before she appeared in Jessie's room to say hello and to find out why we were there. After an emotional, truth-filled update, she seemed undaunted by Jessie's appearance, reaching out to hug me.

"Sister, it's not by chance we bumped into each other."

I nodded, knowing this divine encounter was for this moment of mighty heart chaos.

She proceeded to share a story of a miracle she had recently witnessed with a patient and then voiced her promptings to pray, as she believed God was ready to do more for Jessie Boone. She placed her hands on Jessie's body and began storming the heavens with her powerful commanding voice of love and faith for healing. I felt my soul trying to settle into the comfort of the newly-revealed sanctuary of hope.

Being in this new place with new staff proved difficult for me on our first morning. The morning RN came in without introducing herself or acknowledging Jessie. She just started "doing" tasks to Jessie as if she wasn't there.

My "nurse knowing better" rose up alongside the grief storm of anger that she had awakened and went to her bedside.

"Hello, my name is Lisa, and this is my daughter, Jessie. And who are you?"

Nursing 101, lady. Introduce yourself and acknowledge the patient in the bed.

She looked at me uncomfortably and said, "I am so sorry."

I felt my heart lurch downward as I quickly judged the routine. Reading her history, hearing report, and seeing her current appearance made it easy to assume there wasn't much there. I felt myself reaching for God again as my pain erupted at the way Jessie appeared. Tears flowed as I watched this young nurse go about her routine, never speaking to her once. I didn't confess my truth at that moment, but I did resolve I would never let that happen again. And I didn't.

As I shrank into the corner of grief, gripped in silent anger and wanting to stomp and scream and throw arrows of, "Can't you see her? Hey, lady! She's right here! What is wrong with you?" in walked the pediatric intensivist, Dr. Banner.

He greeted us with an introduction, a smile, and a warm handshake as if he had known us for years. Then he turned to Jessie, touched her foot and said, "Well, hello you, how did you sleep?"

Her looks and lack of response didn't faze him. I could feel my anger releasing, escaping through the cracks of my grief as he disarmed my weapons of anger.

"You aren't going to believe this ... " He began to tell the story of how he was talking to his pediatric doctor friend in Tulsa on his way to work. When he told him he was going to the hospital to see a young girl who had been in a skiing accident in Colorado, his friend had asked, "Is it Jessie Boone?"

Surprised, he had answered, "Yes, as a matter of fact it is," and began to hear more about her story since his friend happened to be the uncle of Jessie's brother, Justin.

Just as quickly as I had been cornered in angry grief, I was redirected right back into the center of His Light, being reminded again of God's intimate presence within all circumstances.

He sees her. He loves her. He knows her. And He has placed her in the hearts and prayers of so many.

A few minutes later another curtain parted as this beam of sunshine of a PT walked in and introduced herself.

"Good morning," she said as she turned to me, "you must be Mom, and this must be Jessie."

The Majestic Cypress

Relief that she "saw" her enabled an expiratory smile and the gentle words, "You guessed right." Her warmness encircled my aching heart.

"Jessie, I know you better than you think I do because my son had a terrible car accident and had a traumatic brain injury too. They told me he wasn't going to make it. And guess what? He is getting ready to mow our yard this morning." She moved with ease at her bedside.

Rivers of comfort and hope flooded my soul.

Mowing your yard? Really? And you are here telling me this right now? Who are you?

I knew God knew I needed someone in flesh to "shore me up" and reorient my heart, as if to say, "Lisa, remember Me? I am here. Look at Me, not at the world. LOOK AT ME."

I watched the young nurse's countenance change before my eyes as she witnessed this masterful PT with personal experience of a brain injured child interacting with Jessie. Just these few moments of impromptu mentoring changed the young nurse's approach to Jessie. From that moment on, each time she entered our room, she heralded acknowledgments of "Hey, girl, how is it going in here?" or, "Hi, Jessie, just coming by to check on you and to see if you needed anything?" I couldn't believe the difference it made within my own spirit, and I believe within Jessie's by the simple acknowledgment that she was there.

During the night shift, I became keenly aware of the attentive male nurse who was assigned to Jessie. During one of his rounding moments, he shared that he had chosen to work in the field of pediatrics because his little brother had died after years of struggling with a birth defect.

He knows deep and complicated grief.

His awakened heart, wounded by his own deep loss, connected spontaneously to our deep woundedness. His gentle words, framing his posture of kindness, provided a profound comforting presence at our bedside.

Ready for Rehab
Integris Baptist Pediatric ICU | Oklahoma City, OK
April 2009

Preparations were being made for the radical move to a different place in hopes of what could come for Jessie's recovery. Her need for intensive care was over and it was time to move her to a new focus of care—rehabilitation.

Having to navigate the decision of a rehab facility from another state had unearthed different challenges for me with the details of her age, the severity of her injury, the extent of her medical needs, insurance approval, finding staff with brain injury experience, and room availability, all intertwining with the complexity of her crucial outcome. Yet I believed the complexity and challenges were continuing to be undergirded by the truth spoken within the promises of Isaiah 40:11 (NIV), "He gathers the lambs in His arms and carries them close to His heart, He gently leads those who have young," a scripture that had been a foundational bedrock of my heart for the last several years.

The heavens outside began thundering with activity on our last night before we were officially transferred to rehab. At some point, a Code Black (emergency protocol for weather danger) was announced throughout the hospital, alerting staff and visitors to be prepared for a radical move to a different place for what might be coming. In a strange way, this disruptive event seemed to foretell the very movements happening within the walls of our lives.

Obstacles and Openings
Acute Rehab | Oklahoma City, OK
April/May 2009

Jessie's age, along with the extraordinary, individualized care she received in Grand Junction from her pediatric trauma surgeon influenced our decision to go to an acute rehabilitation hospital in Oklahoma City. After receiving recommendations and insurance approval for the out of network specialized unit, we were transferred to our new temporary home.

Her room number—4011—was the first welcome mat. Emotions of gratitude and relief were magnified as we crossed the threshold stamped with the stones of my faith. The 40 days and nights' significance was emphasized as we had just survived the wilderness, and those simple integers—11—announced His omnipresence with us, with the gentle guiding light of Isaiah 40:11 (NIV) bidding my heart to speak the blessing that lived within these walls of healing.

May this room, Father, hold Jessie the way You hold each of us. Would You especially tend her, gather her, carry her close to Your heart, and gently lead all here as they care for Your young and bring forth healing in this very room.

Our "first big obstacle" was the unexpected announcement, "Only one parent can stay in the room with the child at night."

Bill and I hadn't been apart since the accident. We looked at each other in disbelief. Immediately, we objected and explained the unique circumstances. There was no way either one of us would be able to leave and we knew it. The evening nurse looked the other way the first night, but we were "educated thoroughly" the next day about this hard boundary and how this was for the good of the parents, ensuring one would get the needed rest for this difficult time.

We immediately felt trapped and controlled by something unnecessary when the rest of our lives were trapped and controlled by what was necessary. Without a choice, Bill reluctantly left alone in the dark to return to the emptiness of our home.

It was brutal on us both. Our emotional comfort and strength that we found together at night was ripped out of our arms.

One morning, I saw him standing outside our window hanging a basket of flowers on a shepherd's hook. He waved and put his hand on his heart. Tears flowed freely at the sight of love in flesh. He later shared he wanted those flowers to be a visual reminder of his closeness with us when he wasn't there. It was such a loving gesture but fell cruelly short of his warm skin and his smell of home.

Rehab moved in full force the next day, seeing OT and PT twice. She spent time with Speech, Education, and Respiratory as a reduction of trach size was being done in preparation for the hopeful removal of her trach tube, with Dietary and Psychology finding tiny windows of time to complete their in-depth evaluations. The pediatric physiatrist and nurse practitioner introduced themselves later in the day to review her history and plan of care.

Our difficult day was unexpectedly brightened when my mom came to see us for the first time since the accident. She brought her two new, tiny Yorkies for some personalized pet therapy. The pause in the day with her loving presence was heart medicine for me. I could feel the comfort steeping my soul. As for Jessie, she was utterly wiped out by the flurry of the day's activity and slept well into the evening.

The young evening aide announced it was time for her bath. She explained bathing was done in the evenings as there wasn't time during the day because of the therapies. I looked at Jessie's pale, empty, and exhausted countenance. She was sleeping like an angel under a quilt of hearts made with love and prayers from the hearts of precious ladies from Grand Junction. It was a comforting beautiful sight to "see" her covered in prayers and resting.

Inviting the aide to "see" her, I said, "Look at her. She's exhausted and I don't think bathing her would be in her best interest now. I will sponge her off in the morning when I dress her." She nodded her head in agreement while jotting something in her chart and left.

The "second obstacle" quickly appeared as I began to "dress" her room with comfort and strength in the form of her posters, scriptures, cards, and photos. We were instructed to take them down, as nothing could be on the walls so as not to ruin the paint. I felt "stripped" of the home environment we had created at Grand Junction with the accumulation of all the love and support that had been sent to us. It took extra energy and effort, but with the help of my dot-n-law, we found creative ways to display a few of her special mementos of love.

Receiving a huge poster from Jessie's boyfriend and signed by all her track team was another heart booster. In big bold letters, it read, "WE RUN 4 JESSIE! KEEP YOUR HEAD UP!" They had no idea those very words were our constant mantra to Jessie. Her inability to hold her head up along with the continuous drooling from her mouth revealed the infancy of her recovery and the depth of our loss.

We knew those words were also meant for us, as our heads had been hanging as low as hers. We were missing

Part 2: The Remnant

her personhood so much. Being "home" had brought a more intense pain, if that was even possible, missing our lives within the frame of familiar surroundings.

Jessie had become less responsive since her arrival, and the therapists were struggling with her inability to give them any reaction or movement. Overstimulation with exhaustion seemed to be overwhelming what tender little brain function she had.

An unexpected opening of resources appeared through a phone call from a concerned RN friend employed by the Oklahoma Health Care Authority. She had been reading Jessie's Carepages and felt prompted to call. She informed us of possible resources available through the state for Jessie due to her devastating injuries and being hospitalized for over thirty days. I would have never known about this type of support had she not reached out to us. It was through her experience and knowledge we were able to apply and get approved for this secondary coverage of insurance to help with the exorbitant medical expenses through the SoonerCare program.

An overload of information regarding outside appointments requiring medical transport was the "third obstacle." I was overwhelmed with the thought of putting her through transport to "see" a doctor in his clinic or obtain ordered medical testing, resulting in a loss of precious paid rehab time and having to navigate the regular world with our fragile, minimally-responsive daughter. It seemed unsafe and not the optimal way to provide care for her.

Issues continued as downsizing her trach tube and replacing her gastrostomy tube became an unwanted source of painful stimulation, causing her face to reveal agony. Her inability to communicate required scrupulous attention to her body which seemed to attempt communication through weary eyes, soiled diapers, an occasional grimacing of her face, and this newly-appearing increasing muscle tone or spasticity being caused by the disrupted signals of her brain.

Sitting at the round table in the rehab conference room, we had our first family conference, providing the opportunity for each team member to share their evaluations and goals for Jessie. It was brutal to hear "all of her" at the same time. My chair endured the load of heaviness that I felt steadily increasing as each person spoke their baseline assessments. Somehow hearing it spoken would no longer allow the coping skill of compartmentalizing her severe deficits to soften the blows. It was all laid on the table as the feast of grief consumed me.

I took the opportunity to openly share some of the immediate obstacles we had encountered, which caused more emotional pain, as well as our concerns of whether we were in the right place—how these difficult boundaries left us feeling unsupported within our own family and our community of love.

We also took the opportunity to request scheduled quiet time for her, her only hour of rest during the day was frequently interrupted by more "interventions," reminding the team how brain injuries require frequent rest periods and extended sleep.

During one of her newly-scheduled rest periods, I escaped outside to find some temporary relief. I found creation medicine within the fresh air, the soft cooing music of the doves, walking barefoot on the freshly cut green grass, reaching down to touch the fresh bloom of a flower offering its gifts freely to whomever walked by, all being overlaid by the expansive blue sky of creation and the warm light of the sun. For a moment, I had encountered a liminal space which brought Julian of Norwich's pondering words of assurance for my heart to bathe in, "But all will be well, and all will be well, and every kind of thing will be well," helping me to ground my heart in the midst of our painful dark night of the soul.

Sentiments of belief and hope wrapped in generous love would frequently arrive through the mail. I had been waiting for Jessie to be alert enough to open her packages, but those moments seemed to be slipping further away. I decided to bravely forge forward in the belief she would "know."

Opening these packages created sacred spaces of shared provision. I was taken aback by the depth of faith buried within the small package sent by a young friend. Enclosed was a letter, a picture, and a necklace. She wrote, "Jessie, as I was searching for the perfect picture to add to the story of St. John Licci's, God sent me this one. I imagined the beautiful dark-haired woman as your mama, and the precious blonde child with the bandage on her head as you. I am constantly praying for you."

Someone had written about St. John Licci, the patron saint of head injuries, earlier in one of the Carepage postings. He was one of the longest living holy men of the Church. He lived to be "111" years old and was known for great healing miracles, especially for the three people whose heads had been crushed in accidents.

The picture she had included was of a dark-haired woman holding a blonde-headed child, limp in her arms, with a bandage on her head. Jesus had His outstretched hand placed on the child's head. The mom was looking up at Jesus, and He was looking at the child.

The Majestic Cypress

This powerful icon branded my soul as it became us, reorienting my gaze, knowing His watchful eye and healing hand was upon her ... upon us.

My heart is flooded with hope. Thank You for this visual of reality before me and bless you, sweet girl, who went to great effort to share with us.

Underneath the picture, I found a St. John Licci medal engraved with his image. I held it against my heart for several minutes, closing my eyes, imagining his holy presence within our room, asking this dear saint to pray for my daughter. It soon found its home dangling above her holy bed of hope.

That night the storms came, pouring down rain from heaven and within my heart. Flooding tears of grief were gushing out of my hurting soul. Lying in a folded-out bed chair, alone in the darkness of my grief, next to this shell of my child, I began to hear something different.

Part 2: The Remnant

Am I hearing soft soothing rhythms of music?
I raised my head to see where it was coming from. My heart quieted as I soon discovered this ethereal music was not coming from a physical dimension but instead arising out of the fissures deep within my spirit.

Thank You, God, for this comforting song from Your heart, holding me and comforting my broken spirit and heart.

Sunday was simply sabbatical, being our day of rest from the outside and giving her a spaciousness of time to awaken and respond. With her favorite playlist bringing the familiar vibrations of worship, we began to gently stimulate her by whispering, "It's time to get ready for church." Sluggishly she began to engage a bit, attempting to reach her arm into her shirt and even lift her leg a few inches for a sock. After getting her dressed and transferred into a wheelchair, we circled around the computer as she looked to be trying to focus on the screen displaying our community gathered in the worship service.

Later in the day, we crawled up into bed with her and watched the movie "Marley and Me," a sweet movie about a family with a "clearance" puppy, emphasizing the highlights to her, hoping to find any kind of response or connection. Bill and I cried bucketloads of tears when Marley went to heaven, giving our hearts a much needed sabbatical from the stoic states we held during these brutal days of recovery.

Anxiety and discomfort had become frequent visitors to my heart. It was difficult to discern what was from her condition and what was coming from our surroundings. All I knew was this unease was mounting. And one night, it reached a pinnacle, a red flag alert to my soul.

Her evening bath routine was going to be different. The aide suggested a warm shower instead of the traditional bed bath, and I jumped at the opportunity after weeks of bed baths. I went to gather her night gown and toiletries, assuming she would be transferred to a shower chair, but instead I found her laid out naked on a towel-covered metal table with sides as they were hosing her down like a piece of meat.

I couldn't find my words to stop what was happening. Glaring cruelly at me was her exposed quiet vulnerability, and the disregarding of the modesty and privacy of my fifteen-year-old daughter, who would have yelled at me to close the door and get out only a few months ago.

I was sickened at the sight and knew this would not happen again. In all my years of nursing, I had never witnessed this type of dehumanizing shower. My heart was splattered all over the floor.

This "fourth obstacle" was another harsh visual, refusing to leave my consciousness, which only furthered my unsettledness.

Every morning, we would be visited by this kind, quiet soul. Her non-intrusive presence was comforting as she emptied the trash and mopped the floors. We had exchanged simple pleasantries with a nodding smile but never had a conversation. Then, one day, it was different.

She slowed her pace and came toward me, "May I tell you something?" She seemed to be aware of my protective state.

I smiled at her warm inquiry and replied, "Of course."

She stepped closer to Jessie's bed and took the bedrail into her hand, "I would like you to know I have been praying for your daughter, Jessie."

Jessie. She called her by her name.

My heart was hugged by this angelic visitor.

Her humble ministry with full access to all those who are in such need was suddenly brought to light, echoing the vibrations of Mother Teresa, whose whole life and labor bore witness to the joy of loving the greatness and dignity of every human person, doing all the little things with such great love.

I felt I was in the presence of greatness as she served the least. Hugging her simple gray scrub covered body, I pressed close as I wanted her to receive the gratitude from my heart instead of my words.

I felt a merging of our spirits as she whispered, "You know God says whatever you ask for in prayer, believe and you have received it."

I nodded.

She pulled away, locking her piercing brown eyes with mine, grasped my hand and bore in even deeper, "Believe it and you have received it."

I took a step back as I felt those sacred words re-engaging my tired spirit.

Her gaze never wavered as she continued, "I believe one day you will have great joy with your daughter."

My body tingled as my tears joined us in receiving her spoken words that I believed were coming from another realm.

Joy with my daughter, one day? Oh Lord, is it really possible? Help me to believe and receive what has been professed so clearly.

Being fully present to the prophetic prayers of this small-framed, large-faith-filled presence who spoke with authority, I began to allow myself to wonder what joy with Jessie might look like.

Reading the Carepages that evening, I came across a posting that resonated with the inner movements of the restlessness and anxiousness I had been feeling over the last several days, wondering if we needed to make a change. It would be a huge change, one I didn't know how or if it could be orchestrated, but the earlier encounter with the housekeeper had changed everything as my heart was still whispering, "Believe it and you have received it."

> ## Carepage Posting
>
> Sometimes in my life when I am uneasy it is because of a big decision that I need to make and until I make that decision, I have no peace. I believe God uses peace and unrest to move us on His path, whether it is a new job, new home, new business venture, or whatever situation we find ourselves struggling with.
>
> Joyce Meyer tells the story about baby eagles that goes something like this. When it is time for baby eagles to leave the nest, the mama eagle begins to take out the feathers and soft grass one by one making the nest harder and harder to sit on. When the nest is down to just thorny sticks, the little eagle can no longer sit in the nest because of the discomfort so they literally throw themselves out of the nest dropping hundreds of feet … nearly to their death before suddenly taking off flying or soaring really. Joyce likens the eagles to humans in that sometimes, not always, God has to make us very uncomfortable about our situation before we will do anything different. Then because we get so anxious or uncomfortable in a situation, we will seek God's face for answers and suddenly take off in the direction He has designed for us all along.
>
> I don't know if that is for you in this situation, but I have felt that it might be. When we are anxious it just may be God telling us it's time to make a change. Let the peace of God rule your hearts and mind.

It was like a doorway had opened for the next right step. After tearful discussions with Bill and extended conversations with God, we made the big decision to change rehabs.

The new facility was wonderful and caring but not meeting our specific needs of seasoned experienced therapists in brain injury rehabilitation and a more conducive environment for our family's non-negotiable needs.

I called my friend, Dr. Shawn Smith, who was a physiatrist with Jim Thorpe Rehab. He agreed to meet with me and have the conversation I was ready to have. Our discussion was open and in-depth as we discussed the details of Jessie's condition with the challenges and concerns of our current status. He talked at length about his experienced brain injury team, assuring me her young age wouldn't be an obstacle to receiving the very best rehabilitation medicine in Oklahoma and accepted her as his patient if all the arrangements could be worked out.

Our next right step was to have a conference with her current pediatric physiatrist, fully disclosing our hearts with him, especially in regards to our personal obstacles and the lack of experience this new team had with brain injuries. It was important for him to know we believed this facility was on its way to becoming an outstanding rehab unit but needed more time to develop and gain more experienced staff in the acute care rehab of traumatic brain injuries. He supported the change in our direction and even prayed a blessing over our family as he began to make arrangements for discharge.

Sweet Reprieve

Jim Thorpe Rehab | Oklahoma City, OK
May 2009

The move to Jim Thorpe Rehab was swift and seamless. Our first encounter upon arrival was a young male nurse, who helped transfer and get Jessie positioned in the bed.

Ugh, not a male nurse on admission.

I could feel my protective mom of a brain injured teenage girl anticipating the full skin assessment which I felt was brutally embarrassing to Jessie if she was aware of anything.

But discernment overruled that instinct, guiding me to surrender into what was being given. My heart struggled to settle as I breathed deep breaths, attempting to relax my tense, exhausted, overstimulated body and mind.

"Hey, Jessie, we're so glad you're here." He introduced himself before turning to the large white communication board hanging by her bed and writing specific information as he asked questions about her and our family.

He is speaking to her by name!

When her fuchsia pink band bracelet around her arm caught his eye, he paused his interview for a moment.

"Jessie, tell me about your bracelet!" His tone was one of excitement like one of her close friends. "Look, I have a bracelet too!" He raised his wrist close to her face.

Oh my gosh! Are you kidding me!? How special is he?

I could feel my entire body relaxing into a more normal posture.

His endearing presence confirmed our decision for transfer within a few minutes of arriving, but what happened next cemented it in stone.

"Her friends from her church had hundreds of them made to show their love and support. It reads, 'We love you, Jessie' on one side and 'Philippians 4:13' (New King James Version) on the other."

"What's that?" he asked.

"Her favorite bible verse, 'I can do all things through Christ who gives me strength.'"

Part 2: The Remnant

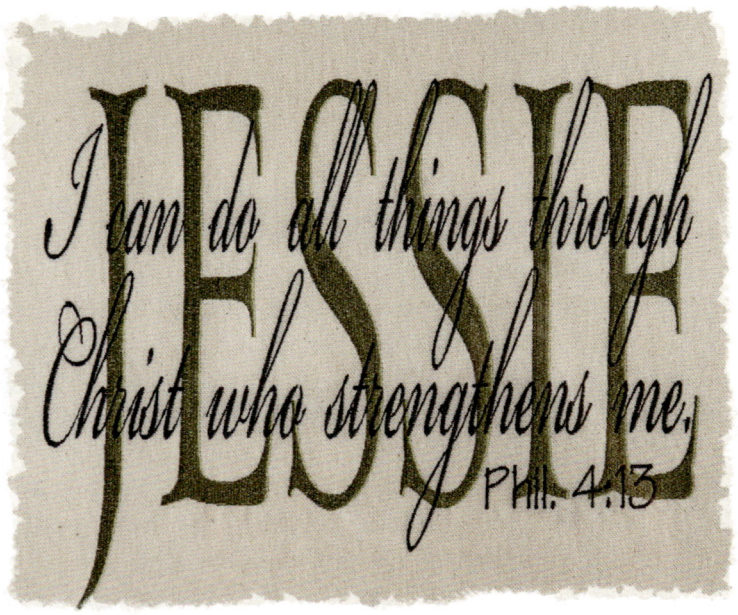

With his blue marker, he reached high to the top of the communication board as if he were reaching for the heavens and wrote her heart's words across the top. He turned and looked directly at Jessie, lifted his hand, and professed, "Praise Jesus, I feel His Spirit in this room." He then boldly called us to agree with him on Jessie's healing in the name of Jesus, and we did exactly that as he recited the ancient words of Isaiah 53:5 (NKJV), "And by His stripes she is healed."

My head reeled as my feet were grounded again into this new landscape of hope with this unexpected young man's anointed welcome and his proclamation of healing. We quickly settled into our new home, and all of us were welcomed as we were "both" tucked in the bedside chair beside Jessie for our first night.

Together again.

Helpers
Jim Thorpe Rehab | Oklahoma City, OK
May 2009

The medical director who had been with Jim Thorpe Rehab for twenty-five years came to our room on our first morning. I relaxed at the sound of his gentle voice as he introduced himself and settled comfortably into a chair at her bedside. His relaxed posture communicated he was in no hurry as he began the conversation.

He wanted to know who Jessie Boone was, and his exploratory questions were settling and appreciated as he even surveyed how we were doing as her parents. He listened intentionally as Bill and I shared our victories and our defeats along with our grief and our hopes, making it a profound moment of deep connection as he witnessed our story.

When our story had been told, he explained in detail what we could expect.

"Rehab is different from any other type of specialty. You will have a team of doctors, PAs, nurses, therapists, and other members coming together with you—the family—focused on overcoming her deficits and helping her regain as much independence as possible. We will help you to identify the many possibilities of her recovery and resources to help you live within the new reality of your lives. Our exceptional team will go beyond all methods and means of striving to get her back on her feet."

My ears were ringing with that proclamation!

Get her back on her feet! We need all the help we can get and we're ready for this team to get started. And yes! Going beyond all methods and means to help Jessie. These words are music to my soul!

My entire body was shaking with affirmation and hope.

His voice softened as he began to share about his own personal experience with his nineteen-year-old daughter who had a massive brain hemorrhage but didn't survive.

"I know how difficult it is to receive the tragic news of a loved one. So I want you to know I have dedicated my life to creating the best team in the best rehab unit to help overcome the greatest deficits, to help people walk and talk again, and regain as much as they can."

Oh my goodness, who is this man? My gosh! He gets us. He knows exactly what we are processing in the midst of searching for the best help available for her. Thank You, God, for this man and for helping us get here.

As he was leaving, he concluded with, "I also want you to hear me on this. Her type of brain injury will not be a sprint but a very long marathon. Patience is your most important tool. You cannot rush the brain. It must heal before it works, and brain healing takes a long time. The brain also needs lots of rest for healing."

We nodded our heads as we attempted to embrace and understand all he had just said. Those words felt familiar yet hopeful and fit so easily within our empty spaces. With hugs and tears, we genuinely thanked him for creating this place to help us. We were at a complete loss of words as I searched Jessie for any signs of a response to all that had been said. Gazing upon her stillness, all I could think was how thankful we were to still be in the race.

We met her team throughout the day. Her speech pathologist was tall and beautiful, filled with grace and experience as she brought detailed information on brain injuries and told us what we could expect from her. The PA was informative and thorough in her evaluation and admission, coordinating all of her medications and medical needs. Her occupational therapist placed her hands upon her as if she were getting personally acquainted with her muscles and joints. She casually asked Jessie to reach out and touch her hand, then touch her nose, and we were astounded as we watched Jessie attempt to follow her directions.

Patience is my most important tool and you must not rush the brain. It needs time to heal, was the mantra that I kept repeating in my head as I began to slow down my unspoken expectations and hope for a quick return home.

Clarity appeared and showed me what I needed to do as I settled into the rehab rhythm of slow and steady wins the race. I quickly became aware of the moments of my impatience and began intentionally developing the muscle of patience. My morning workout for patience included using her therapy time for moments of quiet devotion for me outside the four walls. Another patience builder included adorning her room with her pictures and scriptures, creating a sanctuary of hope filled with the light and love of others once again.

Before PT appeared, Jessie was transported on a carrier to radiology (just down the hall) for pelvis x-rays. An orthopedic doctor came to her room to evaluate her weight-bearing status due to her previous pelvic fracture from the accident.

Obstacles seemed to be falling away as the moment finally came, gaining full weight-bearing status.

The larger than life physical therapist entered her room with a smile and a goal, "Are you ready to stand up, Miss?"

"Wait! What? How is that even possible? She can't even hold her head up," I spoke out, unknowingly voicing limitations to a team that only saw possibilities.

His kind, knowing smile said, "Well, no worries there." His assistant appeared and held her head up as his large masterful hands gently commanded her in an upright fully weight-bearing stance.

For the first time in months, face-to-face, I looked Jessie in the eyes.

"Want to give your mom a hug, Jessie?"

What!?

I stood speechless beholding this moment with all I had. I stepped forward and gave her the most love-filled, proud mom moment hug I had ever given her, wondering if she was feeling the hope I was seeing with my own eyes.

Dr. Smith was extraordinary in his knowledge and experience, educating us on her current clinical picture and his short- and long-term goals for her. His confident professional posture was like a rudder on a ship, steadily guiding my heart through the unknowns of the stormy waters. He wore compassion and kindness like his white lab coat, covering our hearts and bodies with a quiet assuredness of his presence. His compassionate listening, framed within his wisdom, was the powerful medicine of support we needed for our family—knowing he truly had us.

One afternoon, he appeared unexpectedly, wanting us to meet someone special. Within moments, a male nurse aide walked in, warmly greeted us, and shared his personal story of his severe TBI and his journey to recovery. It was astounding as he shared many of the struggles he had overcome right here on this very floor that he was now working on, helping others find their way through the rough times of recovery. He excitedly shared his next goal was to finish nursing school.

As his scars from his single craniotomy were peeking through his shaved head, his story of miraculous recovery held my attention as I marveled at his communication and executive abilities to work within the challenges of providing healthcare to others.
All things are possible indeed.

Hope
Jim Thorpe Rehab | Oklahoma City, OK
May 2009

Our evening nurse quietly introduced herself, "Lisa, do you remember me? You used to be my nurse manager at Bone and Joint Hospital."

"I do remember you, and can I just tell you how thankful I am that you are taking care of us this evening? I feel like an old friend just showed up to help us." I hugged her neck as my mind recaptured memories of what a caring, kind nurse she was.

Each time I encountered someone from my past healthcare management experiences, I would have this moment where I held my breath, reaching back through the years trying to remember them and hoping I had always been kind and supportive. I hoped their experience with me had left them feeling supported and cared for, as my own woundedness was exposing my vulnerability and profound need for others to care for us.

Breathing seemed easier that night as I experienced a moment of peace, feeling like we were in the right place. An oversized picture window overlooked the beautiful gardens below with this open big sky, giving me a higher perspective with unlimited possibilities, thinking about all we had been given up to this point.

We have this new place of hope, brothers and sisters who are praying without ceasing, and more time with Jessie. We have a long journey ahead of us. We have guides and caring companions. We have nourishment with morning breakfasts and evening meals being delivered to our room by a loving community of support. We have unexpected provisions that just appear when we don't know how we will take another step and are always being given what we need to help carry us to the next moment. Our gratitude seems to overwhelm the grief, helping to level our path of intensity, enabling us to move through our days with a little more ease at times, even finding bits of joy scattered throughout.

Mother's Day Communion

Jim Thorpe Rehab | Oklahoma City, OK
May 2009

During the ICU days in Grand Junction, we had Jessie anointed by oil and prayed over as we hoped for survival. Day by day, we had been called to fervent prayer, praying over her therapy sessions, her feedings, her vomiting, her spasms, her medications, her bowel and bladder training, her ability to speak and move, for her joints to remain soft and supple and her liver enzymes to normalize, and for her brain to heal.

As we continued in hopes of healing, on Mother's Day, we asked the elders of our church to come and anoint her with oil and pray over her.

Prayers were uttered in faith that she would be made well as spoken in James 5:14 (BSB); "Is any one of you sick? He should call the elders of the church to pray over him and anoint him with oil in the name of the Lord."

As we circled around her bed, the elders of our church joined our hands and hearts, witnessing the anointing oil marked in a cross upon her wounded head as the holy words of scripture were spoken and held in the hope of healing.

Holy communion had been blessed, and each of us shared the bread and cup in remembrance of His Life given so that we too might have life everlasting.

As it came to Jessie, she opened her precious mouth and received a tiny piece of bread that had been dipped in the juice, resembling a baby bird receiving what was given to sustain and nourish her.

My heart was full of gratitude as His presence was revealed in the breaking of the bread and the prayers over our beloved child being lifted up by our friends to the One who heals.

Gardens of Grace

Jim Thorpe Rehab | Oklahoma City, OK
May 2009

The generous picture window from our second-floor room overlooked the prayer gardens sprinkled with breathtaking life and beauty, deeply inspired by the pain and suffering of others. The sprinkles were the tangible hope of healing and peace to those who find themselves sojourning upon the hallowed ground. Many of the trees and benches were marked with bronze, etching memories of souls who had gone before us. This sacred outdoor sanctuary held us for months, with the communion of saints breathing life and wisdom into our weary souls.

Walks through the gardens during Jessie's therapy sessions illuminated life for me. Watching a mother bird feeding her baby bird high in the nest of the cypress tree rebounded my heart to the day when my "baby bird" Jessie was given Holy Communion by elders, receiving the gift of life from another.

The compelling metal sculptures invited one to sit and reflect. One sculpture had two pieces of tall dark rectangular metal, one piece taller bending over, the smaller piece leaning into the taller one. The inscription read, "The Healing Love of a Mother and a Daughter." What a profound visual to gaze upon seeing "the more" in the bending and the leaning. It was Mother's Day and the very "card" I needed as I felt her leaning as a gift of healing to me. A gift I needed at that moment.

Just a few steps away, metal was erupting from the ground with such power. I stepped back to absorb the impact of the numerous rectangular pieces of all different shapes and sizes. This one was inscribed "The Healing Love of a Family." As I closed my eyes, countless families came rushing in. Families of all different shapes and sizes. My immediate family and the families on the ski trip and in the hospitals, the churches, as well as our neighbors and communities of the Carepages. All these families were pouring healing love over us.

Standing on the arched bridge of wood, questions began to slowly float down the stream below: How does a heart receive and hold such an immenseness of love? What happens to the love being offered with generosity and kindness? When received, does it transform into courage and strength for each step? Could it silently knit together the brokenness hidden under the skin and bones of people? Or perhaps it could become a transfiguration into hope, so mysteries of grace might be uncovered within the sufferings of others? What if that healing love is sticky and holds us together when everything on earth is trying to violently pull us apart into pieces? Or what if each healing

The Majestic Cypress

hand of love comes together in all different colors and forms a beautiful bird with outstretched wings, carrying the one who can no longer fly, where together they can soar above the confined view for a different perspective on the wind of love and hope? The ways of love are infinite and overwhelming.

The benches of the gardens seem to whisper the hallmark of hospitality, begging one to come and sit for a while, elevating one to a meditative space of calling one to "Be Still and Know I Am God."

Sitting on one of those very benches one morning, my eyes were drawn to the Occupational Therapist (gardener) tending the strawberry beds. The boxes were growing healthy, large plants, and she knelt before the soil as if giving thanks for the life of the plants bountifully loaded with unripe fruit. Unexpectedly, she began removing life from its comfortable home and tossing it away. As she worked, she explained to the gray-haired witness in a wheelchair that this "thinning out" was needed to make room for their fruit to grow bigger.

I held her words uncomfortably, reflecting how our lives had been full, beautiful, healthy, and growing with much fruit.

Now some of the most beautiful parts of our lives have been thinned out, tossed out. Could this be a message of hope for us? What if this new space we find ourselves within is being used to help our fruit grow bigger? Our fruit being the Fruit of the Spirit, increasing the size of our love, joy, peace, patience, kindness, goodness, faithfulness, and gentleness. What if?

These tended gardens furnished the outdoor sanctuary needed to provide light revealing moments in the midst of the dark tomb she was buried in.

Finishing therapy for the day was frequently celebrated by rolling Jessie's wheelchair to rest under the shade of the ancient cypress tree that towered over thirty feet tall. Gentle breezes danced through her graceful boughs, bringing refreshing comfort. Sitting under this giant, Jessie felt the wind on her face, heard the sounds of the birds, and warmed her body in the sunlight.

And I believed creation medicine was changing things.

The shade, partnered with the breeze, transformed the suffocating moments of non-movement into movements of breath and life. The "heat" was no longer unbearable. Sweet gifts would adorn moments, like a dove cooing a peace lullaby, as she slept under the healing canopy of God's comfort, painting an outdoor portrait of Psalm 91:4 (NIV), "He will cover you with His feathers, and under His wings you will find refuge." My heart brimmed with gratitude for God's graceful arms covering us, giving us new ways of seeing things, and holding us within a womb of safety, shielding harshness for a brief moment in time.

He sees us. He hears us. He knows us. He holds us.

Renewing grace found me as I relaxed into this open space away from the hospital room filled with the noisy interruptions that disturb the sleeping, replacing it with healing restorative sounds of creation.

"Look at the birds of the air; they do not sow or reap or store away in barns, and yet your heavenly Father feeds them." (Matthew 6:26 NIV)

Goodness Father, this!

Not one time have we had to worry or think about what to eat or drink during this journey, as Your provision comes through the countless numbers of Your people, answering Your call to share their generosity of preparing and placing nourishment directly into our barren hands while touching us and saying, "Get up

and eat. If you don't, the journey will be too hard for you."
(1 Kings 19:7 NIV)

Never has our need been greater, and never have we been given so much. Each meal we have received is like a holy communion of life-giving bread transfusing strength for the next step.

How does one reciprocate such extravagant generosity and grace given so freely with the merciful hope of a miraculous healing? It is more than a handwritten note could even begin to express.

I will attempt to express our gratitude through the Carepages, hoping the ones who are intimately attending to our basic needs of life can hear the deep unspoken groans of gratitude that I am just not able to express sufficiently.

The Father's Hands

Jim Thorpe Rehab | Oklahoma City, OK
May 2009

There was something extraordinary about her physical therapist who everyone called Big Joe. His towering broad presence was even more dramatized up against his newest patient with her petite frame of barely five feet. His countenance brought to mind a thesaurus of words, like steadfast, consistent, unflinching, resolute, faithful, dedicated, immovable, stable, tried and true, dependable, persevering, unwavering, unswerving, diligent, constant, and wholehearted.

He never seemed daunted by her therapy sessions, which many times resulted in her covering him with drool, vomit, or even incontinence of bowel or bladder. He approached her with the same steady kind voice of compassion and confidence in every session.

I was keenly aware of his large, strong hands during her therapy sessions. He would hold her ragdoll frame while using his careful touch to communicate with her body. Using gentle yet firm pressure, he commanded her muscles to initiate movements from memory. I wondered if the pressure caused her pain, yet I trusted this gentle giant to know what her body could endure for the best possible outcome. His presence with her was consistent and safe, maintaining an expert assuredness of his goals for her recovery.

I would sit in silence watching this intimate dance and experiencing moments of spiritual enlightenment—seeing these movements within the spiritual realm of my own life. I could visualize "The Father's Hands" upon me, holding me like a ragdoll, using His touch to communicate with my spirit, trusting He knew how much I could endure for the best possible outcome of His beloved.

One day, after she erupted a volcano of vomit (thank goodness for Mom with a towel in hand that saved her PT from being baptized again), the tomb was opened and she was stood up and then she was stepped out. Holding her head up for the first time, being held with maximum assistance, she took several steps, initiating those movements with great PT expertise.

"We used all that toning to benefit her today," he explained in response to our confused looks as she stood with stiff overextended legs.

Her face was grimaced, her breathing was rapid, and her skin moist and hot. It took everything she had to accomplish this miracle.

At the end of the hallway, he sat her down in a chair for a brief recovery yet within a few minutes, he commanded,

The Majestic Cypress

"*Talitha Koum, little girl,*" or in his own words, "Come on, Jessie, we gotta walk back. No wheelchair today."

I could feel my head shaking no and my faith failing, as I didn't see how that could even be possible after just witnessing the extreme exertion of stamina and energy she had just exhausted. While I closed my eyes and asked God for help, Joe proceeded to stand her up and manipulate her muscles all the way back to the gym.

It was finished. She was finished.

With everything she had endured, God chose that day to give her the impossible gift of holding her head up for the first time by herself, the cued initiation of steps, and the strength to maneuver through the hard sludge of movement—granting the two of us a brief glimpse of a branch that was possibly emerging. My heart and soul surged with the unfettered hope of more as my mind wrestled to comprehend what had just been witnessed—the impossible.

Her recovery from this momentous feat lasted more than just the few minutes she had rested in that chair. A profound fatigue settled over her for the next few days while we celebrated the incredible miracle we had just witnessed.

Traps, Travails, and Time

Jim Thorpe Rehab | Oklahoma City, OK
May 2009

Hope had relocated us to a place where awakenings could happen, briefly opening up this new space of movement.

However, without more than a pause, a claustrophobic cloud descended as the confinement of her fragile condition left little room for relief. Her inability to speak or move, the unpredictable vomiting and toning, incontinence of bowel and bladder, her unprotected brain with unhealed scalp incisions, and the continuous tube feedings strained our continuous attention.

Any awakening movements seemed to be countered with this increasing severity of toning in her muscles. This cruel ritual of hypertonicity exhausted my soul to its core.

I felt trapped in a dark, locked chamber with no way out. If I did find a moment of sleep, it was quickly interrupted by the nurse needing vitals, blood draws, housekeeping, medications, doctors, therapy six times a day, a loud TV, staff laughing, social worker and clergy visits. Sleep deprivation, overstimulation, and care demands combined with grief created a perfect storm of sheer exhaustion with no relief to be found. We had nothing left to give to others.

But the giving of others continued to find its way into our locked chamber. Meals were left outside our door every evening, nourishing what little life we had. Carepage postings along with cards of love and light seeped into our souls, sustaining us with hope, encouragement, and the strength to take the next step.

One evening, I was reading a Carepage response from a prayer warrior who communicated powerful intercessory imagery of, "I won't stop screaming and kicking at that box until something gives way and light streams in." Movement within elicited a memory of a story Margaret Silf told in her book, *Inner Compass*.

I remembered something about how heavy boats would enter a canal lock and the lock gates would firmly close with no way out.

I felt like that heavy boat locked in a deep dark prison, facing walls on every side with no way out. Within a few days, I had found someone to send me the story, as I hoped I could find some insight or hope to anchor to.

Reading the powerful words of "examining my prison walls is futile because it lacks perspective" reminded me to look beyond the obvious. I kept reading, "The locked chamber makes no sense unless you know the canal. It can be seen as the place where God's grace is flowing in to raise me to the place where I must be until God brings me, in His own time and way, to the point of readiness for moving on."

This new perspective invited me to a new patience of waiting and watching as the streams of grace flowed in, believing God would raise us up and release us when it was His time to move us on.

Between the Grief and Suffering
Jim Thorpe Rehab | Oklahoma City, OK
May 2009

Within each day, I would search for the gifts I could find within the emptiness of her life. Finding and writing down each gift of goodness from God veered my heart from the blaring grief of loss to giving thanks for what was being given so graciously to us.

This room, when dark and quiet, and empty of the scheduled stimulation to wake and move, would usher in small, sacred spaces of time for reflection and journaling. Sitting by her bed, my feet up on the rails holding her safely within her place of rest, the soft light of the computer screen would quietly wait for the keys to tell the story.

Closing my eyes, I would start the day over, scene by scene, recounting the moments of good—the many gifts in the midst of the hard. Every single night, I would give way to exhaustion before my list was completed. It was inconceivable to think I could capture in entirety

Part 2: The Remnant

the immeasurable goodness of God. This examen of consciousness every evening would frame the rest of my night with God's peace and goodness. Here is a piece of my Carepages one of those evenings:

Carepages

Post A Message

More relaxed tone, less pain, thirty minute devotion time outside in the sunshine while Jessie was in the shower with OT, no vomiting, a visit by a special friend, a visit by my director of hospice with a much needed discussion about work and insurance, a doctor who cares very much, a nurse who shared a Word with me today, telling me the Holy Spirit moved him to come and talk with me today, giving encouragement and strength, a visitor of another patient stopped by our room to tell me her church was praying for Jessie and to keep the faith, a big basket of snacks delivered, a phone call from one of Jessie's friends, my faithful husband, a nap, a wonderful dinner brought across town in rush hour traffic after being prepared by a kind soul and delivered to our door, watching American Idol with Jessie, watching Jessie in PT and Speech, an evening nurse working out a schedule to increase Jessie's rest time, a patient on this floor shared the elevator with me, text messages from family and friends, Carepage messages, all the prayers being lifted for her, hearing a miracle story from the evening nurse and her openly sharing her faith and prayers, new beautiful nightgowns freshly laundered for Jessie by a special neighbor, love from so many people, a special pink t-shirt from Ireland, no infection in her brain, cards in the mail, a warm shower, and an inpatient rehab facility experienced in brain injuries committed to helping her recover.

Finding and focusing on the moments of goodness helped me look for more each day. Being thankful for what was being given by Him helped me respond with kindness and hope in the chaos and obstacles of our days, but even more powerful was the gratitude for the good that helped me navigate the weight of grief as I groped for hope.

Groping for hope was like riding a roller coaster through the lows of the gut wrenching pain deep inside that grabs, twists, and holds you, refusing to let go. Some mornings, I would have a peace that passeth all understanding, releasing the wrench completely. His fresh and new mercies would start the day with less intensity but as the day progressed, my posture would bend like a tree being pummeled with gale force winds, absorbing the pain of all her struggles into my own canopy of grief.

Daily updates in the Carepages were my ritual of release. Capturing the glimpses of His goodness, revealed through grace, provision, help, and people, I would transcribe the glimpses between the lines of the grief and suffering—altering her story. It changed me. It changed my perspective. It evened the playing field. It released the *all* and made it the *both and*. This powerful rewrite inspired me to daily grope for the hope between the lines. It wasn't pretty, but it was a possible way to see beyond the physical reality we were forced to look at every day.

Resurrection Love

Jim Thorpe Rehab | Oklahoma City, OK
May 2009

In the front of his book, *Touched by Resurrection Love: Finding Hope Beyond Our Tears*, Trevor Hudson had penned, "Lisa, may your life always be touched by resurrection love, Psalm 16:8. (NLT)" Underneath his signature, I had written the words of the verse, "I know the Lord is always with me, I will not be shaken for He is right beside me." Little did I know that God's foundational truths were erecting walls of faith within that would hold me when all else shattered.

In his book, he shares, "Resurrection Love is a deeply moving story of the transformation and hope that can lie beyond our tears. The Risen Christ continues to meet with us at the point of our deepest need. As He came to Mary Magdalene, 2000 years ago, so He comes to us in our dark and difficult places. Sometimes, like Mary herself, we do not recognize Him immediately. But as we open our hearts and our minds to his living presence, and to the message of his resurrection, we find ourselves gradually empowered to live beyond our tears, to go out and connect with those suffering around us."

This Resurrection Love continued to touch us as it weaved its way in and out of the days of this journey. One afternoon, she walked through the front door of the rehabilitation hospital, took the elevator to the second floor, and found our room. A soft knock heralded her presence.

Sister Benedicta soundlessly appeared, bearing in her faith-shaped hands a beautiful tapestry of colors in a quilted fabric square. Her greeting was soft and gentle as she reached for my assaulted spirit. With her deep abiding faith, she began to speak, "This hand pieced square we shall call the Resurrection Cloth. It represents the Cross and the Resurrection. Both are in sight all the time, reminding us that during the intense suffering we must face in this world, Resurrection is coming. But we must stay at the cross for as long as He says."

Her words lingered. This was truly the most difficult and horrendous place to be, one that if I had a choice, I wouldn't have stayed. But in this place, I had no choice. I stayed because my daughter was there. And knowing Christ was there with us, remaining with us, I believed He would lead us out of this place when the time was right.

She ceremoniously spread the blessed cloth over Jessie's feet, who laid as motionless as one in a tomb of death as Bill and I quietly watched. With a Crucifix in one hand and holding Jessie's feet with the other, she humbly bowed her heart and head and silently infused her petitions of Resurrection Love. Time stood still as the silence brought heaven's ears closer.

As she was preparing to leave, she held my heart close to hers as she hugged my crying soul, marking my weary back with the sign of the cross, "Peace and strength be with you." Her spiritual presence of "Christ with us" soothed my excruciating pain that seemed to never subside. She handed me the Benedict Crucifix and said, "All of the Sisters of Red Plains Monastery have been reading your Carepages and praying over Jessie while holding this Crucifix. I will leave it here to hang above her bed containing the prayers for healing and resurrection over this child."

As she turned to leave our room, I caught a glimpse of Divine Mercy marking our door with the sign of the cross and leaving the scent of Resurrection Love trailing behind her.

A Father's Love
Jim Thorpe Rehab | Oklahoma City, OK
May 2009

Two months on the agonizing and gut-wrenching roller coaster of her intense struggles of toning and vomiting, combined with the inability to move or talk, ravaged our hearts. Bill had been attempting to work remotely in the brief moments he could find within the day from our room, but we both knew it was time for him to return to his practice for the sake of our family's financial survival. We were heartbroken but knew we had no choice.

Exhausted grief led the way as I began to face the long, hard days without him, yet there was great solace in the evenings and weekends when he would "come home to his girls."

I was in the midst of a hectic morning routine, getting Jessie ready for her therapy schedule, when an unwanted knock at the door submerged me even deeper.

"There's a man here to see you," the nurse declared.

I CAN'T DO ANOTHER THING!

I kept my screams to myself, but the look on my face must have said it all.

"Do you want me to tell him no?" she asked.

Through gritted teeth, I groaned, "Who is it?"

"Someone by the name of Lee Henry."

"WHAT?" I bolted out of the room, searching for his familiar face.

MY DADDY?

I hadn't seen him since before the accident.

I collapsed into his big ol' bear hug, letting him hold me until I came to the surface.

"I didn't know you were coming. I am so … " Sobbing replaced my words. Everything fell away, leaving a little girl in her daddy's arms.

OT soon came for Jessie's therapy, giving us just a few moments alone. Seizing those precious moments, we found a sunny spot on the patio. An angel of provision had provided bread and juice to share that morning, reminding us of what great love and sacrifice had been given for the life of others.

The Majestic Cypress

Dad couldn't wait to tell me about his vivid dream in which my hair had turned completely gray. "Sissy, I felt it was so real. I just got into my car this morning and drove up here. I needed to come and see for myself. Imagine my relief when I saw your full head of brown hair! Aye, you look pretty good after all you've been through."

Our conversation deepened as he dove deep into his concerns about our well-being given the current reality. It was clear he had spent hours thinking about the enormity of our circumstances.

A fierce and determined patriarch, he had come with questions, thoughts, and ideas about how to survive this catastrophic event. He was always the one to meet difficult challenges head on in life, whether personal, business, or financial. He held my hand and my heart with his face set as flint, committing to do whatever it took to get Jessie back to health in a functional state.

Two hours with my dad was a powerful medicine, filling me with love, strength, hope, and profound courage to carry on. He and Mom had been through a similar journey with my older brother and they knew some of the many challenges we were facing. He assured me that we, too, would get through this rough patch of life.

One of the truths Dad left me with me that day was, "God sends 'love' to help us through times like this." God certainly sent me "love" that day in the form of my daddy.

CHAPTER 7

The Black Trees

Pain Yet Promise

To walk down the aisles of an Art Festival is a miraculous adventure of entering and existing within many others' souls. This vulnerable creative expression is exposed to the receptivity of another, hoping to create an energy of intimate connectedness through a familiar experience or a place yet to be discovered.

Massive black trees caught my eye from two aisles over, disrupting the flow of my step. The unknowing was haunting.

Who paints huge black trees? Why?

"Even though the fig trees have no blossoms, I will rejoice in the Lord! I will be joyful in the God of my salvation." Habakkuk 3:17-18 (NLT) These were the hand-painted words next to the large black trees. Gazing upon this dark yet beautiful expression of "pain yet promise" softened my memory of having whispered those very words.

How is it possible for someone to create a piece of one's heart without knowing her heart?

The younger woman surprised me when she introduced herself as the artist, Bethany Pigott, and shared her story of her journey with Christ and how she paints for Him, using the money to help pay for her college tuition. Her love of God's Word inspires each piece as she expresses hope and faith into the Creator's ear and He expresses His Word through her creative artistic spirit.

As I was handing her my payment, she took my hand, whispered my daughter's name with a prayer of healing, and rejoiced in this moment as God tenderly revealed His presence to us both with provision and hope.

This dictum of faith hangs triumphantly in our home in remembrance that when our world was crumbling—our little tree full of darkness and death—we chose to rejoice and trust in God no matter what. And it continues hanging in hope for each day, because no matter what comes, yet I will rejoice in the Lord and will be joyful in the God of my salvation because in His time, He will deliver His people and fulfill all His promises.

Code Black Tones

Jim Thorpe Rehab | Oklahoma City, OK
May 2009

"Code Black, Code Black, Phase 2" blared throughout the hallways, signaling a weather emergency. Night staff came running into our room, flipped on lights, and commanded us to a safe place. Jessie was wheeled, bed and all, to the center of the nursing station. What a sight Bill and I witnessed on the brain injury floor—twenty-four hospital beds, occupied by patients with families, circled up like a wagon train waiting for the outside rampage to hit. These storm protectors are the heroes of our healthcare system, making sure the vulnerable and injured are safe and out of harm's way with no thoughts to their own safety. It was several hours later when the "All Clear" announcement ushered all the beds and families back to their own rooms to once again face their own individual storms.

The daily storms of spasticity and toning were relentless. Her brain injury had disrupted her normal muscle movements resulting in painful, uncontrollable stiffness and spasms of her arms and legs, which often led to permanent contractures of the muscles and tendons. Any simple command of movement would invoke a response of her arms and legs becoming as stiff as a board as though she was being pulled apart from all directions. Even Jessie's deeply-embedded muscle memory from years in gymnastics was no match for this brutal beast.

My deepest fears of her body becoming twisted and tortuous, fueled by my nursing background, demanded her skin and muscles remain intact with no exceptions. Each stiff declaration met my fierce determination of refusing what the brain injury was inflicting.

Constant "breaking the tone" was my revolt against this evil intruder with no regard of what it might be doing to her precious muscles and tendons. I could see no other way, having personally witnessed the gnarling of bodies this evil had carried to fruition. With the ineffectiveness of the anti-spasmodics, we were vigilantes who monitored and forcefully escorted the toning out of her legs with intentional bending and extending of her legs and arms each time it attempted to take control.

Exposed and Enduring

Jim Thorpe Rehab | Oklahoma City, OK
May 2009

During my early morning quiet time, the word "endured" lifted off the page as my eyes fell to the scripture on my lap. Hebrews 12:2 (KJV), "Jesus, who for the joy that was set before Him, endured the cross." He himself experienced

Part 2: The Remnant

the full intensity of human hatred and brutality. In a real way, he endured another's suffering.

As I ruminated upon the word "endured," Jessie's fragile malfunctioning body laid before me as an icon for my meditation.

Her vulnerability had been fully exposed by all she had immeasurably endured in the multiple surgeries, swelling of her brain, removal of her skull flaps, countless CAT scans, intubation, ventilators, MRSA pneumonia, pelvic fractures, sinus and orbital fractures, acute cholecystitis resulting in an emergency cholecystectomy surgery with a bile duct injury and repair, tracheotomy with suctioning, peg tube placement, paralysis, central lines, PICC lines, blood draws, blood transfusions, uncountable medications and treatments, emergency interventions, incontinence of bowel and bladder, frequent vomiting, muscle toning, countless moves from rooms to facilities, unfamiliar people ... The list was endless.

It was simply incomprehensible to think about all this child had endured, and yet I was deeply comforted knowing she had never been alone for one moment. I knew Christ was with her and had endured it with her. His strength and grace was sufficient for all she needed. His power was made strong through her weakness. And she still remained in His hands.

We all did.

Hell and Hell-no's

Jim Thorpe Rehab | Oklahoma City, OK
May 2009

It was the day before Pentecost, which was a birth out of frailty. The believers were huddled in fear behind closed doors. Yet Pentecost unleashed a courageous power, the very power that transformed their fear to courage as they stepped out into the reality of their world with Truth. It wasn't without pain and suffering, yet they found the courage to move through the *hard*.

That same power continued to sustain us through our frailties, giving us the courage to face our *hard* each day.

After being huddled in fear and grief behind closed doors, I was feeling courageous enough on a Saturday morning to leave Jessie with Bill to walk across the street to Target. With my head held high, I was on a mission to get a few necessary items and thought Target would be a place I could browse and breathe.

I walked into the bright, busy store and my grief unexpectedly ejected from a compartment that I thought I had closed. Motionless, my heart could not take another step when I saw them.

The children. They were laughing and talking, running and screaming.

What was I thinking? Look at their heads! Their skulls are fully in place! My gosh, they are breathtaking!

I felt the urge to yell at every mom walking by me, "DO YOU KNOW HOW INCREDIBLY MIRACULOUS IT IS TO HAVE A CHILD WITH A FULL SKULL WHO CAN MOVE AND TALK AND LAUGH?"

My eyes would not leave their foreheads. Seeing children look "normal" hit me hard like a board in the face, causing my head to spin and my body to refuse to move. It was as if my body knew my heart couldn't bear another step toward the outside world. It wasn't time yet. I gripped the red plastic cart to steady myself and closed my eyes. My lungs filled with the forced deep breaths now taking control as my heart turned around and returned to the only safe place it knew.

"You weren't gone very long," Bill said, reaching out to embrace my traumatized spirit. He didn't ask any questions. It was as if he already knew.

My body remained confined to this circumstance of life. There was no other place I could be. I had attempted a brief trip home and found it was a vacuum of a hollow shell, sucking my soul of what little comfort I had. The unsuccessful trip to Target erupted the pain of what used to be, and it slayed me. Attempting walks outside brought anxiety and the inability to breathe, gripped by fear that she would be in a pain crisis with brutal toning or having spontaneous vomiting with no ability to protect her airway, all with no way for her to voice her sufferings.

Burning tightness gripped my neck and shoulders, and the heavy weight of grief rose and swelled like a tidal wave trying to overtake me. In each therapy session, her lack of response to commands, her feeble attempts of awakening to only find the tone consume her again, and witnessing her not able to connect or initiate movement was enough to make this grown girl cry.

What is she feeling? Is she screaming on the inside like those stories I have read when they know everything that is going on but are unable to move or speak? Does she even know I am here? What is happening within you, child? I can only see from the outside in.

Each moment, I would have the choice to accept what was happening and then I would turn to the Master of the waves, knowing I was not able to steer this ship and how utterly dependent I was upon Him in each moment of every day. When the waves would come, I would choose the Master. Eventually the wave would pass and I could breathe again. And yet before long, another wave would come and again I would choose the Master. One would think I could just automatically lean into the Master, but no. The feelings of intense fear would overtake me, and I would always have to choose.

Do I stay to be swept away or do I look elsewhere? The question was always followed by the same answer, *Where else would I go but to the Master?*

Traveling this unwanted path of devastation and trying to navigate all the debris was illuminating a different aspect of the faith I had professed in the past. Moment by moment, I readily reached for the very source of my strength as I could find none without Him.

Each day felt like a day from hell. Our reprieves of hope and joy were brief as her tone and pain escalated with a vengeance. Even with the arsenal of medications being given, this evil was relentless and unforgiving. I spent days in a physical battle as I witnessed her tiny body ravaged with hypertonia, as her severely injured parts of her brain were contorting her muscle tone, threatening contractures of her extremities with each gripping hold.

Every moment my fierce love demanded a different response by "breaking her tone" over and over with my battle cry of screaming, "Oh hell no, not today!" My very next breath demanding that God put a stop to this cruelty threatening to overtake her entire body.

The searing pain in my heart intensified as these never-ending days of watching my beautiful daughter be physically attacked with no way to stop the assailant's aggression continued.

Even with the excruciating reality of her condition and hard medical facts telling us how extensive the damage was, we still held this deep belief in our hearts that God had the final decision about Jessie. He had plans and hope for her future. He had brought her safe thus far and He wasn't going to leave her now.

As I studied her exhausted tiny frame surrendered upon the bed after an intense day of battle, a memory came forward of a little girl named Ashley who personified the perfect example of childlike faith. This blonde-haired stranger had come to meet us while we were in Grand Junction. She showed up regularly with bright eyes full of excitement and would share how she'd picked out candy for Jessie, or brought a stuffed animal to make her feel better. One afternoon, she'd brought Jessie a big sculptured hand holding a baby angel and declared, "This is God's hand holding Jessie." Out of the mouth of a child!

As my weary, sad eyes fell upon the sculptured hand sitting in her windowsill, my breathing slowed and my heart settled into a quiet space as I witnessed her hospital bed transfigure into His big sculptured hand, assuring my heart that He was cradling her in a rest of safety and mercy.

Tired Smiles

Jim Thorpe Rehab | Oklahoma City, OK
June 2009

My fatigued face was frozen with deep stress and concern, untethered grief breaking through often without warning.

Sitting on the tiny porch outside of her room during one of her morning OT sessions, I began to brood about the article someone had posted on the Carepages.

Maybe they just don't understand the extent of our circumstances ...

I tried to give them the benefit of the doubt as I thought about the article that had shared research data about the health benefits of smiling. They were wanting me to smile

The Black Trees

more for my own good, and I wondered out loud to God about how it could even be possible to smile when my heart had been broken off from that muscle.

Suddenly many high shrills hit my ears, drawing my attention to a "train" of children coming across the street. There were about a dozen ranging from ages one to three. Eight littles were riding in an extended stroller, the rest following behind, holding onto a rope in between the two child care attendants. They appeared content to be led or carried wherever.

Happy chatter and silly giggles reached across the parking lot, eliciting a slow smile to my face. And then it happened, a child made eye contact with me, smiled, and lifted her hand to wave to me. Without thought, I lifted my weary hand up and waved back, engaging with the spirit of this child who was showing me my smile wasn't broken. I then remembered the gift of Jessie's simple wave on her good days and how it brought a huge smile to my face.

I smiled again with my head bowed as I thanked God for the simple example of His care. I asked Him to help me be more content and thankful whether I am being carried or led by a rope. I wanted to be more childlike, trusting and simple, just being content where I was. Smiles came easily the rest of the day as I remembered the "children train" appearing the very moment I was needing help with my smile muscles.

The next morning during a reprieve of the toning attacks, as I was getting Jessie ready for the day, I noticed she was more alert. She was trying to focus on my face and mouth. I began telling her the story about the children's train. It was at that moment I began the quest for her smile. Leaning in very close to her face, I gave her a big smile as I teased her with a silly tone, "Jessie, give your momma a smile. Come on, I might have to tickle you. You remember the tickle monster?" I wiggled my fingers close to her face in hopes of a response.

After a few moments, something changed within her face. There was a subtle softening of her eyes, and her little lips might have turned upward for maybe a brief second. If you weren't searching for it, you couldn't have seen it. But I saw it and knew she had heard me as she gave me the cloaked gift I had teased for. The look on her face was simply angelic with the tiniest hint of tenderness, a respite from battle fatigue, bringing me a deep, true inner smile of comfort.

"Tiny smiles" were beginning to appear from time to time in the form of following a few simple commands like picking out colors and pictures with her eyes, standing with max assist in PT with some head control, and having slight glimpses of initiation with OT as she worked on simple tasks of her activities of daily living.

These moments of hope continued to appear without too much notice.

One particular day, she seemed different. I mean really different than I had ever noticed before. As I was watching her, I could see that she seemed to be present to what was going on around her. She would move her head in the direction we spoke and even appeared to be listening to our voices. We began to intentionally volley our voices across the room at each other in hopes of bringing more connection to her surroundings.

Later in the evening, one of her greatest moments happened while she was sitting up in her wheelchair and I was facing her doing oral therapy. Her OT had left an assortment of flavorings to use to try and stimulate movement of her tongue. When I touched her tongue with a tiny drop of cinnamon, she started coughing. When her coughing stopped, I heard a quiet humming noise. I leaned in closer to listen and it stopped.

"Bill, come over here and listen, quick!"

I would mimic her and she would start humming again. At one point, the humming increased in volume before it was gone. It only lasted for a few seconds, but that beginning vibration was a glimpse of something bigger that was to come, causing me to develop a new prayer language of humming.

The Gravity of Grief

Jim Thorpe Rehab | Oklahoma City, OK
June 2009

Having my mom visit for a few days was soothing, her presence enabling me to be a child burrowed underneath her wing that covered me with great love. Her love has been a constant force in our family, always steadying the storms. She stepped in, shouldered my load, insisting respite for my weary soul.

My heart needed to be rekindled. Grief was consuming me as I surveyed the length of the journey, where we had been and how much further we had to go. Facing the reality that I must return to work soon, watching my beloved husband carry such a heavy load and remain steady in his rhythm of love, and watching Jessie struggle with a body and brain that didn't work right overwhelmed me beyond belief. I just didn't know how much more I could do.

I had hoped finding the dark quiet room down the hall would help me find restorative sleep while Bill and Mom stayed with Jessie. Sleep didn't come, but the tears did. My months of tear reserves were depleted that night, witnessed only by God and the walls that held me.

Part 2: The Remnant

With Mom at Jessie's bedside, Bill and I stepped away from her together for the first time. We made the hard decision to leave, traveling home to check on things and to attempt to spend a few hours away. The thirty-minute drive was foreign to our hearts. We were hoping it would be easier if we both went, but it wasn't. There was nothing easy about anything. The gravity of grief pulled me down to crawling through most of the house. My tears never stopped as we were consumed by the emptiness of our home. The absence of life was deafening as we encountered the harsh visual of "nothing had been disturbed" in months. Eerily cold desolation quickly ushered us out the door as the cord that bound our family was yanking us back to the only home we knew.

All the feelings remained present in the car as we returned to our refuge, both of us reeling from the trauma of the chosen separation.

Mom assured us Jessie had not awakened while we were gone, which was both comforting and alarming. The tension within the "both and" was reaching its breaking point according to my heart.

Still recovering from the emotional assault, I nestled in beside Jessie, relieved to be "back home."

Her room suddenly began to fill with a warm glow. Searching for the source, I looked outside the huge window to discover fire in the sky. I was stunned to silence by the brilliance, privileged to glimpse the miracle of this moment. As the sun dropped, the hand painted oranges, yellows, and reddish display sustained the glow, lingering as embers in a fire. I was captured and held within His beauty. Beauty in the sky, beauty in my mom's presence, and the beauty in this bed I gazed upon as she slept so quietly. The remembered prayer from days past came to my lips, "Come Holy Spirit, fill the hearts of Your faithful and kindle in them the fire of Your Love."

And that is exactly what He did that day. Perhaps the bounty of my tears were the gift to empty and cleanse my soul of fatigue and grief so that space within my heart could be rekindled with His.

CHAPTER 8

As Time Goes By Tree

Hope

A vision of her healing had been created by an unknown artist. Unnamed, it found its way into our home, anchoring hope and blossoming beauty in the desolation of her injury. With a mystical background of muted blues and greens, the small black shoot erupted from a severed root bursting forth a canopy of leaves with opulent alabaster blossoms.

Each blossom represented one of her "firsts." Her first sound, first finger movement, first eye contact, first smile, first humming to first whispers to first word. Eventually, the first reach, first crawl, first stand, first step, first swallow, first bite of food, first time holding her head up, first scribble, first dry diaper, first PEG tube removal, first 5k, first hike, first swim, first ride on Dusty at Coffee Creek stables for rebalancing and restoration. All the "firsts" paved the path of hope to the "nexts."

As I prayed with this vision of hopeful fruitfulness, a name arose in my spirit, "As Time Goes By, Hope." Etching its newly given name into the frame, I could hear the echoes from the past hope that had vibrated in my heart from Isaiah 11:1 (ESV), "Then a shoot will spring from the root of Jesse, and a branch from his roots will bear fruit."

Each blossom impressively displayed His great glory, providing embodiment to the unceasing prayers for her recovery and restoration.

Part 2: The Remnant

A Squall Made Still
Jim Thorpe Rehab | Oklahoma City, OK
June 2009

A frightening threat erupted with a vengeance one weekend afternoon when her unhealed scalp incisions began seeping a foreign drainage. Her skin was extremely thin and fragile from her bilateral craniectomies, creating great concern because she did not have a skull providing protection over her brain. Stat cultures of the purulent fluid were obtained, followed by a stat MRI to determine if the infection was superficial or had found its way to her brain. An urgent SOS code was sent to our community of support, asking for protection and help.

The awareness of her fragility rolled in like a squall with alert sirens going up several decibels within my head with all of the potential threats.

With the Southwest Integris MRI department attached to the Jim Thorpe Rehab, this meant an easy carrier ride down the hallway to the radiology department, not a vehicle transport across the city.

It was there we encountered a God-appointed angel with a kind and compassionate spirit. This woman's assuring demeanor calmed the storms of my incessant concerns about Jessie's inability to lie still long enough for the MRI due to her toning issues. I knew intubation with general sedation was required for those patients who were incapable of stillness, which would mean an increased risk for her and an unwanted delay in getting answers.

In anticipation of her spontaneous muscle toning events, the radiologist tech's experience and wisdom took the necessary steps to ensure she received enough Valium to provide adequate sedation so nothing disrupted her stillness, even with the loud clanking noises of the machine.

It was late when we returned from the MRI. My stillness reflected Jessie's as I was deeply imagining her within the cleft of God's rock being protected from the dangers that were threatening her life while her evening nurse quietly started her IV antibiotics.

During morning rounds the next day, we were given the much hoped and prayed for "All Clear." The storms had passed quickly and there was no further threat. The superficial infection responded to the direct command of the antibiotics.

Lamenting the Light
Jim Thorpe Rehab | Oklahoma City, OK
June 2009

An old *Mustang Times* newspaper arrived in an envelope within our hospital mail. A friend had sent it along with a note of love and directions to check out the sports page. A photo of Jessie running the Putnam City Track Meet in March before her accident was front and center. It was also the last time her dad and I had watched her run. I gasped in shock, not prepared for the agonizing slap of reality hurled at me, featuring her past in living color.

She was stunning and powerful. Seeing her beautiful face set with such determination, her agile body poised with such strength and posture, running full stride in the 400-meter race launched me into a fetal position. This photo I was grasping, next to the bed that was holding her, was now a cruel reality successfully attempting to destroy the protective governor device I had developed within to help manage my grief.

As my body shook in response, my spirit refused this dark assault. Within a few moments, my heart offered a different approach.

Use this picture as a prayer icon. See her running with this determination, strength, and posture as she recovers. She will run again.

I lifted my head and quickly remembered reading Coach Lorenz's comments about Jessie in the Carepages: "Jessie is a diligent, hardworking student who also worked hard at being a track athlete. She gave all she had in practice. She also had a giving heart. I remember one day she traveled across campus just to bring me a cupcake because it was her birthday. She told me she wanted me to share in her celebration." He finished with, "She's just a little beam of light."

Oh how my heart trembled at the truth of his lived experience with her as I remembered just a few days earlier singing over her, "This little light of mine, I'm gonna let it shine," trying to get her to hold her finger up like she did when she was little. It had never sunk in so deeply that "SHE" was this little light of mine.

This was one of the hardest parts of missing "her." She was here but had no beam. This darkness along with her lack of communication, inability to respond, and very little movement reverberated the magnitude of loss our hearts were lamenting.

Battles for Balance

Jim Thorpe Rehab | Oklahoma City, OK
June 2009

The vigil of managing her toning issues and responsiveness with medications continued to be a daily challenge. Bill and I watched her physiatrist use the same advanced skills of grace, power, control, rhythm, flexibility, and mental focus to balance her brain injury the way our little "beam queen" gymnast had balanced on beams for all those years. His adjustments were focused on moving her muscle relaxants upward just enough to release her toning to relieve her excruciating pain, but keep her toned enough to stand, but not too much to over sedate her, adding to his concoctions just the right amount of stimulants to attempt awakening her without stimulating her toning issues or elevating her liver enzymes.

There would be these brief moments when she was "balanced" enough to catch a glimpse of a response of following a command but quickly became unbalanced again by her intense hypertonia and/or profound fatigue.

These battles are brutal for everyone, but especially for you. You have no way to tell me just how brutal they really are. UGH! I hate this so much!

Gentle Guidance
Jim Thorpe Rehab | Oklahoma City, OK
June 2009

Gentleness was the word of the day God had invited me to spend time with. All day, I practiced gentleness. Gentle in my words, my actions, my volume, and my being. Gentle in my spirit, my tears, my thoughts and reactions toward others.

That afternoon, Jessie's case manager (who worked with the insurance company and the rehab) knocked on our door and whispered, "I need to talk with you."

I smiled at her gently.

"Yes, of course."

I had been expecting this visit. She informed me our insurance company had contacted her with the directions of discharge planning since Jessie hadn't been making any notable improvements over the last four weeks.

Part 2: The Remnant

I felt the cracks in my heart extend further but had been prepared to gently respond, "Yes, I knew this would be coming and maybe that is exactly what we need to do. We haven't been home in three months. If she needs a month or two to help her get over these toning issues and more time to heal in order to progress, then that is exactly what needs to happen."

The case manager's eyes swelled with relief.

"Well, thank you for that. I wasn't looking forward to telling you that, but you made that so easy."

Thank You, God, for the spirit of gentleness which makes everything a little easier on everyone.

The thought of going home was full of conflict, saddled with the harsh reality that she wasn't progressing in rehab and the warm thoughts of giving her gentle restful time in the familiar surroundings of our home, knowing it would be healing for us all.

As swarms of details began flying around my head of what it would take to get her home, I paused to still my anxious heart. With some deep breathing of release, I prayed Psalm 121 (NIV), *"I lift my eyes up, where does my help come from? My help comes from the Lord, Maker of heaven and earth."*

Knowing He would guide each step of His way, I closed my eyes and went deeper within the recesses of my soul, remembering the power of the St. Francis de Sales prayer of peace: *"Be at peace. Do not look forward in fear to the changes of life; rather look to them with full hope as they arise. God, whose very own you are, will deliver you from out of them; and when you cannot stand it, God will bury you in His arms. Do not fear what may happen tomorrow; the same understanding Father who cares for you today will take care of you then and every day. He will either shield you from suffering, or will give you unfailing strength to bear it. Be at peace, and put aside all anxious thoughts and imaginations."*

Once again, I had to choose to continue to walk this journey one step at a time. If I looked too far ahead, I was overwhelmed with all the what-ifs. If I looked back, I would find myself so grief-filled with all we had lost. So here I was, staying in this moment, putting one foot in front of the other. And just like Joe, her amazing PT who helped her to take each step completely dependent upon his help, holding her up with his big safe hands, guiding and cuing her, God was helping me. He helped me put one foot in front of the other, holding me up with HIS BIG SAFE HANDS. He guided and cued each step and most importantly, I knew He would never let us go.

As we continued to wait expectantly for the next right step, Grace appeared as our doctor somehow convinced the insurance company to keep her inpatient for another week in hopes she might have notable improvements that would allow her to stay longer. This extra week would also help give the two of us time to explore options of home rehab and provide us with the necessary opportunity for a home outing with her to better prepare for her real homecoming.

Running for a Miracle
Jim Thorpe Rehab | Oklahoma City, OK
June 2009

When we were informed Coach Mount "had it placed upon her heart" to organize "Jessie's Miracle Run" to raise money for medical expenses, overwhelming emotions arose at her desire to "run alongside us." I remembered how Jessie had always felt supported by her coach's constant encouragement and enthusiasm. She was another one of "those" coaches that made a difference in the lives of young people with her words and actions, coming alongside those she "coached." Now she was making a powerful difference in ours.

So many generous souls came together to organize this unimaginable gift to our family. I had all the "feels." I felt gratitude for the magnitude of generosity and caring. I felt grief for Jessie not being able to run and be in the middle of all the activities. I felt the angst of not being able to attend. I felt the love for all the people giving their time and money. And I felt the power in the unified hope of Jessie Boone's recovery.

The day before the actual run, I was with Jessie in physical therapy watching her struggle with maximum assistance to try and move her foot a few inches. I thought of the irony of this "Miracle Run" that was taking place the next day. I began to imagine all the people who were going to "run" or "walk" in faith for Jessie to one day walk on her own again. I had never thought about the miraculous gift of walking as I did now. My heart prayer evolved into envisioning each step taken in the Miracle Run would be a step Jessie would take in the future.

When we got back to her room, one of her nurses came in and handed me an envelope. Inside the envelope was a completed registration form, money, and a note that read,

> Jessie, I will work hard in your honor tomorrow. I won't be able to run/walk but I wanted to participate in the hope of you walking one day.

When I found her to say thank you, she shared she had Jessie on her prayer list from the first day she saw her and would continue to pray for her as long as it took. She told me she was a Catholic and her momma had taught her to bow and beg, and with humility kneel in prayer; and she was doing exactly that for Jessie every day. She was another one of the stunning examples of the outpouring of support we continued to receive within our shattered walls.

Four hundred and fifty-one souls manifested their hope and faith by their presence in the Miracle Run. Her track team, various churches, families and friends, our gymnastic family, people from surrounding communities all came in solidarity for the united call for a miracle. Many of her therapists and nurses included their families to join in on their day off to stand and walk for this child who needed the faith of all who had been called to believe and hope she would one day walk again.

Video clips were sent to us throughout the day of the huge gathering of supporters pounding the pavements, wearing t-shirts proclaiming the "Jessie Boone Miracle Run." This powerful day of hope and love even had the skies responding as streams of light pierced through the overcast gray clouds, shining the light on the path for the runners below.

Some of those streams of light found their way into Jessie's room during the run as I watched tiny movements of her hands reaching out to try and take the toothbrush from mine. Any independent movement was an immense miracle moment as we waited and expected more.

The *Mustang Times* newspaper covered the big event, announcing on the front page in big, bold, black letters, "Miracle Run raises $15,000 for Jessie Boone." The article celebrated, "MHS Girls Track Assistant Coach Andrea

Mount organized the event, which featured a 5K run, a one-mile Spirit Walk, and a one-mile children's run. The community's outpouring response through donations and volunteerism made the day a complete success." Coach Mount was quoted saying, "I had so many people willing to volunteer time and money to make things possible, I was totally shocked at the turnout."

My brother, Mark, who lives in Tulsa, had driven in early for her run. He placed third in his division of the 5K. On his way home, he stopped by the rehab hospital to see Jessie and found us in physical therapy. She was standing with the max assistance of two therapists. As he watched her greatly struggle to move her foot just to take a step, he began to encourage her, telling her about his run he just finished for her and how he wanted her to take that next step for him. He told her how strong she was and he knew she could do it, that he believed in her and was so proud of her.

After the therapists had transferred her back to the wheelchair, he kneeled in front of her and began to tell her stories of what he had witnessed at her Miracle Run. He then took off his winning medal and reached out to her saying, "Here, take it. It's yours. I ran for you, Jess." It took several seconds but she slowly began to move her arm toward him. He waited so patiently. It took everything she had, but she eventually was able to grasp the medal. Words couldn't express how powerful that moment was for us all.

Trial Run at Home

Jim Thorpe Rehab | Oklahoma City, OK
June 2009

Knowing discharge from rehab was in the near future, preparations were made for her first home outing, giving us a first glimpse of what we would encounter if we lived at home with her. We had practiced car transfers in hopes for smooth and safe movements of her in and out of our car and were ready to move forward.

Traveling with her was our first hard lesson as she unexpectedly began erupting vomit from what we assumed was motion sickness. It seemed an awful price for her to pay for just the few short hours we would be there.

I was anxious to get her out of the car in hopes she would get some relief, and it took both of us to begin the awkward routine of transferring her into her chair from the car, especially because her vomiting hadn't stopped.

We slowly wheeled her up the sidewalk as I held her helmet-covered head between my hands to help stabilize the movement. As we neared the front porch, we were grateful for the wheelchair ramp built by one of our neighbors.

After getting us both cleaned up, we rested in the quiet of the living room. She slept as I relished in the silence and isolation, away from the continual stimulation of hospital life. For the next few hours, we absorbed the medicine of home—enjoying our "tended by angels" flower beds in full bloom and freshly mowed lawn gifted by our neighbors, sharing a picnic of food left by a friend, washing clothes, sitting on the porch and watching it rain, listening to the birds gossip about us being home, and seeing that big sky with no boundaries. These moments of rediscovering our sanctuary of privacy and quiet expanded my heart with the hopes of coming home soon for all the "good" that was waiting to help heal us all.

Part 2: The Remnant

Interruptions and Intrusions
Jim Thorpe Rehab | Oklahoma City, OK
June 2009

After our brief four-hour "trial run" at home, we quickly reentered her routine of lack of sleep and muscle toning, which continued to force frequent adjustments of her medications in attempts to relieve or at least lessen the onslaughts. This balancing act was delicate and difficult, as too much medication would over-sedate her and too little would stiffen her like a board.

Our chronic lack of sleep added to the irritation of the unpredictable interruptions within our days and our nights. One night after we'd gotten her settled for sleep, we were sandwiched together next to her bed, listening to the rain pounding on the window and hoping sleep would come.

Please, no more Code Blacks.

Pulling the blanket up around my head, I was wishing for the earplugs I had tucked away in her bedside drawer. An unfamiliar sound suddenly forced me to sit up and whisper, "Bill, it sounds like it's raining *inside.*"

"No, it's just raining hard outside."

"Ummm, listen," I said. "I really think it's inside."

Bill sighed and, with some added grunts, struggled to get out of the single chair bed that we shared.

He turned the lights on, only to discover Niagara Falls was rushing down from the top of the big picture window, pouring water over the fifteen-foot window sill filled with our things, cascading down the walls and flooding the floor. We battled the unwelcomed entertainment with towels, blankets, and bedding, moved furniture, and performed high water rescues of all the adornments on the sill. Reinforcements in the form of nurses soon arrived with additional towels and made phone calls to maintenance. I think the storms and aftermath finally quieted around 4 a.m.

A few nights later, after our nightly routine of a warm bed bath and a complete lotion rub down with range of motion, we tucked Jessie into bed for the night. The nurse connected her continuous tube feeding for the night, administered her evening medications, and turned out the lights around 8:30 p.m.

Around midnight, I woke to the sound of rustling noises from her bed, which happened when her muscles were toning. Moving to her bedside, I could see her body was in full extension. As I pulled her covers back to begin to help her "break the tone," my hand fell into a pool of fluids.

Gosh, Jessie, did you flood the bed?

Thinking it was urine, I turned on the light to discover her tube feeding had become disconnected and had filled her bed, leaving her tummy empty of much needed nutrition.

She was cold, stiff, and shivering as the two of us moved through another full warm bed bath, and linen and gown change, which only increased the relentlessness of the muscle tone. Sleep finally came for her around 2:30 a.m. only to be awakened again at 4:45 a.m.

The lights flipped on as the nurse announced, "I need to get her vital signs, obtain some blood, and get a urine specimen."

Somehow I managed a kind conversation of concern about this early disruption of sleep in light of her being awake for most of the night already, knowing therapy would be knocking on the door soon. She was finally able to drift back off to sleep around 6:00 a.m.

Part 2: The Remnant

My awareness of disruptions was harshly jolted again when a man suddenly opened our door soon after with a loud jovial voice, "Good morning, I am here to do pet therapy, but now I see I can't come in this room because of isolation precautions," and promptly closed the door.

Speechless and frustrated, I could hardly believe the lack of awareness of the most simple need of patients in the midst of demanding schedules of intensive therapies: REST.

Every single morning around 5:30 a.m., I would be awakened by the loud, unconventional alarm clock of the floor buffer polishing the floors on the unit. I would wonder how it was possible to not be aware of the loud whirring machine and how it was interrupting much needed sleep for those in the healing zones. Eventually, I wrote a letter to the administration voicing some opportunities for improvement.

At one point, I became so determined for change, I began to dream of a way to use all these examples to create a consulting business focused on helping hospitals develop quiet zones and quiet times centered around patient care and healing. I had even decided I would require the consultant to spend at least one week living in the different units of the hospital to assess noise interruptions, submit recommendations, and help the facilities implement them.

Lack of sleep was costly, increasing the fatigue and profound drowsiness her injured brain already battled, causing decreased alertness, which resulted in less participation in the crucial rehab sessions and the loss of a productive paid rehab day. I brought my concerns about her frequent sleep interruptions to her physiatrist and wondered how her care might be bundled and restructured to help better protect her sleep during the night.

He willingly wrote an order in her chart to help minimize interruptions at night.

Living fulltime in a rehab hospital resembled fishbowl living. The exposure and magnification within the vessel were necessary yet provided little privacy as we waited in hope for what was to be brought and dropped within the small bowl of our naked, vulnerable lives.

Tubes and Trials
Jim Thorpe Rehab | Oklahoma City, OK
June 2009

Seeing her PEG tube emerging out of her tummy and onto the floor brought great anxiety as I rushed her back to her room for help.

Will they be able to replace it without another surgery? How long do we have before the hole closes?

My face was stinging with tears.

"What do you mean you don't have the right size feeding tube?"

The nurse explained Jessie's was a pediatric size and it would take some time to find one. She called the gastroenterologist for a consultation.

"He recommends placing a foley catheter tube in her tummy hole to keep it open until a feeding tube can be replaced."

Relief settled in as more time was offered. She placed the catheter tubing without any issue. Later that evening as we were getting Jessie ready for bed, I discovered a diaper full of diarrhea. I wondered what might be wrong as I cleaned her up. Then, after getting her tucked in for sleep, I heard it happening again a few minutes later. After several loose stools throughout the night, I notified the nurse of the drastic change. Stool cultures were ordered for further investigation as suspicions arose regarding the dreaded C-diff diagnosis.

I was also concerned about dehydration as she wasn't able to receive any fluids or feedings and continued to have continuous diarrhea stools.

It was late afternoon when the gastroenterologist made his appearance to replace her PEG tube and to evaluate this sudden onset of diarrhea, and thankfully it didn't take him long to discover the hidden culprit. One I would have never imagined. The foley catheter tube had migrated down into her intestine and was causing noxious stimulation to her bowel, as it hadn't been securely taped to maintain placement.

Upon removal of the tubing, her diarrhea stopped immediately. He gently replaced her PEG tube without difficulty and we were able to resume her enteral nutrition and hydration without any further issues.

Routines and Rest

Jim Thorpe Rehab | Oklahoma City, OK
June 2009

Days were an organized schedule of tube feedings, medications, and therapists with the consistency of unorganized responses from Jessie and the never-ending, unexpected interruptions. Her inability to voice her needs demanded that we never left her alone.

Mornings always began with a clean diaper, washing her hands and face, and brushing her teeth before her nurse would arrive with her morning meds. Her meds had to be crushed and mixed with water, and administered through her gastrostomy tube since she was unable to swallow. Many days without warning, she would projectile vomit pills and tube feeding, soiling her clothes and bed. This vicious cycle would prompt a bath and linen change which would cue the painful muscle toning, only to necessitate her being medicated for comfort, resulting in her being sedated for hours. Bowel and bladder training was scheduled every two hours during the day regardless of what activity was happening, which meant two people physically holding her up on a bedside commode for at least fifteen minutes with little success to document.

Morning sessions in occupational therapy revealed a steadfast perseverance and hope from her OT as she assisted Jessie, often celebrating a single movement of her hand or leg as if she had just finished independently dressing herself.

Without time to rest, she would be moved to the next therapy scheduled. Three hours in the morning and three hours in the afternoon with a brief break at noon.

Her speech pathologist was exquisite in her techniques of care. Her focused, gentle demands for speech and cognition held my heart in suspense as I waited for the moment a response might come.

One session, she was trying to get Jessie to say, "I love you," even though she was still completely nonverbal, unable to move her mouth or even pucker her lips to form any movement in an attempt to speak.

I bent down close to her face, as if getting closer might draw something out as her speech pathologist said, "Jessie, say I love you, say I. LOVE. YOU."

We were looking for anything automatic that might come out.

"Jessie, blow me a kiss," I said as I was blowing kisses to her.

Jessie, unable to form the pucker for the kiss, reached up with her little finger and touched my lips and then touched hers.

My heart was wracked with emotions, as I now knew she understood what we were saying. I couldn't even fathom the amount of effort it must have taken for her to touch my lips with her finger.

After her noon rest break, she would repeat the same schedule in the afternoon with adjunct sessions of music therapy in between. Research has shown when words fail, music can potentially be the key to opening the door of speech, and the therapist would use familiar songs with lyrics to help attempt to initiate spontaneous language.

Her full schedule of "life hoped for" was being actively demonstrated and demanded daily by this rehab team of incredible human healers.

Grief and Gratitude

Jim Thorpe Rehab | Oklahoma City, OK
June 2009

Three long months had passed since the unimaginable phone call came, and it was easy to see how far we had come. Yet each day, Bill and I were continually reminded of how much further we still had yet to go, as we waited upon movement, cognition, and the sound of her voice. Our prayers remained fervent for the day of her first word.

When I hit another wall of immovable grief, I decided maybe it would help to try and slip away for a few hours. Bill stayed with Jessie and I went home to a quiet lonely place to pray, sleep, and rest.

It was the first time I'd laid in our bed since her accident, and my thoughts went to our marriage. Our intimacy and time alone had been stripped away with everything else and yet I had never felt closer to another human being. He knew my every moment just by the way I was breathing, or the look on my face, or the tone in my voice, or the pause before answering. He moved in sync with my emotions, balancing the highs and lows like a dance between lovers. The intimacy had moved underneath the physical, deep within the soul of my wounded spirit. His deep woundedness connected to mine had created this unspeakable union of love.

I remembered the day a psychologist had come to our room after her accident and "set us down" to have the conversation about how this type of trauma is known for a high rate of divorce. Bill stood up and abruptly ended the conversation with, "Get the hell out of our room. We have no room for this in our lives at this time or ever." We never saw him again.

Moving to the back porch swing, I quietly watched the family of Kildeers that had always nested on the ground in our backyard. Momma Kildeer was sitting on her eggs while Daddy Kildeer was darting around, bringing her food. I remembered in the years past watching this fierce and protective momma sit on her eggs during torrential rains and fierce winds and never moving. She endured any storm that would threaten to take what was hers. Daddy Kildeer was always close by as the protector and provider. He would spread his wings and let out a loud squawk running at any animal or human that came too close.

Seeing Daddy Kildeer go to their nest and relieve Momma Kildeer tendered my heart, filling it with comfort as I recognized my own story within theirs. Maybe she hit a wall today and just needed a break away. I am always deeply awed at how God speaks in the simplest ways to let me know He is here and He sees me.

Part 2: The Remnant

I soon found myself drawn to the upstairs. Slowly, I climbed the steps, holding tightly to the banister railing. Each step was harder than the last. I passed her darkened room, quiet and waiting, and turned to the right to step across the threshold of my silent prayer room filled with my past life of disciplines and studies. My chair had sat empty for months, when before it was occupied daily for years. My books and journals untouched. The last date in my prayer journal was March 16, 2009, with scriptures and prayers over the life before. It was surreal to be standing in this hidden place where I daily went behind a closed door to be with the only One who could have prepared me for the unthinkable. I touched nothing as I felt a permanent closing of this door, knowing this season was no more.

I stepped outside to the front gardens and sat among the Calla Lilies. They were in full bloom and seemed to be waiting for someone to adore them and sing their praises. I hadn't seen them in over a year and yet there they were in full glory. The bulbs, hidden deep within the frozen ground with no evidence of movement or growth, proved the mystery of God's timing of work bringing beauty and life from what appeared dead. I could hear His quiet, subtle promises within the white petals of His creation.

Walking down the long drive to the mailbox brought such sadness. I knew nothing would ever be the same as I closed my eyes and could see her running barefoot to get the mail regardless of the weather and hear myself yelling, "Get some shoes on!" The memory of her laughing at my unheeded command made my chest ache.

Opening one of the cards in the mailbox, I was buoyed by the meaning of courage.

> Courage is not the towering oak that sees the storms come and go, it is the fragile blossom that opens in the snow.

My fragile blossom. Trying to open in the snow.

I wept as I felt the intensity of this moment, knowing we were being gifted with an unspeakable opportunity to watch Jessie open ever so slowly in the winter snow.

It was painful and difficult to not be able to help her blossom more quickly. Just as nature has revealed to us, she must open on her own within the graces of God's perfect timing, as we wait in patient hope.

God, You are everywhere. Everywhere You are. Thank You for these moments away to be able to see more clearly in these simple moments of life.

Blossoms of Awakening

Jim Thorpe Rehab | Oklahoma City, OK
June 2009

The next few days began to reveal glimpses of blossoms. Even in the midst of the stiffness of toning issues, Jessie somehow pushed through the hard and did tiny things.

I watched her take a toothbrush and put it in her mouth, attempting uncoordinated small brushing movements. After much prompting and encouragement, she raised her legs slightly off the bed. She once held her head up for a few moments and even turned to look around once. With deep intentional muscle manipulation, she took several steps as Joe sweated and groaned, holding her upright

Part 2: The Remnant

and coaxing her along. She reached down to grab her leg to help OT put her shoe on, even reaching down to try and pull up her shorts. She blew me a kiss without the blowing. All these movements amounted to miracle upon miracle as we gave God all honor, glory, and praise for every single one of them.

In speech, she began to nod her head for yes and shake her head for no. It was evident she had some memory, as we witnessed some right answers. Her therapist would write two answers on a piece of paper and ask Jessie a question. She would wait for her to eventually reach out and point at the right answer, which she did most of the time.

At one point, she focused on me, as if her eyes had recognized the familiar face before her.

She reached out to me with her hand as I got very close to her face and said, "Hi, Baby. Yes, I'm your mom and you are so precious. Can you smile for me?"

I could see her lips trying to curl ever so slightly.

When I asked her for a kiss, a slight pursing of her lips appeared as if she was trying to kiss me. She even reached for a pen on the table and chaotically scribbled on a piece of paper. Each tiny little movement was evidence of our hope blossoming.

After her evening bath and nightly lotion rubdown with range of motion, I noticed the sweetest glow about her face. I marveled at this divine radiance, unable to be contained within her body. I was amazed after all she had been through, how beautiful she remained—her skin, her eyes, her face, her body, her hands, her legs, and her feet. All perfectly perfect, a gift I would never take for granted and give thanks for every day.

Drawing near to her face, I began to tell her how beautiful she looked and asked her to smile. And there was that blossom. It was so tiny, but this mom knew it was there—a smile, her smile, her beautiful lips moist from ChapStick, etching upward ever so gently.

Before turning to sleep that night, I searched for the wisdom of Julian of Norwich and found within the pages of her heart a call to joy, "The fullness of Joy is to behold God in everything."

EVERYTHING.

I knew I was being guided to keep finding God in everything about this brain injury as He worked to bring forth healing in the smallest of ways. This foreign way of seeing and trusting the slow work of God wasn't easy, but I believed God's timing was perfect and He knew the plans for her life. And those were the plans I wanted for her—His very best for her.

CHAPTER 9

The Wounded Tree

Pruning

Weeding a front flower bed one windy afternoon, I noticed "The Tree Doctor" van across the street. I'd never met a tree doctor before and watched him measure and examine trees like a child at a wellness visit, even shove a long metal rod into the earth as if taking the temperature of one of the tall, lean, big-armed creatures.

Curiosity enlisted my courage and I walked across the street, intruding upon the privacy of their moment. He was gracious and asked how he could help me. A few simple questions led to an in-depth discussion of the life of trees.

"Just like people, trees need much care and attention, especially when they're young. Watering, mulching, and pruning trees properly provides a lifetime of benefits: improving our health, climate, air, water, and wildlife for generations to come. Did you know that 100 trees remove around fifty-three tons of carbon dioxide and 430 pounds of other air pollutants each year and that tree-filled neighborhoods can lower levels of domestic abuse and make them safer and more sociable?"

Mesmerized by his passion for and knowledge of trees, I found myself asking for a front yard consultation for one of my own, explaining the unhealed weeping wound on its trunk.

His visit was informal yet informative. He explained how to scribe around the wound and shared preventative measures for insect and disease attack. Then his face changed directions.

"Can you see this? Can you see how none of these branches are moving in this wind? This big guy has never been pruned, so he is trapped within his own life. Have you ever been trapped and unable to move?"

Unexpectedly, he joined the wind, moving his arms and body in a liturgical dance, demonstrating how trees were designed to have space between the branches to breathe and move freely, reducing the risk of damage by high winds.

His interpretation of "freedom" deepened my insight to the significance of pruning and started my journey of removing dead, diseased, or unwanted branches that crossed or touched each other. I was thankful to learn how to be part of improving the tree's structure and directing new, healthy growth.

Seizures and Support
Jim Thorpe Rehab to Integris Baptist Pediatric ICU
Oklahoma City, OK | July 2009

Her gradual improvement suddenly crashed during an afternoon PT session when a grand mal seizure overtook her and refused to release her. Within minutes, unexpected neurostorming and seizures developed, rendered her unconscious, and threatened to destroy her community of organs and muscles. (Neurostorming involves a sudden and exaggerated stress response due to dysregulation of the autonomic, central, sympathetic, and the parasympathetic nervous systems after a severe TBI.) Her sudden increased surges of blood pressure, heart rate, and body temperature in unison with the seizures created a perfect storm, broadcasting life-threatening warnings. She was immediately transferred to Integris PICU.

As they do in any emergency, helpers came running. Physicians, nurses, radiologists, and even laboratory staff appeared with the sole purpose of saving her life. With a temperature of 102.4 and a heart rate of 170, the pediatric intensivist used the words, "critically ill with possible sepsis" and began emergency sepsis protocol. Even though she was heavily-medicated, she continued with seizure activity throughout the night.

After the neurologist's thorough examination and EEG, his assessment was dictated, "She is a complex case with multiple issues," recommending continued sedation as he increased the seizure medication in an attempt to halt the seizures.

Status epilepticus was defined by a seizure lasting more than five minutes and hers had been going on for hours. As a nurse, I knew this could lead to further damage to her already injured brain and possibly death.

Our hearts were grateful for the immediate provision of intensive health care and our family responding to our call: "Jessie may not make it through the night and we need you here." Bill and I wanted them to see Jessie and knew we would need a large support of love around us. I urgently reached out through Carepages and gave a quick update on her critical condition and asked for bold prayers, asking God to help her make it through the night.

The battle ensued throughout the night with her sodium and cortisol dysregulation, hypertonia, high fevers, seizures, and blood clotting issues.

As the sun rose, so did our hopes, as she had made it through the night. It was impossible to know her neurological status as she remained heavily sedated, but what we did know was she was still with us as we waited once again for her unknown outcome.

Part 2: The Remnant

Morning rounds with her doctors updated us with her latest status and their goals to stabilize her blood work, keep her seizures and toning under control with heavy sedation, and eventually wean sedation in hopes she would wake up.

Journeying once through this valley of hell should be enough for any family, but having to do it again seemed cruel and impossible. Our hearts were sickened as we continued to watch her helpless body be assaulted by her injured brain.

We had spoken our deepest truths to each other about how much was too much for her to continue to endure. We asked the question out loud, "At what point do we surrender and stop battling?" I knew and believed there were worse things than death.

My wanting her to be free of this suffering and the excruciating pain from this unceasing hypertonia brought me back to begging God again to take her if that meant she would continue in this unbearable suffering, a painful replay of the night on the floor of the chapel in Grand Junction when I begged Him to take our energetic chatty bundle of life if there would be no quality. It was only when Bill had felt that powerful Word upon him of "God would restore her" did we both make the commitment at the foot of the altar to do whatever it took, with God's help, to restore her. We continued to use His powerful Word to help guide our decisions with her, but in our darkest nights, we would find ourselves at the throne of His mercy asking, "How much more, God?"

In this intense moment of dark uncertainty, a single blue balloon with a brown stuffed puppy came quietly to the door, "Delivery for Jessie Boone." Everything stopped as the shiny mylar balloon hovering above the chaos brought the gold-embossed reminder, "With God, all things are possible." My soul was immediately quieted with the answer.

ALL things ARE possible.

A long deep breath allowed those living words to once again sink deep within my soul, "ALL things ARE possible."

No matter what, because God is with us, we are not abandoned and we are not hopeless. He will make a way when there seems to be no way.

We vigiled at her bedside, tending to her constant needs, knowing our only hope was in God, the Creator, the Maker of heaven and earth. So we waited, knowing He is faithful, remembering spring always comes after the harsh winter, rain always falls after the extreme drought, the sun always comes after the flooding rains, and morning comes after the long night of darkness.

We were grateful for our faith, our hope, our family, this hospital and staff, this day with Jessie, for listening ears allowing me to emotionally release my pain, a husband who loved me and Jessie beyond comprehension, for so many people who would do anything for us if we asked or if we didn't, and for God who was holding and carrying us all through this horrific time.

Weary and Worn

Integris Baptist Pediatric ICU | Oklahoma City, OK
July 2009

Each day in the PICU proved increasingly difficult, as she wasn't showing any signs of improvement.

Early one morning as the sun began to rise, a beam of light peeked through the tiny framed window into the darkened walls that held my most precious treasure, hitting my face like a fist. For the first time, I couldn't

Part 2: The Remnant

bring myself to say my usual morning greeting, "Today is the day the Lord hath made, let us rejoice and be glad in it." It just wasn't there. Instead, I said nothing and turned away from the light, from God Himself, and stared at Jessie lying motionless in the bed. I felt dead and empty just like she looked.

I am done, God. I can't do this anymore, and I don't really want to talk to You ever again.

Refusing to move forward, I closed my eyes and held the fetal position well into the morning. Eventually, I found myself scrolling for help once again in the Carepage postings. It didn't take long for my eyes to fall upon living words posted by a friend that seemed to be speaking directly to my darkened, defeated heart. Slowly, my ears began to open and could hear His compassionate mercy pouring upon me.

Carepage Posting

"I am worn out O Lord; have pity on me! Give me strength; I am completely exhausted and my whole being is deeply troubled. How long O Lord, will you wait to help me? I am worn out with grief; every night my bed is damp from my weeping; my pillow is soaked with tears. I can hardly see; my eyes are so swollen from the weeping caused by my enemies. The Lord hears my weeping; he listens to my cry for help and will answer my prayer."

~Psalm 6:2-3, 6-7, 8b, 9 (GNB)~

God heard my cries and within the day's vibrations of love, my heart slowly beat back to the only place I could go—to HIM. Words of gratitude infused my heart and reached up to lift my hanging head, "I am glad this isn't the end of her story. I am glad she has rested today. I am glad for the gift of my precious family. I am glad for all the care she is receiving. I am glad because I believe God has her safely tucked in His arms. I am glad for all the love and prayers that are holding us right now."

Within the mystery of His grace, the abandoned early morning greeting that refused to be spoken was now whispering within my evening vespers, "Today is the day the Lord has made, let us rejoice and be glad in it."

From Hell-no to Hope
Integris Baptist Pediatric ICU | Oklahoma City, OK
July 2009

The doctor's request for a family conference was unexpected but not surprising. He spent several minutes reviewing her complicated medical status, emphasizing her lack of improvement over the last few days, and giving the two of us his recommendation to sign a Do Not Resuscitate.

"This would be a good time to complete one, as you can see her quality of life isn't one you would want for her. Her next crisis, we would just make her comfortable with no aggressive care."

I wouldn't want for her? HE DID NOT JUST SAY THAT! He has no idea what I want for her! All of my previous conversations with God and Bill came flooding forward. *I get it, Doctor, I truly do. But this isn't our call. We have already been there and asked those questions. God gets to make that choice, not me. He has the power to take her at this moment if He chooses. Besides, He has already told us He will restore her.*

As I stood up, my eyes blazed, "We are finished here. There will be no DNR. I know you are doing what you think is right at this time, but we are being led in another direction by God Himself. We have surrendered her life to Him, and we still believe He has other plans. So, we will follow His direction until He leads us otherwise."

Our family conference was over, and we left in silence, holding hands in solidarity but shaking on the inside as we stood on the precipice of faith without seeing, knowing that from a medical point of view, his perspective didn't look wrong.

The next day, her sedation remained the same but the hypertonicity seemed less. After the emotional emptying the night before, there seemed to be a little less suffocation and a little more space to breathe. Great grief was still palpable, but the extra space within my heart seemed to help diffuse it, making it feel a little less oppressive.

Carepage wisdom came from the words of a dear pastor friend, nourishing the dry bones of my heart and helping me to rediscover hope once again. He shared his own devastating personal tragedy ending with,

Carepage Posting

Then slowly, day by day, the light came back, refusing to give up to the darkness. Now it is ten years later and most days are wonderful. There is HOPE!

Today was surely one of those "slowly" days. Slowly, the Light began to peek through the tiniest places, refusing to give up to the darkness and enabled me to find the footing to embrace the "slowly" of HOPE and what was still yet to come.

The Wounded Tree

Discharge planning swiftly plowed through the door the next morning, revealing the question looming in the darkness: "Where do we go from here?" Inpatient rehab was no longer an option due to her current medical status, leaving only two options to consider—a children's long term care facility or home.

Bill and I both already knew the answer without speaking to each other. Our only option was our hearts. We would take her home, even in the midst of the overwhelming challenges to provide care for her complex medical needs, to do whatever it took for her optimal healing.

One of the most pressing concerns was finding a good physician specialist willing to provide complex medical care for her within a private home. I had no idea where to even begin.

The next morning, sunlight streamed into our room once again as Dr. Brannan, a pediatric specialist, suddenly appeared at her bedside, introduced himself, and shared a wealth of information about home care.

"This is what I do," his quiet gentle voice revealed as I watched the one huge obstacle standing in our way to go home fall into the sea. Freely releasing tears, I knew God had made a way once again.

After his agreement to provide medical care for Jessie, we were able to smoothly coordinate with our insurance company for necessary durable medical equipment needs, prescriptions for medications, and referrals for home therapists. It wasn't long before we were headed "home."

Part 2: The Remnant

No Place Like Home

Home | Oklahoma City, OK
July 2009

"Jessie, we are HOME," I whispered in her ear, wondering if she knew.

HOME. So much is different, but we are home. God, thank You for bringing her home.

Faded yellow ribbons were still holding tightly to the trees and structures as they had waited for their hope and purpose to be fulfilled.

The wheelchair ramp offering of love from our neighbor was the cushion of comfort we needed as it greeted our wounded hearts and helped us wheel her across the threshold of this new cocoon.

Our home had been freshly anointed as a huge cross vacuumed in the carpet revealed the healing presence of God. Fresh flowers softened the harshness of reality. Furniture had been rearranged, much like our lives, to accommodate new pathways. The refrigerator was full of the bountiful provisions from friends. The master bedroom downstairs had become our new family room holding a hospital bed draped with a gifted new comforter next to our bed. Feeding pump, suction machine, and a fully-stocked cabinet of medications and medical supplies were in place and readied for the mission ahead.

The reality of being at home with a mute, spastic, quadriplegic daughter with no skull collided with fear and relief. We were returning to our quiet sanctuary of life and spaciousness, yet we still faced the mountainous battles of awakening and healing.

I couldn't consume the quiet fast enough. Even though her care demands were constant, the missing intrusiveness slowly began to soothe my bone-weariness and frazzled nervous system.

Mute, spastic, quadriplegic were the targets of our determined intentions to overcome. We found ourselves at ground zero again, but now we were home and had been prepared and taught what we needed to do. This sacred sanctuary had been readied for the pilgrimage of our hearts and souls in search of the promised land of speech, cognition, and function. Gradually our doors opened to a host of helpers.

Our first visitor was the admission nurse of the home health agency that would be establishing the groundwork for home therapy. It was a short visit, as my exhaustion and grief ushered her out the door when she never looked at or spoke to the precious reason she was visiting. I had vowed to never allow Jessie to be "unseen" again. I simply explained to the nurse as she was leaving, "It is my expectation, as Jessie's mom, that she be acknowledged when a health care professional comes to visit. I need someone who can see her."

Reinforcements of therapists appeared, sharing their expert strategies to stimulate more movement and speech. Friends and family provided meals, organizational skills, companionship, gardening skills, and gifts of prayerful support, bringing light and hope within each day. Because of her profound medical needs, a part-time private duty nurse was provided by the state SoonerCare program to help with the intensiveness of her care, gifting me with an occasional small break away for errands or sleep during the days, as Bill attempted to return to as much of a work routine as her medical condition would allow.

The first day we met Whitney, we quickly discovered a young, cheerful, and chatty presence had returned to our home. Her attentiveness to details, oriented to specific care needs in the shape of optimism and hope, brought a new energy of laughter and play into our darkness and began to expand our lives with tiny bits of air and light.

Signs
Home | Oklahoma City, OK
July 2009

One morning, I caught a glimpse of a plastic-wrapped newspaper at the end of our driveway, surprising me as our delivery had been suspended since her accident. It was strangely comforting to once again "walk out to the driveway" and simply pick up the newspaper. I found myself breathing in the newness of the morning, receiving the expansiveness of the sky as a brief respite.

The front-page headlines were bold: "TEEN CALLED A WALKING MIRACLE."

Stunned, I stopped, staring to make sure I was seeing that correctly. I read each word out loud, "A seventeen-year-old boy was in a coma for two months and, for the last six months, was unable to walk or talk. All of a sudden, a switch flipped and almost overnight he began to make progress and was now walking and talking." I read it out loud again as if my ears and eyes hadn't been able to grasp the sounds of hope within the written announcement.

God, is this a sign from You? Is this by chance? You know I don't believe in coincidences. The first paper delivered to our home? Really, God? Is this yet another miracle You have placed before me to help move us forward with continued perseverance and endurance?

I arranged the prophetic headline on my bedside table next to my simple bookmark, "NEVER, NEVER, NEVER GIVE UP," adding it with my daily intention of determination to press forward in hope, believing for the day when her switch would also be flipped on.

Streams in the Desert, my daily companion since her accident, joined this choir of hope: "May God grant us faith to completely trust His Word, even when every other sign points the other way. When is the time to trust? Is it when hopes beat high, when sunshine gilds the sky, and joy and ecstasy fill all the heart? NO! For the time to trust is when our joy has fled, when sorrow bows the head, and all is cold and dead. All else but God."

These timely words of wisdom and truth reached down into my sunken heart, prying up paths that journeyed around the obvious destruction and devastation into a land revealing hope, trusting and believing there was a "switch" on its way.

Infusions of Love
Home | Oklahoma City, OK
July 2009

The landscape of our days from the outside looked like normal family life. Lights seen through windows, air conditioner units humming, mail being delivered, visitors coming and going, but within the walls painted such a different picture. Hospital bed, tube feedings, repositioning every two hours, medications around the clock, vomiting, toning, skin care, bed bathing, and as much rehab as we could cram safely into a day. We continued to stimulate her, touch her, talk with her, watch movies with her, cook with her, sing with her, hold her, rub her, and read to her, hoping and believing the familiar signs of life, with the grace of God, would make a connection and turn her switch of life back on.

Just as we continued to infuse our lives into Jessie, others continued to infuse their lives into ours. Our emptiness and exhaustion reflected in the Carepages,

Carepages

Post A Message

It has been especially difficult to reach out to others, as our time is completely filled with care for Jessie and we are empty and exhausted. We continue to put one foot in front of the other and wait upon the Lord as He places provision for us.

Infusions of love in so many different forms continued to find their way to us, nourishing and sustaining us for this uncharted journey of the unknown.

The Hope of Restoration

Dr. El Amm's Office | Oklahoma City, OK
July 2009

"I am not sure why we are doing this?" Dr. El Amm's cold response mirrored the room he was examining her in for the first time.

The plastic surgeon had no idea what it took us to just get to his office. The oversized wheelchair holding her lifeless body with an extension to support her head was a feat, even before loading it into the car. He didn't know I had just performed a miracle in the bathroom two doors down, changing her diaper without a changing table fit for a teenager. He had no clue the vomiting episodes in the car on the way required me to frantically pull over, clear her mouth, and clean her up. He couldn't have known the grief in my heart every single moment I gazed upon her, remembering her infectious laugh and beautiful blonde hair, and the sweet chatter that incessantly vibrated the walls within our home since she was born—and the physical pain I experienced every time I realized she was now unrecognizable to me. That *I* needed a bone healer to bring about some physical restoration to my daughter's ravaged head. He didn't know I was searching for hope to take another step toward her restoration, or that her skull was in several chunks stored away, identified only by her name and date of birth in a medical freezer hidden away in the basement of a hospital in Colorado.

He must have known she was at high risk for further brain trauma without the protection of her skull, but those words, "I am not sure why we are doing this?" indicated he didn't know any of this, or he just didn't care.

But Dr. Timothy Mapstone, the chief neurosurgeon, *knew*. His gentle expertise sat with us with the intent to replace her skull, assuring us he knew the surgeon to do it. We left his office with fresh hope and an eagerness to put Jessie back together again. "All the king's horses and all the king's men didn't know how to put Humpty back together again," but Dr. Mapstone knew that Dr. El Amm was just the person to do it.

I began telling Dr. El Amm about Jessie Boone from my momma's heart-shaped perspective. "If you knew her, you would know why. She is a beautiful life force to be reckoned with!" After emptying my heart, repainting the floor and walls of that exam room with her story, we left with her surgery scheduled and many unknowns, including finding her skull pieces and determining whether they were still viable.

Part 2: The Remnant

Hard-won Firsts

Home | Oklahoma City, OK
August 2009

Jessie's finger moved to the beat of music playing in the background while her nurse, Whitney, was moving through the morning routines of bathing, brushing teeth, tube feedings, medications, dressing, and diaper changes. My momma's heart was soothed by this young woman's way of caring. She treated Jessie like they were best friends. Her never-ending chatting and laughing was enough to wake anyone up. "They" would play beauty shop, frequently calling me to come and see a new hairdo. Anyone listening through the door would have never guessed only one was participating.

During a movie they would watch together, she would ask Jessie questions about the plot or character, and then answer like Jessie had asked the question. She would tease her about boys and challenge her with trivia, always finding new and creative ways to stimulate any kind of a response. I would occasionally catch Jessie's eyes following her movements and hold my breath to see what would happen next.

Physical and occupational therapy continued to work endlessly toward improving Jessie's head and trunk control, so she would be able to sit and stand without support.

Gradually, we began seeing intentional movements of her body like a turning of her head to see who was coming in the door or a little wave with her sweet fingers. One day, she became "so active," she pulled her PEG tube out of her belly and we were all rewarded with an urgent trip to the Children's ER to have it replaced.

The Wounded Tree

A floor mat was the new rug in our dayroom, providing the platform for stretching range of motion on all of her extremities. Her toning remained but seemed less fierce with each passing day.

The first day she rolled over onto her belly was the day we began to work toward the goal of crawling. Holding her knees in place, one of us would hold her arms straight as her head would hang down. We would take turns moving her extremities one at a time, helping her to stay up and not collapse to the floor, cheering her on, "Come on, Jessie! You can do this! Just move your arm!"

One afternoon, I overheard the PT say, "Jessie, let's crawl up the stairs."

I came from the kitchen just in time to watch her help Jessie reach for the first step.

What is she doing? She knows she can't even crawl well on the floor!

With maximum assistance, helping her to move one extremity at a time, she crawled up one step at a time until she reached the very top of the landing. This type of expectation demanded results as it fiercely challenged her balance, coordination, and head control. I was stunned silent, not knowing how I felt about this unbelievable accomplished feat.

Movement in her legs slowly began to take root as I watched each struggling step after another. She was held with maximum assistance by her PT who was once again using her muscle memory, eliciting movements with little or no conscious effort.

Eventually the day arrived when she was able to be walked by holding her up with a gait belt and someone on each side of her, ensuring she didn't fall. Being able to walk her to the bed or her chair helped strengthen her legs and increase her mobility by decreasing the time she spent sitting in the wheelchair. Every daily activity was molded therapy for her. Searching for a way to help her stand alone, our physical therapist recommended a home "standing frame," explaining the additional benefits of standing for lengths of time to strengthen and stretch her muscles, prevent contractures, reduce muscle spasms, improve bowel and bladder control, enhance respiratory function, and maintain bone density.

Electrical stimulation of her nerves roused slow, clumsy movements from her hands, arms, and legs through a specialized unit provided by one of our therapist friends. His knowledge and experience with physical therapy and body kinesiology guided our home efforts to expert levels.

Even with all the movement and activity, her quietness was deafening to my heart.

Oh Jessie, to hear your voice, to be able to know what you need or how you feel. Sweet darlin, are you in there?

Her disconnected flat affect and the fatigued look in her eyes left me heartsick.

I will never forget the busy therapy day when I thought I heard faint humming. Instantly turning toward Jessie, my heart pounding and hopeful, I asked, "Is that you?" My answer appeared to be a no. There was no sound, no words, or no facial expressions—just silence.

These decibels of quietness spoke volumes to the depth of her injuries, contrasting the overwhelming sounds of voices rising to heaven in hopes of leveling out the uneven ground.

It was such a paradox to find my strength and comfort in the quietness. Small talk seemed to minimize what was happening and sharing in great lengths about Jessie seemed to magnify the circumstances. My peace was only found sitting in the silence of His presence, being held by His gentleness, falling in sync and coexisting with Jessie's rhythm of life.

One morning, I heard my name being yelled, "Lisa, come in here quick!"

Running to the voice of her nurse, fearful Jessie had fallen or was vomiting, I was instead greeted with a Disney soundtrack. As I opened the French doors to the bedroom, my searching eyes found Jessie sitting up in her chair, fully dressed, and adorned with an overabundance of makeup. Whitney, who resembled an older blonde-haired Jessie, was dancing to "A Dream is a Wish Your Heart Makes."

I held my breath as I caught a glimpse of my "old" Jessie and her wildly creative dancing to the Disney soundtrack with an emphasis on the emotions occurring in the song. What a moment to be invited into as I watched the features of Jessie's stoneface watching the silly choreography of her nurse as my heart laughed in the midst of my tears.

And suddenly, without any warning, I was given the sweetest evidence of connection when I witnessed her face move gently, her eyes soften, and the edges of her perfect pink tinged lips turning upward.

It was our first hope photo op taken with great excitement and joy.

"Her first big smile."

Inspired Steps

Home | Oklahoma City, OK
August 2009

Jessie's suitcase had remained untouched on her bedroom floor. My grief refused to unpack the sweaters and scarves she had colorfully coordinated for the ski trip, as if I could preserve the "before." The upstairs room remained dark and quiet like its missing dweller, and it was the very place I would go to bury my wails and tears of loss. Her "old life" held me deeply submerged in a reality I just couldn't get out from under.

How do I do this, God? How in the world do we move through this? I can't even bear to open her suitcase or the closet that holds her past. When I look back at all we have lost, this crushing grief overwhelms my whole being. When I look forward to all the what-ifs and nevers, I can't breathe as the mountain of fear overtakes me.

God's gentle impressions became my anchors.

"Stay in the present moment with Me. Take the next right step when you can. All we have is this moment. Lisa, you can do right now. Step by step, I will guide you. This is My way of peace for you."

Soon after, her physical therapist challenged, "Come on, let's go!" as we were walking Jessie with the gait belt past the stairs during one of her therapy sessions.

Wide-eyed, I looked at her in disbelief, "The stairs? Really?"

"I think she's ready."

You think she's ready? She can't even lift her foot an inch off the floor and you think she's ready?

"I don't know if *I* am ready," I admitted, halting the forward movement. Reaching up, I adjusted her helmet, looked her in the eyes, and whispered, "Want to go up to your room?"

A response never came, and I could feel my breath being sucked out of my lungs as I remembered how many hundreds of times with different tones she had announced, "I am going up to my room." Grasping her gait belt a little tighter, I took a deep breath, using the moment to ground my fear.

In the moment, Lisa. Stay in the moment.

Up she went, lifting her foot to take the first step. With maximum assistance, she climbed seventeen stairs to the top. Out of breath, she struggled to take another step but refused to quit. I sensed a gentle movement toward the left where her bedroom waited. As she slowly crossed the threshold, she instinctively reached up, "turning the switch on." Light flooded in!

Her newly witnessed determination to go into her room carved a deeper intention into my faith along with a new revelation—Jessie Boone was in there.

She wants to be back in her room! This is the very first "want" we have seen! She wants ... she wants ... Oh God ... she wants ... She is in there and wants to be in her room!

Outpatient Advances

Home | Oklahoma City, OK
September 2009

Jim Thorpe Outpatient was our next stop on this rehab journey. Three times every week, traveling caused car vomiting, and three hours of nonstop therapy manifested profound fatigue with frequent toileting issues. Yet I knew these bigger spaces of advancing therapies were the road we must travel as the next right step.

After several weeks at home with home therapy, stepping into this building with every space created and staffed for the purpose of recovery and gaining independence was like stepping through a new portal of hope. As hard as it was, I knew the valuable equipment and machines, experienced therapists, and a history of healing were exactly what we needed to be immersed in to teach, train, and recover what she had lost.

Her newly assigned physical therapist met her right where she was, determined to bring her back to where she needed to be. The well-equipped gym held stations of potential and challenge where she would have forty-five minutes of intense physical challenges pushing for the mobility and strengthening of her weak muscles, with the ultimate goal of improving the overall movements of her body.

The occupational therapist focused on Jessie's ability to do basic activities of daily living which required regaining memory loss, relearning social and nonverbal cues, improving attention span, increasing hand strength and dexterity, and bettering hand-eye coordination.

Speech therapy utilized many different techniques and computer technology to improve her communication. Electrical stimulation on her face would focus on helping to awaken nerves and muscles to improve her speaking and swallowing abilities. Computer programs challenged her memory and problem-solving skills. Breathing exercises enhanced her breath control to help with verbalization, along with specific exercises to strengthen her oral muscles.

The height, depth, width, and breadth of the benefits of the outpatient therapy was immeasurable, creating so many unexpected moments of connection, support, and education within the community of clients that we spent so much time with. Friendships and connections were forged in this new place of "different," a place of accepting and knowing real brokenness, in the united search for improved quality of life. This left little room for the painful comparison to the "normal," enabling us to move forward in the reality of what was without having to also navigate unnecessary grief and pain.

Six Months of Silence
Home | Oklahoma City, OK
September 2009

Her six-month anniversary was a blaring siren of how long it had been since I'd heard her voice. The inability to communicate with her was full of never-ending questions: How could I know if her head hurt? Or if she was thirsty? Or what she needed? Did she even know what she needed? Was she trapped inside, screaming her thoughts with no way for us to hear her? Or was her silence also within?

Her speech therapist had unsuccessfully been working on an eye blink response but wasn't able to coordinate an intentional blink. The yes/no cards were the next attempt to make contact, but fell short of knowing the accuracy of her pointed response.

With her scheduled left cranioplasty (skull replacement) quickly approaching, I had hoped I would have established a way by now to know what she was feeling, but her steadfast silence and disconnection endured.

The Sweetness of Sixteen
Home | Oklahoma City, OK
October 2009

October 11, 12:00 a.m., her sweet sixteen was ushered in by repositioning her body, changing her diaper, and checking on her PEG feedings. Heartsick and heavy, I remembered Jessie's big plans: driving to church and standing up for the traditional birthday song, having a big sleepover with too many friends, enjoying a fancy dinner with the family, taking a trip to the mall with her birthday money, and going on her first date with her first boyfriend.

Her dreams were replaced by her daddy faithfully sitting by his beautiful, broken daughter, reading these words, "Rejoice in the Lord always. I will say it again. Rejoice! Let your gentleness be evident to all. The Lord is near. Do not be anxious about anything, but 'in everything,' by prayer and petition, with thanksgiving, present your requests to God. And the peace of God which transcends all understanding will guard your hearts and your minds in Christ Jesus. Finally, whatever is true, whatever is noble, whatever is right, whatever is pure, whatever is lovely, whatever is admirable, if anything is excellent or praiseworthy, think about such things." (Philippians 4:4-9 NIV)

Watching as words flowed from his lips to her ears warmed me with his faithful love for us both. He went on, "I have learned to be content whatever the circumstances. I have learned the secret of being content in any and every situation." (Philippians 4:12 NIV)

Leaning back against the bed, those words gave me great pause.

I have learned to be content whatever the circumstances are? Father, I am not content in this situation, and I have no idea how to be, nor do I want to be. Help me to see the deeper meaning underneath the words of Your Truth.

As I began seeking, yet another word appeared for more context—peace.

Nope, still not feeling it. There is absolutely nothing peaceful about this situation. I began to lean harder into the question, asking God, *What is this contentment You are asking of me in this situation? I don't understand.*

Slowly, contentment shifted to fullness. The word fullness filled me with a warmth that sank deeply into the folds of my heart, revealing the truth that I had never felt so full of His help. In every moment, there was always some kind of help that guided me to take the next step. If I could find the good in the moment, I could find God helping, strengthening me to take the next step.

"I can do ALL things through Christ who gives me strength" (Philippians 4:13 NIV) ended his reading with her. Her favorite verse. There she lay, sixteen years old, and living out her life verse unprecedentedly.

Her birthday was brimming with love—lunch with family, a perfect homemade cake from her special friend, complete with sixteen candles and the birthday song with a special emphasis on "many more!" After her serenade, "she took a deep breath" and we all helped her blow them out. So many special gifts of love, phone calls, homemade cards, videos, and roses celebrated the truth we knew—this day could have been so different without her. Gifts of no vomiting, fever, or severe toning helped this day be as perfect and peaceful as it could be. And a most special gift was that she slept with her beloved Toasty, a tiny brown chihuahua who hadn't been with her in seven months.

CHAPTER 10

The Cottonwood Medicine

Signs of Life

"We are on the way to the emergency room right now and he isn't moving or breathing very well." My friend's desperate urgency was obvious in her heaving breaths.

I was in my backyard underneath the sanctuary of trees that stood with me as I could hear her deeper groans coming through the cell phone.

"He isn't even two weeks old! Oh God, help us please!"

"Let's pray now," I answered as the breeze forced the branches to attention. "Father, we need help now. Send your power and angels to this little one, bringing breath and energy to his life. Protect him and keep him safe. Help those caring for him to find out what is wrong and take swift action." I pleaded with my heart and eyes as they opened toward the wide blue heavens above me.

Suddenly in that moment, mystical medicine began filling the air, taking the graceful form of the softness of cotton. It was swirling and building as it quickly became a blizzard overtaking the atmosphere of my prayers.

"You aren't going to believe what is happening at this very moment," I said as I tried to capture this unbelievable mystery on my phone camera. "The heavens just opened and have commenced pouring a manna-like blizzard everywhere! The earth where I stand is covered, the sky is full, and it just keeps coming. I believe God is visibly showing me His grace right now being poured out all over your precious baby. He is so present to you and all that is happening and is sending His power and help right now. "

I stood in the middle of the yard, overwhelmed in the tangible grace, and beheld the beloved cottonwood tree standing over eighty feet tall at the edge of our property pouring out so freely and abundantly. There were no boundaries to its reach.

This sacred tree, also known as the medicine tree to many indigenous Native Americans, grows rapidly and easily reaches over 100 feet in height. The wide and far-reaching branches create architectural wonders on the landscape with flat stemmed leaves rustling softly and shimmering mystically. When the fruit pods ripen, they burst open like popcorn and the billowing seeds of faith become sails on the winds to disperse in efforts to assure future generations will grow. And yet it gives even more, there is a hidden secret this tree holds and can only be discovered through the brokenness of a branch. Deep underneath the wrinkles of growth lines, in the center of the branch, one can find a perfectly formed star, echoing the ancient Star of Bethlehem, the one found in the sky two thousand years ago that revealed and guided others to the One who brings hope to the world.

The Mending Begins
Oklahoma University's Children's Hospital
Oklahoma City, OK | October 2009

When I turned over and saw 1:11 on the clock, it greeted me as my old friend sharing comfort, "I am with you always, side by side." My soul was held in reassurance as my heart pounded with anticipation of her surgery.

 A few hours later, I woke to check on Jessie lying in her bed next to mine, and found her sleeping peacefully

The Cottonwood Medicine

with the alarm close to making the announcement: "It's time."

Lifting her into her chair, her eyes opened and met mine. Feelings shifted from peace to sadness as Isaiah 53:7 (NIV) came to my heart, "He was led like a lamb to the slaughter, and as a sheep before its shearers is silent, so he did not open his mouth." It was like we were leading our beloved lamb to the slaughter and she didn't even know. Her silence was deafening. It had been over seven months since I'd heard her voice.

If she could speak, what would she say? What would she want us to do for her?

What I did know was I believed with all my heart that the deepest love was guiding each step and decision we made for her.

As Bill drove the early drive in the darkness of the unknown, it was haunting. The red neon letters "OU Children's Entrance" helped to guide us into this unfamiliar territory. Within seconds, out through the double doors came the warm and smiling familiar face of the dear beautiful Dana (who I had affectionately named DBD).

Oh my gosh, nothing could have been more perfect.

DBD welcomed and ushered us into our "home" for the next several days. Her offering of comfort was volunteering to work her day off to be in surgery, using her gifts of "scrubbing in" to assist the surgeons. Comfort held me knowing her eyes of love and her expertise were watching over Jessie both physically and spiritually. The way was prepared with such love—we simply had to walk through those doors, and we were even given a personal escort!

Jessie's expansive community of love and support gathered with us, some in person in a small waiting room, helping to hold us steady with great intercessory prayers of hope. Great love flowed like a river out of the waiting room, down the hallways, filling her operating room with the mystery of His Grace touching all within, guiding each moment and movement, all with a peace that passeth all understanding.

It was Dr. Mapstone's face, wrinkled and red from his surgical attire, that appeared first with a tender smile of assurance.

"My part is finished, and she is doing okay. Do you have any questions for me?"

Yes! I have questions. But this one question is the one I don't dare ask because I don't think I could bear the answer.

My eyes were searching his, wanting him to answer the question I couldn't ask. I smiled wearily, shaking my head, pushing out the words, "Thank you, Dr. Mapstone. Thank you."

He patted my shoulder, gently leaving his comfort upon me.

I shall call him Gentleness.

I spent the next few hours pensively massaging the deep echoing question that had been haunting me. Dr. El Amm had discussed the real possibility of having to remove her entire scalp and turning it the other direction to assure enough healthy skin would cover her scalp. The thought left me appalled and in this canyon of unknowing dread. I shuddered to imagine what this would look like, concerned about her hair growth and overall appearance of her head.

I can't bear this, God. I hate this with all my soul. Tears flowed as I wept for my girl. *How did we ever get to this cruel place of awfulness?*

Dr. El Amm halted my downhill fear spiral when he appeared. Shifting my full heart and attention toward this man who had just reconstructed her skull, I listened carefully as he began his dissertation about her surgery.

I heard "no bone graft from the hip or ribs…" *Yes*… "she had plenty of bone…" *Yes*… "no scalp removal or rotation…" *OH MY GOD!* My heart pounded with relief and praise, *YES!*… "We were able to reuse her previous incision…" *Yes*… "the pieces of her skull went together nicely…" *Yes*… "everything went smoothly…" *Yes*… "it will be at least six months before we know how it will heal…" *Yes*… "minimal blood loss…" *Yes*… "no blood transfusions…" *Yes*… "vital signs stable…" *Yes*… "she is on her way to recovery." My tears immersed the beautiful word, "*Yes,*" into a blur of immeasurable relief.

Then he was gone. But what he had left behind was more than I could have ever imagined—a trail of hope.

Just a few minutes later, a smiling Dana appeared, announcing, "She is extubated and off the ventilator."

Yes!

We were ushered into recovery to be with Jessie as she woke up.

Yes.

Nothing could have been more comforting. Nothing could have prepared me for what I was to see and hear next. She was breathtaking. Her face was perfect. The left side of her skull was perfect. Her incision was hidden within her hairline. Her vital signs were perfect. We were awestruck at the vision that laid before us.

There you are, darlin' girl. I see you.

Tears flowing freely, we were getting the first glimpse of seeing our daughter being made whole.

Then came THE moment. The very moment I had been waiting and praying for. The moment that pierced my ears and heart with such great hope. Out of her mouth came a deep guttural groaning, erupting from the depths of her soul.

God! Her voice! I hear her voice! Her first sound revealed such great pain, it was quickly quieted with intravenous morphine, yet that one deep guttural groan continued to echo in the marrow of my bones.

Her voice is there. Deep within, but there!

Divine Encounters
Oklahoma University's Children's Hospital
Oklahoma City, OK | October 2009

There are bumps upon every road we travel as people living in this broken world. Speed bumps are designed to slow us down for the safety and protection of others. The ones on this journey were a jarring experience of vomiting with unwanted air pockets underneath her skull flap, causing increasing pressure on her brain. As a result, hyperoxygenation therapy was given over the next twenty-four hours to attempt to dissolve the trespassing air pockets. This slowing down gave her a full quiet day of rest, also allowing us to simply be by her side with peace.

How is it possible to have peace in the midst of such an unknown?

The living words from Philippians 4:7 were attentively guarding my heart: "The peace of God which transcends all understanding will guard your hearts and your minds in Christ Jesus." Nothing unwanted creeped in that day. Not fear, anxiety, sadness—nothing but gifts of peace rested upon us all day.

I heard her voice today.

In the midst of our peace day were divine encounters.

The first was Sacredness. When the quiet knock came, neither of us wanted any visitors, as we were exhausted by emotions and no sleep. The stranger insisted he wouldn't stay long but after reading her Carepages, he knew he needed to meet us. He introduced himself and shared the story of his fifteen-year-old son who had gone skiing twelve years earlier on a church trip and also had a skiing accident. He immediately had our hearts.

How could this even be? The same scenario?

"How is he now?" I gently asked.

He gently stepped into a space of sharing how his injuries were so severe that the only way he could continue to live was by giving life to others through the sacrificial offering of his organs.

I stepped toward him, reaching out to touch his arm, speaking the only words that would come, "I am so sorry." My heart fell at the feet of this brave, brokenhearted father who came to give us what he could.

He showed unspeakable courage and profound love as he stood before us, offering his humble prayers of healing over our precious child, hoping she would not only live but would heal to an abundant life.

What sacred ground we stood upon as we witnessed love made flesh, hoping and praying for the life of another in the midst of his own unimaginable loss.

Our next encounter was with Healer. She was the director of the PICU and had exceptional nursing staff, using excellent clinical skills with great attention to detail, all with a posture of caring and kindness. Healer entered with such intention, wanting to meet us and check on Jessie. She spoke of great hope and expectation over Jessie's healing, her words flowing like the healing balm of

Gilead. Her great faith and hope brought encouragement and a healing light to this dark path we were gently forging.

The encounter named Love came later that evening through a housekeeper. This devout mother of seven children, working 4 p.m.–12 a.m. came in humming a hymn of praise and began emptying the trash. Her conversation shifted to how she loves her work and prays for the children she encounters.

What great love that she is laying her life down for another and praying for the children.

Then suddenly, her hands outstretched over Jessie's brain and heart with commanding words of healing, hope, graduation, and even a future with grandchildren came pouring out.

Who is this bold woman of Love?

Seeing with the eyes of her heart into the heart and soul of our lives was medicine. We had "church" right at the foot of her bed praising and praying over Jessie. Before she left for her next divine appointment, we hugged and agreed that one day, we would be standing side by side in heaven praising, "Holy, Holy, Holy! Lord God Almighty!" and thanking Him for all He had done.

Many encounters followed. Provision, Connections, Fruit, Life Giver, Marriage Covenant, Standing in the Gap, Prayerful, Hope, Gratitude, all with human faces and hands offering the sustenance of Life to our weary and parched landscape.

Sweetly and intentionally prepared by divine encounters, the bumps slowly began to rise up unknowingly into walls.

Compassion, the nurse, greeted us by telling us she would be Jessie's nurse for the day. She shared that she was in a bible study with one of Jessie's old gymnastic coaches and had been praying for her since the accident. She was touching Jessie today by caring for her with her hands, her heart, and her spirit.

What a gift she is to this momma's heart!

Inwardly smiling at God, I knew He had prepared this moment in time for her to be with Jessie as she ushered her to CT for further evaluation of the air pockets. I was feeling comforted with her presence and hopeful the air pockets were gone based on Jessie's night of no vomiting and well-managed pain.

"The air pockets are now gone, but unfortunately, we have a greater concern. They have been replaced with a pocket of fluid under her skull large enough to push her brain past the right midline." Dr. Mapstone gently continued, "A drain is needed immediately to relieve the pressure and allow the brain to shift back into its normal position."

My heart fell from the peace that had been so present.

Jessie, darlin' girl. I can't stand the thought of you having to go through this again!

I fell into the canyon of what-ifs as my tears filled the raging river below.

I could not have imagined what was coming next.

Reality appeared in her room, with CT films in hand, showing the midline shift to the right. He explained the procedure to Bill and me, along with the risks and how he would be placing the drain in a few minutes.

What does he mean he is placing the drain!?!

"Excuse me, I thought Dr. Mapstone would be placing the drain?"

I could feel my canyon filling with anger as he spoke, "No, this is a routine procedure, so I will be."

What the hell?

Part 2: The Remnant

I could feel my voice rising up and reaching out to his face as if to hit him, "Well, this isn't a routine procedure for us, and I don't want a resident putting a drain in her head!"

Something or Someone shifted this moment.

Instead of resistance or argument, Reality turned to Gentleness, agreeing with a softer voice, "You are right. It isn't a routine procedure, and let me explain."

He sat down on her bed and began telling the story of how he had known about Jessie long before we came. He knew she would be coming here for her surgery, and he would be taking care of her. He then invited me to come closer to a bedside computer screen as he opened up his personal email, showing me the email from his sister that very morning. She had told him about our journey, our faith, and the preciousness of Jessie Boone. It was so beautifully written by the heart of someone who had followed her journey and wanted her brother to know the sacred ground upon which he stood. At the bottom of the email was last night's posting of Carepages. He read those words with great tenderness and compassion. His last words to me were reassuring me that he would take good care of our daughter and he knew God would be guiding his hands.

Silence walked with me out of Jessie's room. My tears were not shy. I didn't want her to have to go through this. I didn't want the resident to do it. I didn't want to be in this hospital anymore. I didn't want complications. I didn't want her to have a brain injury. I ... I ... I ... I ... I ... I took a deep breath, closed my eyes, and began to replay the last few minutes with this chief resident.

How great is our God revealing His presence to me through the resident, reminding me once again that God is in charge, not me! That this young man has dedicated his life to the science of medicine and neurosurgery, and that God chose him to place this drain. I felt my heart releasing and opening to receive the gift of this special resident touching my daughter's life, doing all he could to help correct this life-threatening complication. Peace slowly edged out the fear and anger, making room for gratitude to flow again. *I shall rename him God's Hands.*

Moments after my peace had returned, Sweetness appeared, calling our names, "Lisa? Bill?"

Turning, I saw a young woman in a nursing uniform from OU College of Nursing. She had been a part of our youth group when Bill and I had volunteered as youth leaders. She told me she was in a rotation at Children's and wanted to check on how Jessie was doing, how she felt God was calling her into a ministry of nursing out of this country. Before she returned back to her rotation, she insisted on praying for us. These moments of sweet, holy encounters were calming in the midst of the current storm on the other side of the door.

Shortly after we were able to return to her room, another nurse appeared. I will call her Prayerful. We didn't know her, but she knew us, telling us how Jessie's Carepages were so powerful and spoke to her each morning. She used the words "my morning devotions" and wanted us to know that since the accident, she had been praying boldly and wouldn't stop. Somehow seeing these beautiful young Godly girls helped me to catch a glimpse of how I imagined Jessie could be in ten years and it was strangely comforting to my exposed heart.

Jessie was to lie flat for the next forty-eight hours with her crown of bandages covering this temporary weapon aimed at knocking down the wall of pressure. The hiddenness of the weapon seemed to ease my heart as these God sightings throughout this day wove numerous strands of hope into the strength to continue this precarious quest for Jessie's restoration.

With Us
Oklahoma University's Children's Hospital
Oklahoma City, OK | October 2009

Rest came and went as she remained stable throughout the night. Our church's prayer calendar had comforted and held me while gingerly awaiting her CT results. The words were taken from Isaiah 43:1-4 (NIV). "Fear not, Lisa, when you pass through the waters, I will be with you. When you pass through the rivers, they will not sweep over you. When you walk through the fire, you will not be burned; the flames will not set you ablaze. You are precious and honored in my sight, and I love you."

This familiar scripture of my heart was now the very lifeline to my own survival. Meditating on the words "I will be with you," no matter what happens, or "He will be with me, so I will not be overtaken," helped my feet find firm footing upon the Rock, giving me His assured presence in the midst of these flooding fiery waters.

Her latest CT scan results showed marked improvement. Much of the fluid had been removed by the drain, enabling her brain to shift back in proper alignment. Her facial swelling was receding and so was our fear as we leaned into the encouraging report of, "We will remove her drain tomorrow if her next CT looks as good as this one."

Bill read Lamentations 3:22-26 as we celebrated the breathtaking news of her drain to be removed later on that day, "The steadfast love of the Lord never ceases,

His mercies never come to an end; they are new every morning; GREAT IS YOUR FAITHFULNESS!"

The song rose up within me and my heart fueled my voice as I sang the ancient hymn of His faithfulness and mercy found in each day.

Yet even in the midst of such praise, feelings of "I don't want to do this anymore" were present and threatening to overtake me again and again. As if witnessing her having to endure so much with this surgery and then the unexpected placement of the drain wasn't enough, the drain removal procedure took me to my knees when I heard her deep guttural groans of pain.

The trauma of her suffering was cutting deep into my strength of endurance. We made it through, but my thoughts were consumed with *I am done, I don't want to play anymore, I want to go home and this to be all over for her. She has had enough.*

Her beautiful blue eyes were locked onto mine, as if asking, "What is happening? Why am I being hurt over and over again? Help me, Mom. Please stop this."

I stood quietly at her bed, holding her hand and telling her how sorry I was, how precious she was to me, and how much I loved her. I promised her I would never leave her, and I would help her however she needed help. I could hear the echoes from God's promises to me flowing through to her as this peace began to arise from within. His love deepened the river. His grace soothed my soul.

I began to see me as Jessie with my eyes looking directly into His face, immobilized in this circumstance, pleading with my Father, "What is happening? Why is she being hurt over and over again? Help me, Father. Help me to stop this."

I felt Him holding me, telling me how sorry He was, that He would never leave me, that He would help carry us through all the things—to not fear, but to stay the course, to hold on. That His Love never ceases. To wait and good would come. That I can face every morning because He is there. He has NEW mercy for us every day and it never ends—never ever ends.

With His words of love, this strength appeared, giving me the ability to take the next right step, to do the next right thing, to continue to move forward with the power of the Almighty Creator of this earth, to continue seeking Him in all things knowing He would bring Good, Light, Life, Hope, Strength, Courage, Peace, and Joy.

My heart shifted to gratitude for His promises as I shifted my gaze to Him and away from the circumstances that seemed to consume us.

Our next right step was being moved out of the PICU to a regular room on the surgery floor, one step closer to home. Her swelling was less each day, her pain seemed minimal, and her movements a little more as she so perfectly demonstrated while reaching for the thermometer placed under her arm. I told her to give it to the nurse and she did exactly that. I watched her precious hand lift the thermometer up and reach it out toward the nurse, releasing it into her hand.

My goodness, what a vision of embodied hope!

Next to our room was a beautiful Hispanic mama with her sick baby. I had been aware of her since we had arrived. She had been faithful and constant, present to all that was happening to her little one. Her grief and fear had been made public one evening with her wailing begging to be shared. I cried in solidarity with her as I knew intimately the pool of tears deep within her "I want my baby to be okay" momma heart. I wanted to go next door and hold her, but instead I fervently prayed with tears for His Comfort and Mercy to pour over her. I began to envision His Arms reaching for her and embracing her tightly. Her wails slowly lessened to a sob, then to a whimper and silence. I knew she was being comforted by Love. *Thank You, Father. You do that so beautifully, as I well know. You are the God of all comfort. Thank You for our comfort tonight. Two mommas, two rooms, two babies, side by side.* Nothing is impossible with God, and I mean ABSOLUTELY NOTHING.

Home was coming like a train on tracks. Our day was overwhelming with the continuous care of her never-ceasing needs. Her nurse was busy with our discharge plans as we were encountering her specialty physicians with residents making their last rounds, PT getting her onto the side of the bed and into the chair, medication administrations, tube feedings, bathing, bowel and bladder care, putting her AFO's (ankle-foot orthoses, which prevents the feet from dragging and helps to maintain proper positioning, alignment, and stability, as well as improve weight bearing) on and off several times, washing her head for the first time after surgery which took over two hours, applying bacitracin to her head wounds, linen changes, range of motion, and repositioning, all within the scope of her being hyped up from the steroids she was receiving to decrease her brain swelling.

It didn't take us long the next morning to load our car. Our last night was as overwhelming as our day. The precious baby next door cried nonstop, our room was a revolving door of every two-hour neuro checks, vital signs, IV antibiotics, alarms from monitors refusing to give up their voice, with the steroids demanding no swelling along with no sleep. Neuro-stimulation overload was pushing us home. I couldn't even imagine what Jessie was having to endure.

Part 2: The Remnant

Uninformed Impatience

Home | Oklahoma City, OK
October 2009

As we left the children's hospital Sunday midmorning, our hearts were settled and relieved to be headed home with her. Bill was driving with extreme caution while I sat in the backseat holding Jessie's head, trying to help her avoid the frequent vomiting that came with car rides.

A black Cadillac sped up right behind us honking and honking. I turned around to see what was happening and saw a very agitated woman, shaking her head and talking at us. I watched as she got more and more animated, especially with her hands.

An unexpected construction zone had forced the traffic down to one lane, which slowed everyone down even more. The impatient driver behind us sped up and zoomed around our car, leaving her trail of anger and frustration. She had no idea where we had been the last week, much less the last seven months; no idea the burden we were carrying on our shoulders nor the precious cargo in our car that we were trying to protect at all cost. My tender heart was saddened even more, and then I wondered how many times I had responded with impatience, not having all the information I needed to choose the better way.

My pearl of wisdom from that day forward was, "May we all go a little slower, listen a little more closely, and know that every person in this world has a pool of tears inside. Patience and love go a long way in this hurtful world."

Healing, quiet rest was waiting for us to arrive home, as we soon discovered quiet angels had appeared during the week to clean and prepare our home for our return. Momma Boone had nourishing food in the oven. The mail was stacked high on our table and filled with healing light and love. Reading words of prayer, hopes, and thoughts filled our hearts with the presence of those sojourning with us. After encountering the words to an old song I had sung for years in three different cards, I joined the chorus singing over us, "God will make a way when there seems to be no way. He works in ways we cannot see. He will make a way for me."

And that He did. He made a way for us to come home with Jessie once again.

My three-hour nap came easy as I snuggled with our cat Henry, next to Jessie, under the large red OU blanket and Bill's watchful eye. He was never far from us, ensuring we were safe and had all we needed.

Recovery in Routine

Home | Oklahoma City, OK
November 2009

The standing frame became the hallmark to the many aspects of her continued recovery.

After placing Jessie in an upright position, the attachable tray provided a perfect surface for coloring and writing. Placing a jumbo crayon in her right hand, we would guide her movements, creating masterpieces of scribbles on the pages of the coloring book. The slightest mark of color by her own movement would raise the cheering section of my heart.

Helping her trace over a large number or letter confirmed visual challenges that still remained clearly undefined. Using her "old" glasses was the only help I knew.

This intentional type of "schooling" continued every time she was "standing" while we searched together for a bridge or connection to writing. Her scribbles slowly

Part 2: The Remnant

became hints of structures hidden within the fog in which she lived.

Before the dense fog of her brain injury, her past dabbles and scribbles had been fascinating to explore as they exposed an artistic talent beginning to emerge. Her journals, filled with the intimate details of her heart and mind, now lay untouched, yet could unwillingly be opened for anyone to glimpse. The untouched of all she had touched was frozen in time, collecting the dust of her future that was no longer her future. I found myself in this unwanted dimension of immovable time with no idea what to do with any of the sacred evidence remaining, knowing it would no longer move forward. So I did nothing.

Threading large colored beads on yarn and playing Candyland and Slapjack filled many minutes of our days. Every moment was directed with the demand for her healing. A rehab nurse/friend sent numerous different therapeutic activities to add to our toolbox, including a rod with a steel ball used for stimulating the back of her throat to prompt swallowing. (What an awful thought, right?) Several times throughout each day, I would dip the steel ball in ice water and touch the back of her throat, hoping this would awaken the nerves that refused to respond.

Potty-training was scheduled every two hours with a simple reward of 3 M&Ms if she was successful. She loved candy. I wasn't sure if she was able to connect the incentive with the expectation, but what I did know was she wanted that candy. While waiting in the bathroom with her, we would sing familiar songs like "Jingle Bells" or "Happy Birthday" to stimulate her subconscious mind, trying to help her to find just one word within.

Standing with minimal assistance offered invitations to even more complicated activities. Warm, homemade, sourdough biscuits in the Boone household was a weekly standing date for deliciousness. Bill and I walked Jessie into the kitchen early one morning where she sat down and reached for the biscuit cutter sitting beside the freshly patted biscuit dough. She automatically began to cut circles. With some gentle assistance, she put them in the baking pan like she had done since she was a toddler. Slowly, circles of progress appeared through the flour of our lives, sifting our hearts.

Watching her brush her teeth at the sink sparked memories of walking down the long hall passing the "wall of fame" in the rehab hospital. I would study each portrait revealing these overcomers of great tragedy, with a narration of their sacred journey of survival. I would linger tearfully at the student whose brain was injured by falling off the back of a stadium wall, tracing the words with my finger, "And he is now brushing his teeth." Weeping I would yearn to God, "Is it possible she too will brush her teeth one day? Will Jessie's picture ever be on this wall of fame?" As I gazed upon this overcomer of great tragedy, I ruminated, "Maybe just maybe, one day."

Nibbles on cookies or small sips of chocolate milk were a carrot to get her attention as she lacked the ability to hold focus. The challenge continued as she struggled to open her mouth or swallow correctly. Her sippy cup created a perfect combination of practicing hand-eye coordination with attempts to swallow.

Independence was sparked as we were getting ready to stand her in the standing frame one day.

"Would you like to go to your room?"

Part 2: The Remnant

She grabbed the yes card, stood wobbly with minimal assistance, and began taking drunken steps. With Bill and I companioning her on each side, she climbed the stairs better than the day before. She was now grasping the rails and taking a step up, following with the other foot. She would slide her hand up the rail and do it again. Instead of her room this particular time, she headed to the computer room and took a seat, and reached for the mouse. Her attempts to move the mouse squiggled across the screen, as she tried to connect with the icons—another triumphal glimpse of forward gain.

Holding her head up had been a relentlessly fierce battle, mirroring our own hearts. This heavy downward force refused to release her. Fighting for the daily lifting, using props and pillows, kept all of our heads up as we waited for the rising of her head to overcome this cruel obstacle.

Her hand-waving motions struck me the way a first-time mom seeing "the first wave" does. I was so elated she was making a connection and could see me from a distance. Yet as she would simply reach for something in front of her, she would miss, confirming depth perception issues.

Her spoken word remained unspoken as she continued struggling to move her lips and mouth, as we steered every conversation in our home in the direction of speech recovery.

We made the decision it was time for her dog, Toasty, to come home for good. Jessie's attentiveness toward her was uplifting, as Toasty's faithfulness wouldn't leave her side. Jessie reciprocated with her hand, never leaving Toasty's body. What beautiful companionship of therapy God provided through the life of this tiny, perfect, brown chihuahua.

Functional improvements after her first cranioplasty were momentous as we continued with our intensive home and outpatient therapy schedule. Astounded at her progress, her plastic surgeon insisted we schedule the second surgery as soon as possible in hopes of more recovery. We continued to celebrate her progress in the Carepages:

Carepages

Post A Message

Every day for the last week, we have watched Jessie do new things. Some are huge and some are so tiny, each and every one a pure gift from God. We watched Jessie reach out and turn the light switch on and off as we walked by, snap her fingers, stir cornmeal, hold a mixer to mash potatoes, write her numbers and her complete name when asking her. She has played tic-tac-toe (and beat me!) and drew a picture of a flower. She has shown us sitting balance, side lying balance, and standing from sitting to standing with standby assist, and one of the biggest gifts is head control. She is finally able to HOLD HER HEAD UP!!! Can I just tell you how wonderful that is!!! She has used a fork to pick up pieces of pear and put them into her mouth and is able to pick up a cup, putting it to her mouth to get a small drink, tossed stuffed animals out of her bed, and given her precious dog, Toasty, a treat. She has tapped her fingers to music, turned pages in a magazine, reached out for the remote control, wiped off a counter, helped with her shower, put her socks on with some help, and even tried to tie her shoe strings. She wrapped her arms around me,

> hugged me, and reached out to give me a kiss, She has scratched her nose and head and leg, put her mouth under the faucet after teeth brushing to attempt to get a drink, caught a ball, spelled out a couple of simple words with letters, sat up in the bed, and reached down to take off Velcro straps on her leg braces. She mimics everything we ask her to do, except speech and facial movements. She reached for her seat belt, strapped it over her, and snapped it in, and later took it off. She put her sunglasses on and reached for the visor in the car to look at herself. She will reach out and shake your hand and give you a thumbs up or a thumbs down or an OK with her fingers, even helping get herself dressed and undressed. It has been miraculous.

The next week was chock-full of celebrations as we would witness her clumsy attempts to use the fork to put nutrition into her mouth and incessant chewing, as her sluggish swallowing would try to catch up. The bib around her neck would hold the bits and pieces of leftover victory as her sippy cup waited for its turn.

Her slow assisted sauntering to the mailbox was her daily marathon, being awarded with mail she would carry like friends waiting to visit. We would sit together and read, using my hand to hold her finger, pointing to each word as I pronounced each slowly and intentionally.

Homeschooling became a cornerstone in her days of recovery. From her ABCs to 123s, using the primary writing tablet as the placemat of learning, to writing her way to the Times Table, she sat victoriously with her head upright. Her coordination drifted into alignment with simple directions as I continued to glimpse some of her past accomplishments peeking out to see if it was safe to emerge.

Each movement, each connection, each moment was double-gated, providing entry to either grief or celebration. Celebration was my choice. The other gate was massive, pitch-black, and looked utterly impassable, so I avoided it at all costs.

Her miraculous gains further cocooned me away from any of the hopes of reclaiming the intimacy of my own life's dreams and desires, as I was consumed with her care, impelled forward to help her regain as much as possible. Studies, hobbies, music, self-care, travel, and even close relationships were collateral losses as I navigated the loss of my daughter and how she was, to all the gains of how she was becoming. She became my life as I became hers, taking over the empty spaces within her, living, moving, and being her being.

Bursts of Progress

Home | Oklahoma City, OK
November 2009

Then came the day we found a small package addressed to Jessie in our mailbox. She struggled as she ceremoniously carried it down the long driveway as if it were an offering, challenging the core of her balance to a new level. Watching these moments unfold in slow motion invited patience to come in and do what she does best. As Jessie sluggishly tore the strips of paper as if in a slow motion reel, patience was tearing my walls of time down, making it impossible to escape this type of remodeling.

This eventually unwrapped gift of love was from a Texas artist, Amy Havern, whom we had never met. In her note of great support, she revealed she had learned of Jessie's journey through a family member and was following her on the Carepages. Her creation burst forth beauty and hope within the new structured crucible of our lives.

Part 2: The Remnant

This simple 6 x 8 brown canvas displayed a striking hand painted pinkish cross with embossing that resembled an untraditional labyrinth of movements and was intentionally hung close by Jessie's bed.

Moments like this caressed my aching heart, as her generous offering declared the promise of hope, "I am making all things new." (Revelation 21:5 NLT)

One afternoon, I asked Jessie if she was hungry and she raised her hand and made a sign for a little. This simple yet earth-moving motion revealed she was beginning to know things, and she even began to communicate what she wanted in the smallest ways. She was beginning to answer yes or no by the subtle movements of her head.

Her re-creation and restoration was happening before our very eyes by the one and only Creator and Restorer of our lives.

At bedtime as I was tucking her in, I kissed her and whispered, "Jessie Boone, I love you."

She looked at me, and with her hand, slowly patted her heart, pointed to me, and then held up two of her fingers, communicating, "I love you too."

"Jessie Boone, did you just tell your mom you love her too?"

She nodded her head, "Yes."

My heart flashed.

"Oh my goodness! You are the sweetest!"

Love made flesh right before my very eyes.

With these celebrations came the rewards of the new awakenings, but also some exhausting and disheartening challenges of impulsivity and uncontrollable movements, like nonstop scratching of the sutures in her head. Her new movements were rapid and repetitive and appeared unstoppable.

Her continued unsuccessful attempts at swallowing food turned into pocketing in the cheeks, as her tongue struggled with the coordination of moving the food toward the back of her throat.

Her impulsive movements of her arms and legs were new safety threats disrupting our days and nights, as evidenced by the horrific night when I accidentally left her bed rail down and was awakened by a silent hard thud, only to find her face down on the carpet, unable to yell out or get herself turned over. My sickened feelings lasted days as I watched her for signs of another brain injury.

One late night, as I was checking on her, the nightlight shadows reflected rapid movements of her hand. As I got

Part 2: The Remnant

closer, I could see her finger speedily writing messages on her pillow. She was trying to communicate something, but I couldn't make out the confusing scribbles. The next morning, this erratic moving continued as she "wrote" in the air, on her pillow, on the table, even on her leg. I eventually witnessed this incessant movement organized into sign language, which she had known before. She was beginning to make letters with her fingers, opening up the first two-way communication with her besides the eye blinks or head nods.

Wondrous Whispers
Home | Oklahoma City, OK
January 2010

Ten months from the day of her accident, Jessie and I were playing War with our hands—the game where one holds their hands on top of another's hands and tries to move them before the person hits them. We played this game daily, as it seemed to provide a fun opportunity for hand eye coordination therapy. I continued to be concerned by her severely compromised vision yet still had been unable to ascertain specifics. Each time, I would be slow to move my hands away, letting her hit my hand with hers. I would respond dramatically with, "Ow." She would smile and appear to be so pleased with her triumphant hit. Eventually, the moment happened when I hit her slow withdrawing hands and she spontaneously responded with her first long-awaited whispered word, "Ow."

"Jessie Boone! Did you just say 'ow'???" My heart freefell in relief. That bridge finally found a connection as the deep prayer of my heart was answered.

Thank you, God.

The Cottonwood Medicine

As I tucked her into bed that evening, I leaned close to her face and asked her to say "mom." As I repeatedly whispered "mom," this command steeped in love and hope pierced the veil, and out of her mouth came a quiet but assuredly whispered "mom" in my ear.

Within the week, the gateway of her lips had parted and found the connection with the passage of her voice. Her new posture became one of leaning her face into mine, whispering the words, "I love you so much," along with, "My head hurts, Oh my goodness, I want to go upstairs, How are you?" and "No" over and over again. It was remarkable to witness these long-awaited wisps of air beginning the assemblance of what we hoped would transform into spoken conversation.

One evening, I asked her, "Are you ready for bed?"

She whispered, "No."

I then asked, "Do you want to go to the living room?"

She whispered, "No."

Puzzled, I glanced at Bill before I looked at her and asked, "Where do you want to go?" In the quietest whisper with gentle movements of her lips, I heard, "Upstairs."

"You want to go upstairs to your room?" I clarified.

"Yes," she whispered and nodded her head. We helped her upstairs. She was so determined, she was even trying to take two steps at a time, echoing her early years of stair climbing. Her recovery was beginning to reflect that same determination.

During this time, I was reading *My Stroke of Insight* by Jill Bolte Taylor, an autobiography of a thirty-seven-year-old Harvard trained neuroanatomist who experienced a massive hemorrhagic stroke. She observed her own mind completely deteriorate, losing all function within four hours. Over the course of eight years, she recovered and wrote this most fascinating book. I loved every word, but these struck me deeply: "For a successful recovery, it was important that we focus on my ability, not my disability ... celebrate the triumphs I made every day because my successes, no matter how small, inspired me ... I needed to welcome support, love, and help from others ... break every task down into smaller and simpler steps of action. I needed everyone to assume that I knew nothing so that I could relearn everything from the beginning ... to teach me with patience ... to come close and not be afraid of me ... to bring me their positive energy ... I needed people to love me, not for the person I had been, but for who I might now become ... to believe in the plasticity of my brain and its ability to grow, learn, and recover ... to treat me as though I would recover completely."

Her insightful experience was a powerful witness, positively affirming our way of recovering life with Jessie as we continued our daily lived experiences of those exact needs for her. Anything less was non-negotiable.

Equine Medicine
Home | Oklahoma City, OK
January 2010

Eventually her increasing ability to sit and stand with assistance opened the door to equine therapy—using the movement of the horse to engage certain muscles to gain core strength and balance.

Stepping into the therapeutic Coffee Creek Equine Stables with my severely compromised daughter was like being transported into a comforting, dirt-filled stable of hope. Their mission on the wall read, "We are going to help children with disabilities gain strength, coordination, balance, and self-image, utilizing the horse as a motivator in therapeutic riding classes." This place of belonging was filled with the smells of resurrection love.

Standing on the outer edge of the arena looking in, I watched the helpers, with the powerful healing presence of the horses, transform the experience of being different. Disability was embraced, held, and gently guided into a motion toward a new direction.

With every step Dusty took, Jessie's pelvis moved exactly as though she were walking. Her helmet, now a common fashion, no longer looked out of place. Her hands on the reins were a reminder that she held her own power in her recovery. There in the midst of the dirt, manure, and disability rose a champion being carried in a circle of upright victory.

The stables became a weekly outing, providing not only physical but spiritual and psychological healing for us all. I mean, who doesn't love to be around those strong, sensitive creatures with attentive ears and large expressive eyes, breathing in their earthly smell of goodness and grace.

Slow but Steady

Home | Oklahoma City, OK
January 2010

Every movement she made manifested a tiny sprout of hope, as her stillness now sluggishly moved through the thick oil of brain recovery. Time changed again as any effort of timeliness became an enemy to her recovery. Slow repetitive movements painstakingly etched new roads and bridges in an attempt to reconnect pathways of function and thought.

Candy remained an engine, getting her attention, and helping to drive any other movement she might have. One day as she deliberately reached for a red sucker being offered, her far left reach continued to reveal visual challenges in perception. Guiding her hand was all it took as she found her mouth. The red sticky on her face made me smile as I watched her tongue struggle to emerge. If it hadn't been so painful, it would have been a fascinating documentary to watch how a simple red lollipop could be used as a powerful tool to stimulate the awakening of her tongue and throat muscles.

Vocal Victories
Home | Oklahoma City, OK
January 2010

Jessie's whispers continued increasing little by little each day. Over a lunch of butternut squash soup and a grilled cheese sandwich, we were negotiating the spoon filled with warm soup together when she looked me right in the eyes, touched my arm so gently, and whispered, "I love you."

I whispered back, "I love you too."

She surprised me, "Do you really?"

I almost burst out laughing at the absurdity of her question, but instead I melted into the complexity of the thought for her. I watched her waiting for my response, as if there might be another answer, "Yes, I really, really do." Then I couldn't resist and responded in a whisper, "Do you really love me?"

She whispered with such seriousness, "I really, really do, Mom."

My heart burst with this new way of such great love being revealed in the most miraculous tone.

Later that evening, I detected a different expression on her face.

The Cottonwood Medicine

"Are you okay?"

She shook her head, whispering, "No, my head hurts."

"Where does it hurt?" I whispered back, wondering if loud noises hurt her head. She reached for her forehead and rubbed it.

I reached out and touched her hand.

"I am so sorry, Jess. Want me to get you some Tylenol to help with that?"

She nodded her head in agreement as I stumbled over my own disbelief of what I was hearing—her first time being able to verbalize her own discomfort.

I learned of Melody Gardot when one of the Carepage followers shared a posting about her. She was an American jazz singer, guitarist, and pianist who at the age of nineteen, was involved in a severe car/bicycle accident, sustaining a significant brain injury. Realizing how music played a critical role in her recovery, helping her to reconnect in ways therapy and drugs could not, she became an advocate of music therapy, touring universities and hospitals with her story of recovery.

Hence we began our journey of music therapy.

Bill started by bringing home an instrument she had once loved. The newly acquired keyboard became another instrument of help in the search of reaching and reconnecting Jessie's pathways of life. She had taken piano lessons in the past and then had moved to the flute instead.

As her long beautiful fingers slowly found the keys, she touched each one, up and then back down. This created an unsynchronized melody resembling her brain waves, yet revealed the most beautiful sounds we could have ever hoped for. Playing and singing simple songs with her brought rhythms of comfort and joy into my soul while hoping to bring rhythms of organization to hers.

Reuniting her with her cell phone was challenging as we were both unsuccessful in remembering her password. Forced to do a factory reset was excruciating as it seemed to mimic her own reset. With one push of a button, everything was erased—all the past numbers, information, and music that had been intentionally saved by her—immediately surrendering her precious past life musings that were no more. The correlation was hauntingly painful.

Her fingers would find a clumsy familiarity as she struggled to see and type a response to my texts. Increasing the font size came with another realization, her phone was now another "mine." Taking over the administrator of her account, it was just like her life, absorbed in the background of mine.

One morning, I received a phone call from a friend checking up on how we were doing, which prompted me to turn on the speaker phone so Jessie could hear our conversation.

"Jess, tell her hi."

For the first time, out came this small, tiny, not a whisper but her no longer hidden voice.

"Hi."

Proclamations and Perseverations

Home | Oklahoma City, OK
February 2010

Sitting in the familiar chair of observation, I watched with uncertain anticipation as her speech therapist immersed her in the finding of words and voice, strategically placing the white foam electrodes on each side of her face. As her cheeks twitched with the command of, "Wake up! Wake

The Cottonwood Medicine

up!" I was quietly hoping the transcutaneous electrical stimulation was only stimulating the nerves and muscles to help her speak and swallow more effectively and not subjecting her to more discomfort.

One afternoon, the speech therapist took a list of twenty words and asked Jessie to say the opposite word of whichever one she said. Every word the therapist said, Jessie would immediately mouth the correct answer, every single time. "Hot." "Cold." "Up." "Down." "Happy." "Sad." It was simply a fascinating mechanism of grace to behold as we wondered what was held within the remnants trying to emerge through this fractured landscape of her mind.

"Oooh m ... my g ... goodness," Jessie began to whisper and write over and over. What a beautiful phrase for her perseveration to present, capturing my heart's proclamation of the reality of every second of her awakening. Perseveration is when a brain injury patient continuously repeats words, actions, or thoughts. It's caused by damage to the frontal cortex, the part responsible for awareness and inhibition. They are unaware they have perseveration, and it can keep them from being able to multitask or hold a conversation simultaneously. These symptoms are very challenging and difficult to manage and obviously cause great distress for all.

Her perseveration intensified as she grew in awareness and awakeness.

"W ... What t ... time is it?" could have been easily said one hundred times within an hour in harmony with her "ABC, 123." Strategies with treatment plans fell short in managing this intrusive, obnoxious symptom that appeared without warning, and seemed to be in no hurry to leave, making sure it disrupted any moment of peace we might find or the precious sleep we all so desperately needed. Each step forward to the more seemed to be at a great cost of a new battle on the horizon of the unknown.

Sleep and Surprises
Home | Oklahoma City, OK
February 2010

Profound fatigue had been the most debilitating and the most challenging for her in this recovery journey on every front. Reasons for this type of fatigue included endocrine dysfunctions, the need for her brain to work harder to compensate for the brain injury deficits, and changes to the brain structures. This type of fatigue appeared as mental or physical tiredness, exhaustion, lack of energy, and low vitality. She would yawn, appear to have "brain fog," and easily lose what little attention and concentration she might have. She was unable to verbalize her fatigue but could speak volumes through her glazed eyes, slower movements, decreased coordination, and difficulty staying awake.

Sleep was major medicine for her healing which had to be balanced with her schedule of rehab therapies and her intensive training on normal activities of daily living. The balancing of rehabilitation with sleep looked like my neglected checkbook, overdrawn due to the overwhelming cost of what was supposed to be a fun spring break ski trip and disheartening attempts to navigate this brain injury cornucopia.

The Oklahoma winter seemed to answer one of my unspoken prayers one weary day, providing a blizzard that snowed us in for four days. This intense quiet and lack of activity provided deep restorative days of quiet rest for us all. A true reset. All perfectly timed in preparation for her second cranioplasty.

When asked how I felt about this upcoming surgery, truthfully, I hadn't thought about it. Remembering what I had learned from her last surgery, I knew whatever grace I would need would be given during that time. Meanwhile I continued to live in the moment, taking one day at a time, as it seemed the only place I could function. How easy it was for me to lose my emotional balance if I leaned too far into the future, or leaned too far back into the past. It bore a striking resemblance to the way Jessie walked. She, too, could easily lose her balance if she leaned too far forward or too far backward, requiring her to stay centered in order to stay upright.

Our nightly ritual of tucking her into bed consisted of the usual routines and ended with prayers of thankfulness. This particular night, she kept rapidly firing the same words over and over again, but I couldn't understand what she was saying. When she wasn't able to slow her speech down, I would make her write it down. Her scribbles were somewhat legible at times, at least giving me a better chance of understanding what she was attempting to communicate.

Her hand gripped the pencil as I held the notebook.

"Jessie, I can't understand you. Will you write down what you are trying to tell us?"

Within a few moments, her racing thoughts were revealed.

"Why is it below two degrees in here?"

Bill and I both burst out in laughter as he threw the blame, "Because your mom won't turn up the heat!"

What a moment that was, as we both felt it—a moment of normalcy. A moment of joy.

Part 2: The Remnant

All I could think about the rest of the evening was how grateful I was to witness any moment she was able to express anything about the way she felt.

Intimate Inventory
Home | Oklahoma City, OK
February 2010

One afternoon, as Jess and I were in a very close space for an extended period of time, she unexpectedly reached out with her hands and cupped my face, taking a verbal inventory of what she loved about me in her newly discovered rhythm of voice, "Mom, I love you. I love your face, your hair, your eyes, your cheeks, your chin, your nose, your hands, your fingers, your fingernails, your jacket, your rings, your necklace," gently touching each place she spoke of. Speechless, this holy, intimate moment was deeply ethereal, as I could sense Christ's presence loving me through Jessie's words and hands.

The Final Mending
Oklahoma University's Children's Hospital
Oklahoma City, OK | February 2010

'Twas the night before surgery and all through the house, not a fear or hesitation was stirring, our faith would not be doused. The bags were packed and the animals were in care, and sweet Jessie Boone was all settled in and surrounded with prayer.

When her plastic surgeon, Dr. El Amm, saw Jessie, all he could say was, "This is remarkable, just remarkable." He lit up the 3D CT scan showing the newly reconstructed left side of her skull, and declared, "Ninety-nine percent healed! This is more than I ever expected. This is just remarkable." He was giddy, such a stark contrast from the first time he met her. "Her functional improvements are shocking from the last time I saw her. I am now wondering just how much putting half her skull back in place has contributed to her overall improved functioning." He watched in wonderment as she slowly screwed the round plastic lid on the water bottle she held in her other hand. "Just look at her."

Bill and I both nodded in agreement.

He went on to explain, "Think of how a furniture leg indents the carpet, pressing it down flat. Now think of how her brain is being pressed down without the protection of her skull." Pointing to her films, he continued, "Look at how the brain has risen back up and realigned within the structure of her repaired skull. I believe this expansion back to its original state has allowed her brain to regain more function. Now let's reconstruct her other half. I am eager to see how much more function she can regain."

His conversation moved to another level when he asked our permission to use her medical records and recovery in a case study that would be presented in Grand Rounds and written up in an article for a medical journal. The article would bring focus to how vital it is for timely cranioplasties to be performed in hopes of the brain being returned to its original state for the optimum recovery of the patient. He continued with how impressed he was over her functional improvements but specifically regarding her diabetes insipidus resolving so quickly after surgery.

I adjusted for a brief moment as his words echoed in my memory. "I am not sure why we are doing this?" and found myself truly immersed in a sea of gratitude.

Only You, God, can heal this magnificently. Thank You for this man—I shall call him the "bone mender extraordinaire."

It was heart-stopping to behold, all of it. I stood mesmerized, looking at the scans of the left side of her skull, whole and completely healed.

Only God and His helpers.

Shifting to a quieter, resolute tone, he began to outline his detailed plan for the next step with her right-sided reconstruction.

"These risks will be more complicated, as there are several bone chunks that will be put together like a jigsaw puzzle. There's a greater risk of the bone being contaminated due to this side being the one of trauma, increasing her risk of infection, and even a greater concern is the reality of the extensive brain swelling after closure due to not having the benefit of her other side still being open."

My body received the impact of truth as I reached for the wall to steady myself, feeling my stomach revolt at what I was hearing, yet something else was happening within my body. My breathing took over and released my spirit to claim a bigger Truth. The more complicated, the greater risk, and the greater concerns seemed to be propelling my heart higher to the heavens, knowing how far God had brought us and where our help comes from.

Surrounded in a circle of love within the private waiting room, we found the close intimacy comforting while we waited in hushed hope, suspended in time as the most intricate, meandering expertise was being fully executed upon the most cherished treasure of our hearts.

Five hours later, it was finished. Dr. Mapstone gently guided us through the two hours of tediously separating her scalp from the dura (covering of her brain) and repairing three holes in the dura. He was very pleased with the results. Dr. El Amm then took over, reporting he chose to throw away the frontal part of her skull due to his concerns of possible contamination. He had reconstructed her frontal lobe using a part of the back of her skull, piecing the rest of her skull together with hardware. He was able to successfully close her scalp with no skin grafts. He paused to reiterate the potential complications that could occur but overall felt it was a successful surgery.

Being ushered into the recovery room as she awakened was a much-needed respite for both of us. Seeing her alive and moving, holding her hand, and being able to speak whispers of soothing comfort in her ear displaced the agonizing visuals that had been streaming in my head during her surgery.

Oh, my goodness. This moment I have waited for. God, You did it. You made her whole again. How do I ever thank You? You have my whole life forever. Forever. Thank You for saving her. For helping us in such inconceivable ways.

Jessie was whole for the first time in "11" months. She was breathtaking. I couldn't take my eyes off her porcelain face in perfect dimensional symmetry. The protection of her white plastic helmet was no longer needed as the substitute, as most of her displaced pieces of white cranium had now taken their rightful place.

My unceasing prayers of protection and help were being swept up within the deafening cries of thanksgiving. I could no longer hold the power of love inside as it came forging out in the waves of sobs proclaiming relief at her bedside.

The bumps and battles immediately appeared post-operatively as we were informed there was no bed for her in the ICU—not the room but the actual bed—due to a bed shortage. Eventually a bed did appear and was followed

Part 2: The Remnant

with the huge production of transferring Jessie into the bed with her tubes, monitors, drains, and lines only to discover the bed was broken, making it impossible to raise her head to the 30 degrees required to minimize brain swelling.

Her nurse was intent on helping me get her propped up on pillows as she began to share how she was called in to work today due to a staffing shortage. She confessed she didn't want to work her day off, as she was home playing with her two-year-old daughter. I could feel apathy and anger knocking. *Your words of confession don't seem to be fitting in a time such as this and aren't making this situation any better.*

She then paused, gently reaching for my daughter's hand, which shifted my taut spirit. Looking directly into Jessie's face, she continued, "After getting the morning report on your daughter, I stepped into the hallway and there was Tim Travers, our minister who had baptized our daughter. He told me he was coming to see Jessie Boone and her parents. It was at that moment I knew God had called me to work today so I could be the one to care for your daughter."

There you are, God.

I breathed her connected spirit deeply in, relaxing my nurse posture into her care, enabling me to just be with my sixteen-year-old daughter today as her mom. What comfort intermingled within my anxious heart.

An ancient bed from the basement appeared a few hours later to replace the broken one. Another great production ensued as we maneuvered and moved Jessie with all of her paraphernalia, finally getting her head elevated where it was supposed to be. Within minutes, projectile vomiting had us scrambling to get her turned to her side and suctioned. Then, without warning a grand mal seizure overtook her entire body. This volley of cruelty was met with the skill of our "chosen" nurse who quickly intervened with IV medications, bringing all the chaos to a halt.

Radiology and her nurse escorted this now sleeping child for a stat CT to evaluate her for the anticipated complications of increased intracranial pressure. Upon her return, the ancient bed no longer worked, meaning we could no longer elevate her head once again.

What is happening, God? Why does the problem of a broken bed keep appearing, preventing the crucial proper positioning of her head?

Our prayers became demanding and in full force, specifically addressing the results of the CT scan, the broken bed ritual, and protection from the inevitable swelling that seemed to be gaining momentum.

The maintenance man who had brought the first bed up came to investigate the ancient bed, telling us he had located a new "ICU" bed and would be bringing it up as soon as it was cleaned. Staying in the moment and breathing, I thanked him for any help he could give us. It was then that I "saw" him. His countenance of kindness and compassion, his gentle eyes, and his concern and determination to get it right. All his mannerisms were that of love. His caring helped to calm the erupting storm in my heart.

We repeated the major production of moving Jessie again to the new bed. But this time, the maintenance man stayed, focused on making all things right. As we were ready to transfer her over, the nurse placed the pink bed pads on the bed. In that moment, the maintenance man stepped forward in the path of the transfer, tenderly reached out, and smoothed and patted the pads with both of his hands as if anointing her bed with his hope and compassion—going beyond the call of his work to prepare a place for Jess. Bill and I exchanged glances as both our hearts recognized Jesus at that moment in the maintenance man.

Thank You for being with us.

He has such a way of entering our lives at the perfect moment and making things right again. As love made flesh left the room, the words "God bless you" came off his lips and landed on both of our hearts, bringing a new comfort and light to our weary souls.

As we continued to breathe in what had just happened, giving thanks for the bed and the correct elevation of her head, the results of the CT scan were brought to us by our nurse. No massive swelling was found, leaving plenty of room in her ventricles. All was well.

How beautiful are the hands and feet of Christ.

Love is such a gift, one in which we have received so much. Sitting in the much needed calm next to Jessie as she slept, I opened my laptop to find these meditative words waiting for me: "If you are filled with fearful emotions today, close your eyes and picture Jesus walking in the fog, straight toward you, with eyes full of love, a heart full of compassion, and a smile that melts your heart."

That day, Jesus walked toward us in the fog of all the chaos of events and emotions, straight toward us, with eyes full of love, a heart full of compassion, and a patting of a pink bed pad that melted our hearts. Our hearts were melted into comfort by His love.

Our night watch continued being immersed in calm, only interrupted by a few episodes of vomiting. When her neurology team made morning rounds, they further assessed concerns of her seizure and now her prolonged inability to wake up, requiring further testing, including an

EEG to evaluate her brain activity. As they were prepping her skin to apply the electrodes to her head, she began to rouse ever so gently as if emerging from a cocoon. The gentleness and peacefulness of her awakening revealed a deeper dimension of this angelic restful peace permeating her and this room, being present since the maintenance man's appearance, intensifying the urge to remove my shoes as I was fully aware of the holy ground upon which I stood.

Unthinkable Blessings and Solutions
Oklahoma University's Children's Hospital
Oklahoma City, OK | February 2010

Standing in a tiny, pale blue, tiled shower in the recesses of the hospital, I found the perfect silence with the warm pounding water consoling my skin after twenty-four hours of direct combat, wondering how it was possible to be asked to endure so much. Witnessing the unthinkable over and over. Every unthinkable was answered with an unthinkable. As my eyes closed, my gratitude began to run off my heart for all the unthinkables.

This hospital, the staff, the "bed" in PICU, the surgeons and their expertise, the medications, the lab tests showing stability, the monitors watching over her, the EEGs and CT scans, the medications, the life-giving blood, the SCD's, all the testing that revealed her brain, bone grafting, and surgery successes helping Jessie to come this far. The IV fluids, suction systems, oxygen, anesthesia, catheters, linens, nutrition, pressure monitoring devices and drainage systems, the handwashing, alcohol gel, the shower, the laundry available free of cost to those in need, the electricity, the water, the computers, the phones that enable updates, family and friends, the ability of reading the prayers of His people through the Carepages, and a list that can never be finished.

This wellspring of water continued washing over me with the remembrance of all that had been given, enabling me to stand in this baptismal font of life with the assurance that because God is present, all is well.

Renewed and refreshed, I was making my way back to the PICU when I passed the hospital chapel. Entering this quiet peaceful sanctuary, I noticed a familiar picture of Christ behind the pulpit. He was standing at the door knocking. The door was missing the knob, giving the perfect example of how He patiently waits on us to open our hearts to receive Him. My eyes fell to the different. All around the inside of the frame were pictures of children tucked in around Jesus, by mothers who had come before me, bringing their children to Him for healing and love, following His blessed command in Matthew 19:14 (NIV), "Let the little children come to Me, do not hinder them, for the kingdom of heaven belongs to such as these."

Quietly and intentionally, I placed my heart's picture of Jessie next to the others, feeling such a calming peace, knowing He continues to invite with His loving voice, "Bring Jessie to me. Bring ALL the children to Me."

In the same echoes, I could hear Him softly calling, "Come to Me, all you who are weary and burdened, and I will give you rest." (Matthew 11:28 NIV) He is faithful to keep His word, this I know because He had just given me such a moment of beautiful rest.

This road of cranioplasty continued to be a treacherous route. We encountered severe headaches, swelling of her face and eyes, diarrhea, IV pumps beeping, continuous alarms of monitors, hourly vital signs, blood work, neuro checks, repositioning, and no sleep. IV Morphine and

Zofran were of no help. When neurology was consulted, the order to lay her flat caused a red alert in our room. I couldn't reconcile the risk of increased intracranial pressure that Dr. El Amm had deeply planted in my list of non-negotiables. After much consternation in both discussion and research, we surrendered and laid her flat. Within moments, the new "forbidden" position brought instant relief, and she fell asleep for several hours, confirming that the culprit of the chaos was a spinal headache and that she was in desperate need of a spinal blood patch repair, a procedure which was done within a few hours.

Celebrations of Love
Oklahoma University's Children's Hospital
Oklahoma City, OK | February 2010

Being transferred out of PICU brought us one step closer to home, so Bill and I decided to have a special celebratory dinner in her room. We celebrated Jessie and how special she is, celebrated her wholeness and future, celebrated each other as husband and wife, celebrated the love and support we had received from so many, celebrated another day with our daughter, and celebrated LIFE as we knew it in that moment.

When a young, kind nurse made her evening rounds, we recognized her from the last time Jessie was on this floor. Her countenance was strikingly different, so I asked her, "What has happened in your life? You seem different."

She gushed, "I got married last month!"

"Congratulations! What is your favorite thing about being married?"

Her smile was as sweet as her words, "Living with my best friend."

Her words resonated deep within as my eyes found Bill Boone's. Warmth traveled the distance of my head down to my toes, as I am also living with my very best friend. This man, who has been with me every step of this harrowing, awful journey, reaching, holding, and helping in ways one couldn't imagine.

Thank You, God, for this man of great faith, strength, stability, and love.

The Long Dark Night
Oklahoma University's Children's Hospital
Oklahoma City, OK | February 2010

As we were preparing our hearts and packing to go home the next day, the walls came crashing down. Vomiting with her temperature spiking to 102, heart rate rising to the 160's, and respirations becoming rapid and shallow. She was pale and her extremities were ice cold. Her body and head were drenched from sweating radiating heat.

The resident on call wasn't happy to be awakened in the middle of the night with our concerns and expressed his frustration with the tone of his voice and his actions of indifference, not seeing the need for any tests.

I pushed hard for blood work and a CT scan, demands I am sure didn't help his attitude, as evidenced when he begrudgingly took her to CT himself and refused to allow us to be with her. My fears of her vomiting and aspiration carried through my voice, begging him to let me come with her. His frustrated, hurried refusal caused him to crash her carrier into the door of the elevator, leaving me fuming with fear and anger as the doors closed in front of us.

God, doesn't he know the fragility of this child he is angrily shoving around?

When the doors of the elevator finally reopened, my lips could form no words for this tired, overworked, inexperienced, insensitive boy dressed in wrinkled scrubs who obviously had a lot to learn.

He pushed out the curt words, "The CT is clear like I thought it would be."

I couldn't bring myself to look at him or answer him, as I was too angry to acknowledge his apathetic and reckless behavior. He would never be allowed near Jessie again, and I would make an official complaint with his superiors in the near future. I reached out to take control of the stretcher as I searched her face and body for any obvious signs of damage that could have happened while she was gone.

Soon after returning to her room, a grand mal seizure found its way in, as other symptoms raged on. All night, Bill and I vigiled and prayed over her, hoping to keep her safe as possible, refusing to see or talk with the night resident again. By morning, our nurse was finally able to reach a neurology resident and place an urgent request to evaluate Jessie's escalating symptoms.

After such a dark and long night, it was surreal to watch the resident enter our room wearing her white winter coat and gloves. She resembled an angel, gently stepping into the chaos and darkness to take control of the storm. She notified neurosurgery, contacted the Infectious Doctor for a consult, and readmitted Jess to the PICU, canceling our discharge plans. Her reassuring voice helped to guide us safely back into the right harbor.

Blood cultures, lumbar puncture, CT with contrast, chemistries, urine and stool samples were executed swiftly. It was obvious Jessie was suffering with so many issues.

What has happened? Thank God we weren't already home when all this began.

Part 2: The Remnant

The Infectious Disease doctor spent a great deal of time with us detailing the many possibilities of what was happening. We had to re-don the sacred yellow gowns, which paradoxically brought hope and praise to our visual fields, as she was placed on isolation precautions while awaiting test results.

Exhaustion and confusion were met with the comfort and expertise of the PICU bringing her seizures and other symptoms back under control. Still trying to find some footing, I reached for *Jesus Calling* and found the words, "Keep your eyes focused on Me. Waves of adversity are washing over you, and you feel tempted to give up. As your circumstances consume more and more of your attention, you are losing sight of Me. Yet I AM with you always holding you by your right hand. I AM fully aware of your situation and I WILL NOT allow you to bear any more than you can bear."

You know everything about this situation. Thank You.

My heart responded to these powerful, timely words as I knelt beside her bed, my face in my lap, acknowledging His presence and power we have intimately experienced and known.

How much more, Lord? How much more will You allow her to bear?

I fell prostrate onto my face, bone-weary, and cried, "Abba, faithful loving Father, I come to You again with Jessie in my arms, laying her at Your feet. I know You have been carrying her for her entire life and continue to know what plans You have for her. I praise You for never leaving nor forsaking us. I need Your strength to get through these awful moments and hold me when I fall apart. I know this story isn't over yet. I know You are able to do far more than I could ever imagine or hope for. I know because You have already done it. You know how much my heart hurts for Jessie and the continuing pain and battle of this injury, yet she continues to conquer these things with You. I know with Your help, she will overcome, for Your great right hand has not been shortened. Forgive me for getting ahead of this moment, and thank You for allowing me to slide back into the present and fall totally and utterly dependent into Your arms again. Thank You for the powerful provision that was ushered into our room this morning after such a long, raging night. The care that communicated, 'Peace, be still,' allowing us to remove our hands and let the PICU staff take over. Thank You for their loving, professional, consistent care—for the intensivists that step right up and get to work. Thank You we weren't home but instead just down the hall. Thank You for the resident who still needs to learn a lot about bedside manner and care, and for showing me today to pray for him and not be angry, so that he might 'get it' and not ever be 'bothered' by after hour issues, so he can reassure and comfort parents that are scared about their children. Thank You that he listened anyway and got a CT scan. I am so thankful for all that has helped us through the last twenty-four hours. I thank You that we are still sitting beside her bed and she is able to wake up and say, 'I love you, Mom and Dad.' Thank You, Father, for having the last word and, in the midst of all of this, teaching and loving me into Your image, helping me to stay focused on You, and the timely reminder, 'Yet I AM with you always holding you by your right hand and I AM fully aware of your situation, and I WILL NOT allow you to bear any more than you can bear. Amen."

 I lay quietly on the floor, hoping the words and meditations from my heart seeped deeply within the foundation of my life, cementing the fractures from the quakes of this journey. The emptiness was haunting, as our lives had been stripped bare of everything other than just living moment to moment.

Part 2: The Remnant

Morning came and so did my heart's first words, "Today is the day the Lord hath made and we are rejoicing in it." As I walked down the hallway to go to the showers, I passed by the chapel again. This time, the door opened and out came several young people with tousled hair, sleepy eyes, all carrying blankets and pillows.

"Was that a great place to sleep or what?" I asked, impressed with their choice of a resting place.

"Yes, it was. The pews were cushioned and it was so quiet," one of them answered.

Memories of the youth of our church came unexpectedly flooding in. All the retreats, the camps, the overnight campouts. I smiled as I thought how cool it was that in this big hospital with all the waiting rooms, the youth camped out in the chapel. What a safe place where God's arms cushioned the tired and weary youth, giving them a peaceful place of rest.

My thoughts continued as I stood under the warm, life-giving waters, "God, You have been doing the exact same thing for Bill and me, even though it looks a little different. You have cushioned us deep within the pews of your heart, helping us to find safety and peaceful rest in the midst of the raging storms of life."

Test after test came back negative. Still awaiting the final culture reports, it was decided to discontinue isolation precautions. Her fever was gone, and all her vital signs were within normal range. She had been out of bed several times, sitting in a chair and even able to eat small amounts of food. She was awake and alert, whispering nonstop. Each doctor had rounded and ruled out many possible complications or infections. Her "brutal" antibiotics with the side effect of significant diarrhea continued until the final culture was back. The swelling in her face was resolving, her incisions were healing, and she was having no complaints of head or stomach pain.

The evening ended with the ultimate gift of Jessie whispering her broken wants to her dad, "I a ... a ... am r ... r ... ready to g ... g ... go home."

Dad smiled and said, "Baby, so are we."

The movement forward was beginning again as we once again turned the final corner toward home. Taking a deep breath in, breathing out, "God, we thank You."

God said, "No."
Oklahoma University's Children's Hospital
Oklahoma City, OK | March 2010

Moving out of PICU, we were so thankful that every test that was done on Jessie over the last few days was negative. NEGATIVE, NEGATIVE, AND NEGATIVE! God said NO to infection and we were so grateful to not have to travel that road anymore.

Reading through the many Carepage postings that night flooded my weary and tired soul. I was shaking my head in awe of the faithfulness of God's people to fight this battle with us. Every single posting was a prayer for Jessie.

Our earlier preoperative visit with Dr. El Amm before this last surgery made it obvious he was impressed with how well Jessie recovered from her first surgery with him. He had left the room with his arms outstretched as if he were surfing, making an unusual yet hope-filled declaration, "Let's ride this wave!!!"

Well, what a ride it was, as we were able to finally land that wave and end up on the beach of our home still intact after so many unexpected squalls.

Part 2: The Remnant

Exhaustion, Excitement, and Expansion
Home | Oklahoma City, OK
March 2010

Off to bed we went to rest, so thankful that God held us on that wave, thankful for all those who were a part of that wave, and thankful the ride wasn't over yet as I was sure other waves were on the horizon.

What a privilege we had to be able to watch and see how Jessie Boone healed and grew stronger, our hope that she would rehab 100% to her potential expanding. To God be all glory, honor, and praise—we were so thankful to be nestled in the sweetness of home that night.

Recovery was needed for all of us, as the depth of physical and emotional toil we experienced had been torturous. This last hospitalization was brutal, like the rest, and took us to a new extreme of exhaustion if that was even possible.

There is no place like home.

Jessie's brain activity was in full throttle from the minute we arrived home. Her agitation, restlessness, and inability to sleep were merciless. Her incessant whispering required continual attention to understand what she needed. Her demonstrative actions displayed her head or stomach hurt, with repetitive stuttering loops of "I ... I ... n ... need to p ... p ... pee," or "w ... w ... wh ... what t ... t ... ti ... time is it?" Her perseveration of the words "leave" or "bye" could have been revealing a deeper cry for pain relief or wanting all the continuous brain activity, the new awakenings, to go away. Or maybe she wanted some alone time (less stimulation) away from her parents, as she had started shooing us off with her hand. This unbelievable time of hyperdrive awakening continued to leave us with more questions than answers.

She had not been this awake since before her injury.

Dr. Mapstone explained her brain had re-expanded into a new environment, and now it was as if millions of neurons were firing. These millions of neurons also sparked my imagination of hope soaring to the heights of the Milky Way galaxy holding over one hundred thousand million stars extending over billions of light years.

With that door of hope open, I believed that as her overstimulated brain began to reorganize and settle into her recreated brain space, she would be able to think more clearly, speak more effectively, and move with more coordination. I believed there was so much more to come. But until then, we would trudge on.

One Year of Miracles
Home | Oklahoma City, OK
March 2010

The one-year anniversary was nothing short of miraculous. Her new occupational therapist who specializes in neuro spent forty-five minutes in one session with her and ended with these exact words, "Jessie's rehab potential is unlimited."

Those five words exploded my expectations.

Unlimited potential sounds like infinite hope.

Therapy routines were reestablished slowly, intentionally balancing her overstimulation with downtime. She spontaneously accomplished so many little things she couldn't do before surgery, like using a straw, blowing bubbles, and being able to drink small amounts of water.

Her mobility progress had enabled her to stand up independently and walk with a walker and standby assistance as she continued to work on balance.

She had gone from whispering to now speaking with four to five words in a row, carrying a simple conversation

Part 2: The Remnant

if you spoke slowly. She even answered a few texts on my phone, as I still hadn't gotten her a new phone. Her repetition was extreme in her speech. Some of the phrases she repeated over and over included, "What time is it right now, Mom? I love you, Dad, I love you. Leave. Come back. My head and face hurts," demonstrating with her hands where she hurt, and "I need to pee." She continued to have some difficulty in focusing on one task for a period of time, but gentle reminders helped. She asked for a McDonald's hamburger with mustard. She blew the harmonica and continued to hum. We sang worship songs together and when she couldn't voice the words, she would whisper them.

Agitation and overstimulation continued and was reflected by her wishes of no TV or music, preferring to sit in a quiet room by the warm fireplace as she struggled with being cold due to poor temperature regulation. We followed her lead as to what she needed and didn't need. Her pain in her head and face was intense most days. She didn't sleep for more than two hours a night, leaving her dad and I to tag team her care. Her short-term memory loss was evident, but much of her long-term we were finding as her communication capacity improved.

Her awareness and speech continued to slowly appear in unpredictable moments. The scalp incisions were healing beautifully and we hoped that within the next month, we could begin to entertain having a few visitors to help her begin to re-enter a social realm.

An appointment with Dr. Samuel Oliphant, a pediatric vision specialist and development doctor of optometry, was gifted to us by his wife, Tina, an OT who specializes in visual rehabilitation and had been following Jessie's progress on Carepages. She unexpectedly reached out to me in a personal email offering her husband's services to Jessie. She strongly felt that he would be able to do a comprehensive assessment of her vision in the midst of her challenging issues of perception and communication. I was astounded, excited, and completely unaware of this type of specialized vision therapy located in Oklahoma City. His expert experience helped us to determine the extent of her visual loss and worked extensively to help maximize what vision she did have.

Lightening Steps
Home | Oklahoma City, OK
March 2010

One morning, I reached for my coat and purse to run some errands, and she unexpectedly struggled to speak, "W ... w ... where are y ... yo ... you go ... g ... going?"

"What?" I asked, abruptly stopping to turn and look at her.

My heart couldn't take the normalcy of the moment and laughter burst forth. She looked confused as I reached down to hug her, explaining to her why her mom was so euphoric.

A mantle of wonderment and elation enveloped me as I went out the front door, my steps a little lighter and my heart cushioned, preparing me for a brief reentry to the "normal functioning" world we had left behind.

Walking quietly past my neglected gardens, another unexpected moment reached in and lifted my heart. My eyes fell upon the many bulbs that had broken through the hard cold ground, with a few already in bloom. The new life deeply contrasted the reality of the season, revealing a deeper truth of what was coming. In the harsh dead of winter, it seemed as if nothing would survive, and yet here they were, coming forth with glimpses of promises of their beauty and presence.

I hear You, God. I can see Jessie Boone, a beautiful, fragrant, pure, white flower breaking through the hard, cold, dark ground. She is growing and beginning to bloom in ways we have hoped, trusted, and waited for. With many, many miles to go, we move forward in hope, gratitude, trust, and patience. To say thank You just doesn't seem enough. Thank You for bringing forth new life in this beautiful child of Yours.

My steps seemed to shift from a heavy trudging to a lighter plodding.

Grief Shared
Home | Oklahoma City, OK
March 2010

Watching the news one evening, we saw the report of the thirteen-year-old girl who went skiing with her parents during spring break in Vail, Colorado, one year after Jessie's accident. My heart shuddered as Bill and I sat motionless and turned the volume up on the TV.

She was life-flighted to St. Mary's Hospital in Grand Junction with a massive brain injury. I closed my eyes and felt the breath leave my body and my chest burn with grief, imagining everything that was happening to the child, her parents, the staff at St. Mary's, the sounds of the monitors, the room in which she laid all came crashing in on me before the absolute worst part—she didn't survive. She was brain dead and her family was having to do the unimaginable and make the decision to donate her perfect, precious, living organs.

Oh, God, have mercy on this beloved family.

My stomach churned with sudden waves of dark nausea.

The Cottonwood Medicine

And then their unthinkable next step. They walked out of the hospital without her—without their beloved daughter. Somehow they were carried to their car, carrying her treasured sacred belongings but without her, driving with an empty seat hours to their home. Their community, heartbroken and grieving, met them and surrounded them, helping them to hold their unimaginable grief. Purple balloons were released as they drove down their street to their house.

They said purple was her favorite color—the color of royalty that will forever be tattooed on their shattered hearts.

I can't imagine the profound grief of their hearts. God of comfort, pour forth abundant comfort for this precious family.

Grief came rushing in and overtook me as I wept for the loss of their beautiful daughter. Words from my heart were etched on the paper card in effort to share my deepest sadness for theirs. Hoping they received it, I knew my crumb of an offering was severely inadequate for the mountain of pain upon them but trusted it would join all the other hearts broken for this family in effort to hold them up until they were able to find their footing within the raw grief of such a tragic death.

I don't know why Jessie survived, and the precious thirteen-year-old didn't. It makes no sense how one child can die and another survive with such great devastation. But what I do know is the God of all is with us every step of the way no matter what we are asked to face. And He will either shield us from suffering or give us unfailing strength to bear it. For Great is His Faithfulness in every moment of every day, even if we are unable to see it or understand it.

Part 2: The Remnant

Consistent Progress
Home | Oklahoma City, OK
March 2010

Palm Sunday, one year after the accident, Jessie woke with the sweetest expression on her face.

"Good morning, Jessie Boone," I spoke as the morning light from her window bathed her beginning blooms.

"G ... g ... g ... g ... good mo ... morning, M ... m ... mom ... momma, I ... I ... l ... l ... love y ... y ... you," as she struggled to find a way to get her words out.

My heart of gratitude skipped a beat as I beheld the great gift before me. Her loving spirit infused the space surrounding us.

"Today is Palm Sunday. Do you remember what you have always said?"

Puzzled, she looked at me but remained silent.

I leaned in close and whispered, "Hosanna."

Spontaneously, she recited slowly with stuttering, pauses, and broken words, "Hosanna in the highest, blessed is He who comes in the name of the Lord."

Her remembrance brought comfort and thanksgiving as my remembrance of how far she has come continued to fuel my hope for the more to come.

The more was so much more as we witnessed small bits of newness each day like walking a bit more balanced, speaking with a bit more volume, and hearing her become a bit more conversational. In her conversations, she would get into a loop, like mom, mom, mom, mom, mom. I would attempt to stop the looping by "shhhhhhhhhing" her. She would respond with a "Shhhhhhhh" back to me and voice her angst, "S ... s ... stop it, Mom, y ... you are an ... an ... annoying me," which motivated me to keep it up. My daughter's attempt to have an attitude with me

The Cottonwood Medicine

was my very favorite, helping me to catch brief glimpses of her former independent self.

Singing the alphabet song was a part of her homeschooling. One morning she was singing it as fast as she could. When I asked her why, she told me that was how fast it was going in her head. So off we went singing it as fast as we possibly could. These moments of discovery helped to give me brief glimpses of what her brain was experiencing.

While practicing counting, she suddenly switched between broken French and English from one to ten. Moments like this intrigued me, as it evidenced she was able to find some old memory while much still remained absent or hidden.

Baking, playing games, and singing were becoming a part of her daily rehab-focused schedule. Witnessing her gradual improvements, Bill and I began to talk about what it would look like to get her back into a school-based educational  routine to begin making progress toward potentially graduating. One of my deepest aches was the thought of not seeing her walk across the stage and receive her diploma. Knowing traditional school wasn't an option, I coordinated a meeting with the special education department of her school.

After a short informational meeting, I learned they required a neuropsychologist evaluation for direction on what was needed for an IEP (individual educational plan). The thought of getting an evaluation to see what educational support she would need in the classroom created anxiety. I didn't want to see all the "what she can't do" written in one report. My focus and comfort had always been found in what she was able to do.

Setting my anxiety and fear aside, I made an appointment for her neuro-evaluation, and then felt concerned about her endurance when I was told it included eight hours of testing. I had no idea if she would be able to complete the testing, as she required several naps during the day.

It was a long, hard day of testing, but she did it. And now, we had what we needed to be able to move forward in her educational journey. Seeing the detailed report of all the assistance she would need, touring the special education area of her school, and seeing the complex needs of the current students with one teacher and one assistant paused my momentum with the public education route. I was concerned she wouldn't get the needed attention to help her with individual progress. It became clear that continued homeschooling would be the best choice in maximizing her recovery in hopes of completing her high school requirements.

Counting Blessings
Home | Oklahoma City, OK
April 2010

Our first Easter home was celebrated with the traditional Easter cake she had always helped her grandma bake and decorate. With great assistance, she and Grandma finished their masterpiece by adorning the top with the well-recognized rabbit Peeps and the green coconut nest filled with the different colored jelly beans. It was followed by the entertaining coloring of the eggs, as she wasn't happy getting her fingers stained. We ended the day with a newly-revised Easter egg hunt in the living room. She picked up her basket and started hunting for the "openly" hidden eggs. It was a slow motion hunt, but she did it and counted every egg she had found. We celebrated so many resurrections that day.

Seeing movements from the past reappear in slow motion emphasized what was most important in life. Sharing in the most simple rituals were the holy ground we walked upon each day. Watching her explore and take inventory of her goodies in her Easter basket was like a burning bush experience of seeing God's hand of re-creation. Each movement was so unbelievable, rising out of the ashes, miraculously reentering our lives. Most days, I couldn't find the words to adequately express the miracles I was beholding, as I had witnessed firsthand the horrific diffuse brain injury and the devastation it left behind with death lurking in the shadows.

Run, Jessie, Run

Home | Oklahoma City, OK
April 2010

Watching her work during outpatient physical therapy, strapped into a harness to hold her upright and steady as she practiced walking on the treadmill, led us to the idea of getting our own frame built to put over our treadmill at home.

At some point each day, we would harness her safely to the frame and cheer her on as the treadmill slowly insisted on a step by step motion. We hoped the consistency of walking her one mile each day would build balance, endurance, and perseverance.

Our goal for her to independently walk was extended into a family goal of all of us running a 5K together as a family one day, remembering the special "Jessie Boone Miracle Run" that was held to unite hearts in prayer and financial support for the belief and hope one day she would run again. One afternoon in her outpatient physical

Part 2: The Remnant

therapy session, her PT, a young man named Scott, made the announcement that Jessie Boone was going to run.

Yes, she is!

I smiled with absolute certainty, wondering just how fast he was going to make that treadmill go!

He stood her up, holding her gait belt and steadied her. Instead of going toward the treadmill, he walked her toward the long hallway off the therapy gym. Then he turned and looked me directly in the eyes and proclaimed, "Today!"

WHAT? How?

"Mom, come watch our Jessie Boone!"

His grasp tightened on her gait belt around her waist as he spoke his words into action, "On the count of three, I want you to run, Jessie. One, two, three, GO!"

Wobbly, she took off like a new foal just getting up for the first time, clumsily trying to find her balance and sea legs, almost falling at one point, as he was pacing behind her, holding her upright, maneuvering her sways, demanding this goal be recognized as attainable by her unsteady body and mind.

Reaching the end of the hallway, he turned her around and without hesitation said, "Again! Run, Jessie, run."

My heart couldn't keep up with her new pace.

It was over in sixteen seconds. JESSIE BOONE HAD HER OWN MIRACLE RUN!

Her face was priceless. The exhilaration was showing as her face lit up. She was breathing hard and leaned over with her hands on her knees like I had seen her before after she had run a race.

When she looked up, our eyes met. I was laughing and breathing as hard as she was and asked, "How was that for you, Jessie?"

Her slow response was winded but clear as day, "That was amazing!"

My heart unearthed during that sixteen-second window of time. Something extraordinary had just happened. Something miraculous that no words could touch. Something that could only unfold within the furrows of everyone's love, prayers, and presence at the Miracle Run that had taken place in her name when she was still not able to even take a step. I knew I was witnessing this prophetic act of faith come into fruition.

Celebrating Independence
Home | Oklahoma City, OK
July 2010

Independence Day was nearing as harrowing memories jarred me back to the last when I had refused to sign the pediatric intensivist's omen of the DNR within the darkened walls of the PICU at Baptist, and he had promptly begun making discharge arrangements for Jessie as a mute, spastic quadriplegic, giving us little hope as he recommended a long-term care facility for children. Our faith chose differently. We chose home.

During that difficult stay, I do remember one visit in particular, sharply contrasting the DNR meeting we had just walked away from. Unexpectedly appearing at our door, with warm pizza in hand, our faith-filled friends had courageously shared their brutal story of how they'd spent the previous Fourth of July in the hospital battling for their own son's life and how this one was so much better. They had boldly spoken the words of hope over our shattered lives, proclaiming, "Your next one will be better, too."

And it surely was.

Part 2: The Remnant

Jessie had begun asking about going to church, and my answer was always, "Soon, sweet girl."

But the truth was I didn't know when, as my heart was still unable to face her beautiful youthful friends, seeing their lives so full of what Jessie's wasn't.

Her recovery was monumental within the sheltered walls of our lives, but stepping out crushed the sense of progress within my heart, revealing the harshest comparison to what she wasn't. It was a luminous darkness as her miraculous life was still in diapers. A feeding tube bulged under her shirt, her communication was broken and repetitive, she walked slowly with a walker, and her blonde hair was still not able to cover the obvious widened jagged tracks of her past surgeries.

As Bill and I began to discuss how we might celebrate this upcoming day of freedom which fell on a Sunday, her recent visit to her physiatrist made it possible for me to consider answering her church question differently. Because her blood work had stabilized, he moved her from weekly blood draws to biyearly and explained that with her increased oral intake and weight maintenance, her PEG (feeding) tube was no longer needed.

That Sunday morning, in honor of Independence Day, we chose to remove her feeding tube when she woke up, proclaiming thanks for this new freedom of no longer depending on it for her nutrition. It took only her taking one deep breath for this life-giving tube to be removed from her belly and our lives.

At that moment, a strange courage arose within my weary heart, along with the immense gratitude of her newfound freedom.

"Would you like to go to church this morning to celebrate?"

The Cottonwood Medicine

Her eyes lit up and in slow stuttering words, she said, "Y ... y ... yes, v ... ve ... very b ... ba ... badly."

The voiced need of her heart surpassed the vigilant protection of mine as we began getting her ready to attend church in person for the first time since her accident.

One can only imagine the sheer joy and celebration we encountered when we "walked" back into church together. And imagine the tears from all of us, as so many walked up to Jessie to give her a big hug, telling her how incredibly thankful they were to see her.

Her journey back to the youth area was met with intense emotional moments as her youth ministers and friends greeted her with great excitement and love. Her monumental walk to the celebration center was slow, full of emotional hugs, words of thanksgiving, and the visual power of prayer presenting itself as a child who had answered the call, "Talitha Koum, little girl, I say arise."

We sat where Jessie had always sat, in the youth area. Our pastor took a moment to recognize her, sharing a part of her miraculous story. As we helped her stand, the congregation gave her a standing ovation, clapping in celebration of the life before them as they had prayed, fasted, and provided for our family since the accident. She beamed with a smile, waving joy and love to all through that sanctuary of grace. And for a brief moment, all of the crushing grief quieted as we were lifted and held in the winged love of His people.

Grounding hit me hard as we made our way to the women's bathroom with necessities strapped on my back. Her bowel incontinence was the reality of our world, and I found myself struggling to clean her in the small bathroom stall. Tears were blurring my efforts to avoid any further messes as she struggled to stand upright, trying to brace

Part 2: The Remnant

herself against the tiny wall of the stall. I could hear a couple of the youth girls laughing and chatting while they washed their hands, oblivious to what was happening just a few feet away. The very bathroom that Jess had used independently her entire life in this church was now holding her—us—in a different way.

What is she thinking at this very moment? Is she embarrassed? Is she unaware of the reality outside of her? These moments hidden behind walls reveal the deepest reality of what we are having to bear. Oh God, You know exactly where we are. I need Your help now.

The celebration of her life and the humility of her condition collided in my heart as I asked God for strength to get her cleaned and to the car without encountering more conversations from our loving community. My heart couldn't absorb the paradoxical juncture and needed to escape back to the hidden sanctuary of space we called home.

As Bill drove us home, all I felt was relief to be out of the large fluid space of others, no longer worrying about her bowel and bladder incontinence, unpredictable vomiting, or having to navigate conversations with others while needing to tend to her instead. Exhaustion and grief forced a much needed nap, and I curled up beside Jessie on her bed in hopes of sleeping some of the pain away.

Later that evening, my heart was replaying our first attempt of reentry to church. Even though my heart took a beating, I was deeply comforted by the caring of our community. I also realized if anyone had known what was going on within the stall of the bathroom and the recesses of my heart, there would have been a line out the door to help me. It never even once occurred to me to ask for help, as I was overwhelmed with my own grief and trying to survive the harsh reality of her injuries while attempting to maintain my own fractured composure.

Jessie's Wings

Home | Oklahoma City, OK
July 2010

Much more time was needed before we stepped back into church, as it was obvious my heart wasn't ready for all the extra and unpredictables, but what I did know was how thankful I was for these collective wings of so many souls that had helped carry us through such unimaginable darkness.

Hanging on my wall is a visual icon of those collective wings of so many souls.

This impressive watercolor painting called "Winged Flight" was creatively captured by Susan Gainen and gifted to us by friends. It is a treasured Ebenezer Stone—a sign God has helped us—a stunning hope-filled imagery of six hundred and seventy multi-colored, hand-like figures coming together to create a birdlike image flying upward, depicting the lifting up by others within Jessie's brokenness, helping her and helping us regain flight. The frame displaying the words, "Jessie's Wings."

As the hued sunset broadcasted the closing of such an emotional day, we gathered Jessie between the two of us on our front porch rockers as our neighbors were preparing for their annual fireworks display. Having a front row view to this spectacular celebration of freedom, partaking in the shared homemade ice cream, and being nestled closely in the safety of home was the most comforting way to end our freedom day. Earlier in the week, Bill had taken Jessie to buy a few special fireworks in an effort to reestablish one of his favorite daddy-daughter routines. Watching him light the Chinese paper lantern, we were mesmerized, watching the mystery of the glowing orange lantern rise slowly. As it freely floated heavenwards, her tiny, broken, stuttering voice pierced the darkened silence, "Th ... th ... thank Y ... Y ... You, God," drawing our grateful hearts in response to the luminous mystery that was also lifting her slowly.

Yes, thank You, God.

An Unexpected Side Effect

Home | Oklahoma City, OK
July 2010

One morning, I was sorting through stacks of love when I came across one of the letters we had received in Grand Junction from a manager of an Oklahoma City restaurant with an enclosed generous gift certificate. His words were simple, "Please have a meal on me when you return home. I am praying for your daughter. Please let me know how else I can help."

I had remembered reading his Carepage postings and prayers for our family and wondered how this kind stranger had learned about Jessie and what brought such generous love to our table.

Sending a long past due thank you note through email, I shared my deep gratitude for his generous gift of a meal, one we would be using soon because now she was finally able to eat! His unexpected response later that evening fell right into my crevassed heart.

> "Dear Lisa, I was so glad to read that Jessie and your family were able to come home. I know you have a long road ahead of you but I continue to pray for her recovery. I am so happy you are going to have a meal from my restaurant. I wanted to share something with you, as you and Jessie have been a very big part of my life these last few months. My wife and I have been separated. I love my wife and we have beautiful children which left my heart broken. I had spent too much time working and staying away from home and it drove our marriage to its breaking point so she left me. When I discovered your Carepages and the profound tragedy your family was going through, I too was going through one of the darkest times of my life. Your words of faith and great hope through the absolute worst circumstances gave me great strength and hope to move through mine. Every night I would come home from work anxious to read your updates about Jessie. Somehow your updates would overlay on my life circumstances and give me direction or comfort and help guide me to pray about my own family and the hopes of a reconciliation. I

> wanted you to know I have changed. My life has changed because of God showing me so much through your family's journey. I will no longer put work before my family. I want you to know my wife and I are back together. I could have never imagined this happening but I know God helped us through you and I want to say Thank you for being so willing to share your journey. I am eternally grateful."

My heart paused, then trembled and quaked with thanksgiving at the witness of such a miraculous healing within his marriage. I couldn't even begin to imagine the relief his children felt as they were reunited as a family again—the beautiful joy that had been breathed back into their young hearts.

"My life has changed because of God showing me so much through your family's journey," held me suspended as I gazed at the "good" coming out of our ashes, revealing the power of God's grace spilling over and healing this man and his beloved family. His next words are embedded in my heart forever: "Thank you for being so willing to share your journey."

His own family had been severed at the root and with grace he had found our story, helping to heal his own.

Delicious Milestones

Home | Oklahoma City, OK
July 2010

Glimpses of new re-entry would come in the unexpected places of our day. Before her accident, a Taco Bell burrito was a staple meal in the midst of her after school activities. Since, each drive by a Taco Bell taunted my grief-filled heart, "Your daughter isn't living anymore!" Tears and pain took an abrupt revolt to never stop at another Taco Bell until she was with me and able to eat her own burrito with no onions.

Driving up to the banned drive thru with Jessie Boone in the passenger seat, was a victorious moment as I wept, proudly ordering, "Two bean burritos with no onions, please." Although the window attendant had no idea what a monumental proclamation was being announced through the speaker, I knew at this moment, that hurtful voice was silenced forever as Jessie Boone was now about to eat the forbidden meal, reclaiming yet another part of her life.

In the parking lot, we shared this great moment as I savored each morsel of victory within the miraculous moments of watching her chew and swallow the hallowed bean burrito, celebrating the drippings of the reality of truth before me.

Water therapy had not been an option due to her unhealed head incisions and the presence of her feeding tube. A fully healed scalp and freedom from the feeding tube welcomed an arrangement with a friend who had a well-loved pool that had been the venue for hundreds of fun-loving and loud youth during church activities over the past summers.

Today the water was quiet and still, warmed by the summer sun as if it knew exactly the special assignment it had been given. The swimming suit that had laid untouched in her dresser drawer was now in its rightful place on her moving upright body.

Our friend Shelley was already in the pool splashing and wooing Jessie to join her, both of us deeply curious yet cautious of how Jessie would respond to the water.

Part 2: The Remnant

Her years at Kanakuk and her friends with pools had formed her love for water, but we didn't know what was going to happen. Would she be able to swim and hold her breath to go underwater? Would the water help her move more smoothly and effectively? Would it be soothing for her or induce more unwanted agitation?

It was a tranquil afternoon, as I watched Jessie and Shelley gently floating in the buoyancy of the water. Silly laughs would bring smiles to my heart as they would simultaneously put their faces in the water and blow bubbles. Her gentle encouragement for Jessie to move her arms and legs in rhythmic motions was effortless and ended with the synchronized swimming event of both of them going underwater without hesitation. It was all there. She just needed the sacred space created with loving encouragement, inviting her to find her way back to what she had left behind. I became acutely aware of how water therapy could now be another essential part of her recovery, which sparked endless ideas and conversations with Bill about a pool building project, which would soon be on the horizon of our hope for more to come.

PART 3

Reseeding the Forest

—

7 Years of Reclaiming Capacities

CHAPTER 11

Planting Big Trees

Planting Possibilities

Our Clayton Park Road home was an intimate, secluded sanctuary of healing and hope. Witnessing Jessie's mobility increasing in the great reclamation of independence was changing each day as a new reality was being realized: our two-story home was no longer a safe haven. Our continuous efforts to keep Jessie in her room were therapeutically intended but came at a great cost. With increasing mobility came safety concerns like her "unaware wandering" in the house. The staircase at night was a daunting concern, as we knew a fall could be fatal.

Bill and I slept on the floor of her room within ear range of her spontaneous vomiting, fearing she would aspirate. Our pallet, complete with futon mattresses, was also the barrier she would have to pass to reach the perilous stairs.

Months of sleeping on the floor with no end in sight evoked the desperate search for a better way. Early one morning, as I was sitting on the back porch pondering and listening to the song of the doves, I heard the word, "MOVE."

What, God? Move? Move where? We can't move. We love our healing sanctuary. Besides we are barely able to do what we do with Jess. How can we possibly move? If it is to happen, You are going to have to make us move because I don't think I can.

Even as I sat there, my thoughts of moving slowly began to shift.

We could move closer to our kids and our church. How good would it be to have a one-story house where I didn't have to worry about her falling down the stairs? Sleeping in my bed again would be a heaven-sent luxury.

This sanctuary that had held our fragile lives and hearts was now feeling tomblike. The immobility of our lives had settled deep within the walls of merely existing, with much of the environmental and emotional stuff hoarded and crammed, leaving no space for the wind to blow freely through.

Gosh God, we could use a good pruning.

Scrolling through Zillow, looking at new potential homes, I came across the words, "Make Me Move." I laughed as I thought of my last conversation with God. My fingers hesitated as my mind was searching for the connection, clicking to see what came next.

It all happened so quickly. That evening, I took pictures of every room in the house, the front porch, the pool and outdoor building, with a panoramic view of the land. Within two hours, I had our home listed for sale. Bill and I had an interesting and lively discussion when he got home from work that evening, as he hadn't heard the news yet!

Within a short period of time, we had sold our home to a family who had accepted the challenge of making us move without us knowing where. Once again it didn't take long before we were preparing for a big move into a home that was all that I could have hoped and dreamed for.

Moving was hard, but everything was hard. Yet on the other side of hard was a new canvas of hope waiting for our presence to stroke the colors of our lives onto the sacred landscape, creating a reflection of gratitude for each day we had been given with her.

Planting Big Trees

The new house's open floor plan provided unexpected spaciousness to life. Stepping outside on the two and a half acres welcomed a 360-view of sky and field, bringing the freedom we needed for the next chapter of her recovery. It was as though the stone was being rolled away and the burial linens were falling off. The bright rays of the sun revealed new life being birthed. Such life demanded more life. My heart soon began to yearn for a sacred forest of hope to be planted on the beautiful clean canvas found within our new backyard.

Pondering and visualizing trees being planted on the desolate land became a daily devotional for months until the day I began colonizing my dream. Each tree I planted was a living stake of hope buried deep in the earth, believing the roots would grow downward, stabilizing and holding firm against the storms to come.

The forest began to slowly rise up, bringing dimension and life to the barrenness of the land. Birds became curious, visiting the branches that filled the previously empty spaces. Their rejoicing songs were audible to the dancing wind that was finding a new resistance and being challenged in its direction. Their colors of green burst out in laughter as they spread out their cloaks in the sky with each passing year. The seasons were captivated by their new playground, giving and boldly taking away their outward appearances while deeply transforming the hidden life within. What profound life one can find and experience in a forest!

Tending and listening to the trees deepened my love for them as I witnessed their battles with drought, insects, weather, and soil challenges. They stand firm and still receive all that life gives them with open branches. They breathe in the harsh elements the world gives and breathe out life-giving breath for the life of others, generously providing shade and homes without thought to how it might affect them. Branches reach upward, giving praise to the Creator who gives them life.

Learning the language of trees and hearing God speak to me through His creation was one of the deep ways He communicated with my heart in the midst of such grief. Their saintly presence in the backyard of my life whispered these words to my heart:

> **Mystery**
> *by Lisa Boone*
>
> *Oh sacred giants on this living earth,*
> *Your selfless acts of love are undeniable,*
> *And yet without thought we receive.*
> *Giver of hope and healing,*
> *Nurturer of life,*
> *We raise our hearts to your hallowed canopies,*
> *Giving thanks for your strength and sanctified presence through all.*

My new forest of "Visio Divina" offered this beautiful invitation to a "sacred seeing," an ancient form of Christian prayer which allows hearts and imaginations into a sacred image while waiting in silence to see what God might say. These timbered icons of creation nourished healing and hope into the deep wounds of my soul, tending me as I tended them.

Return in Repair
Grand Junction, CO
August 2010

Heart murmurings is one way the Spirit speaks within me. Those murmurings had me yearning for a reunion trip to Grand Junction, to visit our "chosen family" who had carried us through the worst forty days of our lives. Jessie's recovery had been so remarkable that I couldn't wait to see her give hugs and thank yous to all those who had cared for her. I wanted her life-saving physicians to witness their brilliant "work" walking and talking, experiencing her hugs while hearing her sweet angelic thank yous.

Bill and I decided this return trip would be a sacred pilgrimage—a hallowed walk into the past to encounter the sacred footprints of the love and generosity that held our very lives—giving us the unique opportunity to look each person in the face, thank them for their life-saving love, and never forget the immense generosity that was heaped upon our shattered lives.

As the plane made its descent, the familiar white peaks of the snow-capped Rocky Mountains came into clear view. Our landing was as easy as our hearts, despite the lingering memories of our last landing in Denver. But this time was different. She was safe and bundled up right between us.

We strolled like tourists through an outdoor mall, breathing in the cool crisp air as we window-shopped. In an attempt to re-create Jessie's past shopping habits, we teased her with a darling dress and a colorful scarf for her to try on.

"Hey, Jessie, look at this! Do you like it?" I danced with it in front of her.

She smiled, slowly reaching out to touch it. "Yes, I do."

"Let's try it on and maybe we can get your dad to buy it for you," I playfully encouraged her.

The dressing room was entered as a therapeutic outing, overcoming the difficult challenges of the tiny new environment. "All in the name of rehab" was my mantra, which helped to redefine the expectations of my heart. How encouraging it was to see her look at herself in the full-length mirror, take the scarf in both her hands and smile at herself, answering my question, "Do you like it?" clearly with, "Yes, I do." It didn't take us long to purchase the priceless Ebenezer Stone of her first shopping trip while feeling a sweet triumph of helping her re-experience a moment of her "girliness."

Driving through the majestic mountain passes of such extraordinary scenery and seeing the Colorado River pulsating through the expansive open lands awakened my senses to my adventurous spirit that had been buried beneath the tonnage of the devastation of a traumatic brain injury.

As we neared Grand Junction, the approach was different, driving to a different destination in the daylight. We were different. Even the thoughts and memories resurrected as we passed by "the" airport, "the" hospitality inn, "the" hospital, "the" intersection, "the" helicopter on "the" landing pad, and "the" coffee shop were now just shadows in our lives.

The first site we visited was the restaurant our friends had taken us to for a meal attempting to give us a moment away from the hospital. I remember the brutality of that moment with intense anxiety—unable to hold my head up and sickened to the point of vomiting in the bathroom.

This time was different as we walked in with our heads and hearts up and shared a meal with Jessie. We feasted on the gratitude of being given this rarefied moment to rewrite tragedy with a new memory.

Driving down the familiar road by St. Mary's hospital, we went in search of the ministering angel who had opened her heart and coordinated the mission to care and feed us for the forty days and forty nights we had battled demons in the desert.

Diane opened her home to us and invited us to stay with her and her husband, hosting a beautiful evening reunion of food, fellowship, and worship with all those light-filled souls that had served alongside her.

Her backyard was a sprawling green oasis of hills and water, the feast featuring assorted dishes created from the loving kitchens we had once been sustained by. But this time it was different as we were able to see each one of them, share the meal and cup, and show them the immense gratitude our hearts were needing to empty as we introduced them to the living miracle they were a part of ushering forth.

We were glimpsing heaven on earth as God's family sat on blankets, eating and sharing the goodness of life. The youth led us in praise and worship underneath the open blue skies of freedom. Doug Clayton, our minister of the desert, stood and read the Word of God, feeding our hungry souls with the Bread of Life.

After the deep immersion of grace and gratitude, our next destination was the sacred womb of St. Mary's Hospital, a place that held us deep in its bowels, infusing life into the child who had lost most of hers. Just driving into the parking lot was different, bringing flooding emotions and tears for ALL that had been given to us within this hallowed structure. Walking with Jessie up each concrete step to the glass entrance of this sanctuary of healing was like an out of body experience, wondering how it was even possible, yet seeing it was happening at that very moment. I found myself wanting to proclaim, "Jessie Boone is in the house!" Instead, I walked beside her, with my hand in hers, quietly telling her stories of why we were here and how incredibly significant this place was for our family.

"Welcome Home, Boone Family" was the welcoming message written in green buttercream icing on top of the confetti-sprinkled cake in the nurse's lounge awaiting our arrival. "Our" nurses, the warriors and life sustainers, greeted us with open arms of excitement as each one reached out to hug and encounter "their" Jessie in a new way. Tears flowed and laughter lifted as pictures were taken, celebrating the victory of life.

Her sweet face and quiet voice recaptured their hearts once again as they witnessed the resurrection of this dear child's life. To be able to re-encounter each one of them with a different posture, knowing they had seen us all at our very worst, was another healing rebirth for us all.

So much had changed in the neuro ICU since we had been there. They had undergone a complete remodel, transforming it into a completely different place, no longer recognizable by our experiences. And now here Jessie stood, a complete remodel, walking and talking with blue eyes now open and looking around. Smiling beneath her locks of blonde hair that had once again taken their rightful place. She was no longer recognizable by their experiences.

The cake had said it all, and how true it felt. We were home, in the very place that life was given back to Jessie Boone. The home that cared, nourished, protected, and held the most precious thing in our lives—our child. Our hearts are forever woven in the very fabric of St. Mary's and their saintly staff of love.

My heart began pounding to a very different rhythm when it was finally time to journey to the next site of this pilgrimage, reuniting with her trauma surgeon. I didn't know how my heart was going to hold this moment.

I had always jokingly told Bill each time he had left our hospital room, "Gosh, I love him, and I want to marry him." Bill would smile and say, "I know, honey. I know you do." He knew it was the Jesus within him that drew me so fiercely to him.

Dr. Breaux had been the closest I had ever been to "Jesus on earth." I watched him through my "devastated" mom eyes and my "expectations of the best" nursing eyes for forty days and forty nights. He was our "consistent" guiding star, our "present" compassionate healer, our "never give up" fierce lion, and our "loving" gentle lamb carrying our child and us across the harsh and brutal land to the stable of birth. He never once faltered on his mission to get her through to the other side. We owed him everything, yet he wanted nothing but life for her.

We stepped into his humble office space and I noticed a few children waiting with their parents for their time with this miracle man.

I wonder if they knew the depths of this man? The depths of love he has for his profession and the children he cares for? The depths of his wisdom, knowledge, and experience in the field of pediatric trauma? The depths he would go to help others? I do. I know.

His wife was behind the desk, "May I help you?" Her eyes were kind and gentle like her husband's.

I stood staring at her.

So you are his wife. You must know what a special man he is. You must also live such a profound life of sacrifice with him as you have continued to witness and share his extraordinary life of service.

"May I help you?" she asked again with a gentle smile, her spirit nearing mine.

I stepped closer, finding my footing, and quietly said, "Hello," as the tears began to fall. I looked at her and then toward Jessie, finding my way back to hers. "We are here to see Dr. Breaux. I had called to let him know we would be coming by to say hello. This is Jessie Boone."

"Come on back. He's waiting for you," she said, leading us to an exam room.

Jessie was unaware of all the movements pounding fiercely within my heart as we waited in silence for his arrival. I held my breath as the door opened, and the gentle spirit that had always cloaked him made my gratitude fall to the ground like cut branches.

Jessie slowly rose up out of her chair, taking steps toward him, her arms reaching for a hug as she recited her practiced phrase, "Hello, doctor."

We all beamed with joy, and his joy hugged her back.

"Hello, Jessie Boone. It's so good to see you."

The next several moments suspended time for me as we emotionally shared her progress, our gratitude, our hopes, and how deeply he had impacted our lives by giving us our daughter back. The pictures of Jessie standing by his side, marking this very special moment forever are the keepsakes for my heart. And PS, I still wanted to marry him.

We traveled on to visit our next site of re-creation. Dr. Witwer greeted her with a hug and a huge smile as he playfully teased her. This tall, thin, tousled blonde, adventurous husband and father of two knew the depth of the gift we had received. With these few sacred moments of a joyful reunion with his heart, we did our best to share our deepest gratitude for his life-changing work and the forever impact he'd had on our family. The pictures we took of them together looked more like he was her big brother instead of the exceptional, dedicated, and experienced neurosurgeon he was.

With our itinerary coming to a close, it was time to leave Grand Junction. We had been able to come full circle and finish the most important part of a miracle—being able to say thank you. Our hearts were full of the richness of our adopted family, knowing they were chosen to help our little family in a time of great need. These great acts in the face of such great tragedy were the needles of love knitting all of our hearts eternally together, as we all moved forward transformed by a greater Truth, Emmanuel, God with us.

Sacred Slopes
Glenwood Springs, CO
August 2010

We headed east on I-70 to Sunlight Ski Resort in Glenwood Springs, the place where the ski patrol had stabilized and transported her to a level one trauma center. The manager, Erin, had followed Jessie's progress on Carepages, and upon reading about our planned return trip, she messaged me through Carepages asking if we would want to stop by for a reunion with the ski patrol.

"We would love to," I had responded, thankful for this unique invitation.

As we pulled into the parking lot, Erin, the manager, was sitting on the steps waiting. She introduced herself and offered to drive Jessie around the side if she couldn't climb the twenty-five stairs leading to the resort.

Bill and I both smiled, thinking the same thing, and I said, "No, we will climb those steps and meet you at the top."

Part 3: Reseeding the Forest

We were stunned by the number of ski patrol and staff waiting to greet Jessie. They clapped and hugged her, telling her how incredible she was, and what a wonderful sight she was to behold.

A young man approached us and shared how deeply Jessie's journey had impacted his own, leading him to become an EMT. After witnessing her injuries, he wanted to have as many skills as possible to render care to the people who had catastrophic accidents. I looked at his young face with his big, compassionate heart readied for his mission in this world and reached out to touch his shoulder as I deeply thanked him, not only for myself but for all those who would come after us.

Before leaving, this tremendous group of compassionate, kind servants presented her with her own official "ski patrol" hat, claiming her as one of their own. In closing, we gathered in a large circle with enjoined hearts and hands, praying and giving thanks together as a family.

We counted each step out loud as we made our way back down to the parking lot. It was another way we wove rehab into our daily life. Erin walked with us, this time gifting us with her in-person presence, not just through the Carepages. So many people have walked with us this entire journey, and we have never met them face to face. That day helped to change that story just a bit.

"Jessie, I have something for you," Erin told her. She reached into her car parked next to ours and pulled out a large, colorful afghan. "My friends and I hand crocheted this for you and prayed over every stitch as you continue on your healing journey." She lovingly wrapped Jessie up in the stitches of love and gave her a big ol' bear hug.

Jessie smiled as the sweetest words found their way out, "Awwww, thank you very much."

Erin's parting words to us on that day were, "I will never forget that day. I had hundreds of group skiers on the hill. I was sitting at my desk when a walkie crackled to life and reported that a skier had hit a tree. 'Please don't let it be one of my kids' was the only thought I could hear in my head. I found out it was Jessie. We had chatted briefly in the rental shop as she was being fitted for boots. I remember being drawn to her immediately because she radiated a beautiful light. You know that kind of light that can't be contained?"

Oh, boy, do I know that!

"I went back to my office and wept. A few minutes later, a youth pastor from another group of seventy came to my office and asked what they could do. I told him they could pray, and he said they were already on it. The praying began in the lodge and swept across the resort in ALL the groups as they joined forces in the ballroom, praying all night. And I haven't stopped praying for this special light, Jessie Boone," she finished her story as she reached out and touched Jessie's face with such a tenderness of love.

How beautiful are the hands and feet of Christ reaching out to help others ...

We were flooded with such powerful love along this road we had traveled. This power resembled the hard-working Colorado River, both a servant and scenic wonder flowing faithfully along the road we were traveling toward home. This lifeline keeps coming and coming, pouring forth unselfishly the water, food, recreation and energy for the lives of others.

We returned home safe and sound from our pilgrimage, thankful for all of the encounters with the sudden realization that Jessie never complained or had one sick spell the entire time we were gone. What a magnificent gift of grace! She was such a trooper, but goodness, I was pretty sure we already knew that!

Celebration of Courage
Cowboy Hall of Fame | Oklahoma City, OK
August 2010

The time within each day resembled a life-sized building block game. One activity would build upon another, working on balancing and stabilizing structures for more building. Our home had been recreated as an individualized rehab center set up to practice whatever she was working on during her outpatient therapy. Therapeutic activities of exercise, play, and creativity, with others designed to enhance her fine and gross motor skills, problem-solving abilities, mathematics, language, and communication skills were the blocks. Rest periods were scheduled throughout to balance her active rehabilitation time with healing downtime.

We were notified unexpectedly that Jessie was chosen as one of the three 2010 Jim Thorpe Rehabilitation Courage Award recipients. Stunned with disbelief, I listened as the Director of Jim Thorpe Rehab further explained, "This award was established to recognize and honor people who have overcome disabilities caused by a catastrophic injury or illness by facing the physical and mental challenges of rehabilitation with courage, determination, and an indomitable human spirit. She will be honored at the banquet held at the Cowboy Hall of Fame with the other two recipients. This annual banquet invites the attendees to support and witness the courage and strength of our award winners and their success in overcoming unimaginable trauma. To make it even more personal, a personalized video will be created for each one, giving a brief glimpse of their story of recovery for all to witness their victories."

"I don't know what to say," I nearly whispered, as I stared in wonderment at this fatigued, little, blonde girl curled up on the sofa under a blanket with her eyes closed, clueless of the impact she was having on other people's hearts.

"Oh, I almost forgot the best part! All of her therapists will be there to celebrate her," she said with excitement.

I felt my heart melting into those two words, "her therapists."

Her therapists! I can't even begin to express what incredible life-givers these human saints are!

Over the last several months, I had witnessed their selfless dedication to serving us and other people who had suffered the "unimaginable." They helped each one regain and bring forward life in the best possible way with such deep compassion and kindness. This life-giving work is visionary, seeing the unseen, believing and demanding a calling forth of what has been lost. These life regifters are living examples of walking by faith, and not by sight!

"Oh my goodness, I love her therapists and would treasure spending a whole evening with them," I gushed, imagining all the feel-goods that would come with that.

"Is that a yes?" she asked.

"Let me talk with Bill and get back to you, but I can't imagine us not coming to such a significant evening for so many different reasons." I still was not able to absorb the magnanimity of the invitation.

"Great, I look forward to hearing from you soon," she replied.

"Jessie Boone, you are cordially invited as one of the three guests of honor awarded the Jim Thorpe Courage Award to attend this Black Tie gala," is how the invitation read, emphasizing how the silent and live auctions would help raise money to support unique therapies that otherwise couldn't be offered, such as aquatic therapy, community outings, horticulture therapy, music therapy, and recreational therapy.

Each one of these has been an important part of her recovery journey.

Jessie smiled enthusiastically as I shared this special invitation and award she had been chosen to receive. When I asked if she would like to attend, she nodded her head and raised her hands.

"What do you think you should wear to this formal occasion?"

Her smile didn't change as she searched me for the answer.

The prom dress, hand chosen by Jessie before her accident, came to my mind.

I wonder.

Having previously gazed upon that abandoned dress with a deep sadness in my heart, my hope reignited in a different way. Perhaps this could be the "one" for a different type of prom?

Family and friends quickly joined in this unique opportunity to celebrate all of Jessie's victories and to support the successes and progress of this remarkable rehabilitation haven. We began to hear of entire tables being bought by friends, and many would purchase extra tickets and send them to us, enabling us to have more of her friends by her side. Our community of support, all reaching out and over the top to continue to pray, provide, stand, and give praise for this monumental event. Cards, notes, and messages poured in, celebrating what God had done for Jessie. I knew this "prom" party was ultimately being hosted by God in celebration for all who supported us either in word, deed, presence, prayers, or spirit.

The event preparations began with Jess being gifted a manicure and a pedicure. Flowers were delivered in celebration as her friends arrived to start the party early. Laughter and giggles traveled down the stairs as they styled her hair and applied makeup. My heart tendered to the past when those same friends were having sleepovers, watching "A Walk to Remember" for the umpteenth time as they swooned and cried over the love-filled drama, filling our home once again with those familiar noises of lifegiving youthfulness. And finally, the moment arrived when the cherished turquoise satin memento was now no longer on the hanger, tucked away in her darkened closet, but delightfully hanging and reflecting the light-filled grace on her newfound frame of freedom.

The tables were elegantly dressed and readied for the hundreds of guests gathering in collective hope for the "more" that was always the centerpiece of rehab. The food was plated and served to each guest while we waited to see how the silent bidding ended. The ceiling was lifted with conversations, feasting on the generosity and compassion of humanity.

Watching the video stories of the three recipients who had battled fiercely and triumphantly to overcome the impossible was powerfully convicting hearts with rising hope for the more. We witnessed a college football player who suffered a  brutal spinal cord injury, finding his way back to a life of quality; a firefighter hit on a bicycle by a car going 60 mph, suffering a brain injury with multiple broken bones, who is now riding his bicycle again; and sweet Jessie's massive brain injury, fighting her way back to walking and talking again. All three families were surrounded and embraced within a sea of love and support. It was a golden opportunity to celebrate with joy and generosity at life being won back with such fierce determination, with an emphasis to never, never give up regardless of how futile it seems.

When the emcee called Jessie's name, she stood up, her turquoise Cinderella dress glistening underneath the spotlight, her low heels recording each step as if a book was being written one word at a time. With all eyes on this vision of grace, she climbed each step unassisted until she reached the stage, close between Bill and me. She stepped toward her incredible physiatrist, Dr. Shawn Smith, who gave her a warm hug. She reached out and took her award in hand, stepped up to the microphone, and offered her practiced words, which came out like a torpedoed speech, making it difficult to understand, "Thank you very much for the Jim Thorpe Courage Award, guys." We didn't care. We knew each and every movement was miraculous. Her dad finished her "acceptance speech," his trembling voice uttering heartfelt words of deep gratitude.

What a profound moment in time—this sacred pause to remember the "all " as we looked out over this sea of saints giving our girl a standing ovation. All the while, my heart peeked over the veil, seeing the more ... The standing ovation was for the all—the all who had gone before us, the all who helped, and the all to come.

ALL.

She "talked" to many different people throughout the night with her muffled, swift, and choppy new language, making it difficult for most to understand, but it didn't matter. We relished witnessing her smiles and engaging the best she could with those who came up to her with congratulations and hugs.

Her therapists were adorned with such magnificent ball gowns, extravagant makeup, and stunning updos.

Watching them transfigured in this venue only deepened my knowing of their true identity of royalty in service to others.

A magical moment happened later that evening when she had a "daddy daughter" dance. Time stood still as I watched this incredible man of great love and faith hold our beloved daughter in his supportive arms, gently swaying her back and forth in her new life with her *opened* blue eyes locked on his, gazing a radiant love back to him.

This celebration of life was monumental, an Ebenezer Stone of sorts, being fully immersed in this sea of "seeing," "believing," and "becoming." This powerful medicine fueled my heart onward along this challenging quest of finding the "more" and helping it to find its way out.

CHAPTER 12

The Golden Rain Trees

Letting Go

The long drive to Kansas felt so different this time. Sister Benedicta was in hospice care, in the wing of Mount St. Scholastica Benedictine monastery that holds the saints as they prepare for their ultimate homecoming. Her wish for no visitors was deeply respected by all, but it only took a phone call from her requesting our presence, and we were on our way.

As Bobbie and I traveled north, my heart drifted to memories of my first encounter with her at the Red Plains Monastery in Piedmont, Oklahoma, to talk about the Spiritual Exercises of St. Ignatian, a 16th century Spanish priest, theologian, and founder of the Jesuits.

As I pulled into the graveled parking lot that first day, I was welcomed by the massive canopies of the trees that shaded the manicured grounds. I remembered her warm greeting, her deep listening, and the sacred gift of the first meditation book that taught me how to listen in silence.

Each mile driven toward our last earthly encounter seemed to be clicking a counter of each gift I had received from her along the way. Mile after mile, gift after gift, memory after memory ... Goodness, what a life of fontality! (That was her word for abundant love.) Her life resembled the Tree of Life with roots buried deeply within the soul of God, drinking in the nutrients of His Living Word and

His Living Waters. Her trunk was solid and firmly planted in the deeply fertilized soil of Truth, with an unshakeable faith despite the storms of life attempting to uproot and destroy. Her branches were far reaching, so lovely and full of leaves—beautiful, breathtaking leaves used for the healing of the nations or simply just the one ... this one soul who couldn't have known the powerful impact she would have on my life.

Her limbs of love had carried me through the toughest seasons of my life, especially after Jessie had her accident. Sister Benedicta's deep listening allowed me to find and share the grief that continued to appear at every step on our journey.

Her comfort of great love was one of her massive limbs of life, I mused as I recalled the last conversation we had shared about Jessie. She had gently probed into the deep grief within my heart, asking what was I struggling with the most about Jessie at that moment. The familiar cosmic space she always held was sacred and waiting, wanting the question to submerge beneath the surface.

As my heart memory relaxed into an inward journey of seeking, the Silence birthed words I had never spoken out loud, "Receiving a wedding invitation from one of Jessie's close friends recently brought the wound of her brain injury into a magnified future reality of never seeing her fall in love, get married, have children, or grandchildren. I just cannot grasp her not getting to experience those treasured moments of her life."

Sister Benedicta never moved. She held her listening, leaned-in posture in perfect stillness and waited for more. The stillness brought the hidden tears to the surface, ushering in the sobbing words, "My poor baby will never marry."

Her wise heart reached into my grief, speaking ever so softly in the sacred space of love, "Well, I've never been married in a traditional sense." Her words raised my head to see her soft, gentle eyes holding me as my eyes were being challenged to a new perception of seeing. Her covenantal words soothed the gaping wound of my heart, "My marriage has always been to Jesus."

My heart gasped, embarrassed of what I might have unintentionally implied, and then grasped her discerning words of truth, using them as a medicine to heal my conditioned perspective of how one's child must be married to another human to have treasured moments of family. I vowed to never let go of her golden words of comfort as I leaned into a new way of seeing Jessie's future and not defining her happiness so narrowly.

Arriving at the monastery for this farewell created an opposing tension within my heart. Her journey was ending in the physical realm. It would be the very last time her fragrance of divinity would envelop me as I had known it for eleven years. Yet the greater tension was rooted in her readiness of being birthed fully into the freedom within the spiritual realm she had so faithfully prepared for her entire life. She was noticeably fatigued but insisted on sharing a few last moments together.

Sitting in her wheelchair, her paling complexion speaking above her whispered voice, she began sharing a story of the massive tree outside her window. Speaking of this Mother Raintree with a quiet respect, she shared the deep significance of the tree watching over all of the monastery as a great protector and nurturer of life. She revealed her gardening adventures of digging some of its seedlings, attempting to grow them in hopes she could share them, so we too could have "mother" raintrees

Part 3: Reseeding the Forest

watching over us. Smiling weakly, she admitted that despite all the prayers and love, the little trees died.

I couldn't believe what I was hearing! *How is it even possible for anything to die in her presence? She breathes life with every breath.* I shook my head in such disbelief, smiling, relishing being embraced by her gentle humor and warm storytelling one last time.

"Well since it seems to be confessional time, I will now share a story with you. Once upon a time, after you and the Sisters moved from Oklahoma to Kansas, Bobbie called me with a hope that *we* could take some cuttings of the wisteria tree of 'fontality' at your previous monastery and root them. She hoped to bring a little piece of your Oklahoma roots to grow in your new place within a spirit of remembrance. I eagerly accepted her challenge and trespassed onto the newly sold property. I took clippers and quietly slipped in the backyard behind the much-cherished wisteria tree of 'fontality.' After several cuttings, I gathered my contraband and smuggled them home, undiscovered by the new property owners. I nurtured more than ten cuttings for weeks, trying to get them to take root. One by one, they all succumbed to death, leaving a trail of disappointment and sadness. I was sure the sheer holiness of you alone would guarantee the life of anything that was being done in your honor!"

We enjoyed a few light moments of laughter at our futile attempts to bring each other gifts from the earth, all with the loving intentions of somehow bridging the great distance between us.

After we had said our final goodbyes and were walking to the car, we were drawn to take one last walk under the Mother Raintree outside of her bedroom window. We took several moments to breathe in this giant massive presence overlooking and protecting, raining down prayers of love,

The Golden Rain Trees

calling one to come and rest for a while, to sit and listen for wisdom and truth within, pouring out its very life to others.

It was at that very moment I was struck with a divine revelation—Sister Benedicta was our Mother Raintree and we were her seedlings—and suddenly my eyes were opened to the tiny seedlings at our feet. The closer we looked, the more abundant they appeared. They were everywhere! Tiny sprouts were peeking through the cracks of the sidewalk, scattered throughout the grounds, hidden within the mounds of grassy carpet. The "fontality" of them all demonstrating the power to give abundant life.

I knew what I had to do. My heart lifted and beat fast as I ran back to the main house and found a Styrofoam coffee cup and a spoon. Returning, I knelt down at the feet of the Mother Raintree asking permission to gently dig up several of her tiny seedlings. When I had a cup full, I gave thanks and tucked them safely in the car and began the journey back home, fiercely hoping they would take root in my sacred forest.

For three years, the seedlings were carefully tended and nurtured in the safe grow-light-covered garden of my bathtub, only coming out in the spring for repotting and fresh sunshine and an occasional light rain. I felt her presence so tangibly through her tiny offspring. I knew the time was nearing to prepare them (and me) for an outdoor move. Each seedling was two to three feet tall, covered with leaves, and yearning for their true freedom—to live fully where they were created to live.

I consulted with an expert at the local nursery, telling him the hope-filled story of the raintrees, how they had come to be in my bathtub in Oklahoma, and now I was seeking advice on how to safely transplant them outside.

His instructions were clear and easy, but I could feel the resistance rising up within me.

UGHHHHH!

Suddenly, I blurted, "I just don't think I can put them outside!"

I know what happens when you put things outside! I thought as the images of Jessie, our beloved Toasty, and dozens of past trees raced through my mind.

He looked at me sideways and scoffed, "Lady, you just told me this incredible story of these trees and their journey of life. Now I am going to say to you, Where is YOUR faith? Put them outside where they can do what God made them to do! GROW!"

Ouch, right!??

I felt myself take a couple of steps back as my heart paused to catch up to what he had just said. Nodding my head to his words of truth, I simply answered with, "Take me to the stakes and soil conditioner."

The word GROW continued to reverberate in my soul and touch my lips each day I looked at the raintrees. Each hole was dug, conditioned, and prepared for the planting, watering, mulching, and staking in hopes their first night alone would be spent comforted under the moon and stars. I wondered how they felt. I wondered what they thought. I hoped they felt safe and nurtured, believing Sister Benedicta also had her watchful eye upon them and upon me.

My intention and prayers had been well-established, and now it was time to release once again—to trust and surrender them to do what they were created to do ... "GROW."

Ready for School

Home | Oklahoma City, OK
September 2010

Promptings resembled mini alarm clocks, waking me at night with the message, "It is time for Jessie to go back to school." I would lay awake asking God to show me what that could look like. I knew traditional school wasn't an option for her and special education wasn't an option for me. I had researched homeschooling and even ordered some curriculum but wasn't feeling I had the energy or the time needed for such an important part of her recovery, as my schedule was already brimming over with her continuous care, home rehab, and my full-time hospice work at night.

Back to school commercials announced all that my heart had been dreading. Seeing Facebook postings from her friends excited to explore a new high school campus wrenched a new pain I couldn't soothe. Seeing the long, yellow buses filled with students split my heart in two. One direction was in the heartache of knowing she wouldn't be entering her first day of high school with her friends and the other direction was knowing it was time for her to go back to some unknown kind of structured education.

Across the street from our home lived a special family of faith. Their footprint upon this earth was God and family. Mike and Anne had raised and homeschooled four incredible young men, who were grown and married with families of their own and had touched countless others with their generosity and great spirit of love.

Anne's loving and attentive presence had kept our home alive while we were away at the hospital. Upon our return, her daily presence of compassion and attention comforted and held our family steady. She spent countless hours being a nurse, helping me tend to Jessie and her complex medical needs, sharing countless meals of warm, nutritious food with her now claimed extended family.

One afternoon, we were sitting on the front porch with Jessie. I am not even sure what our conversation was, but what I do remember is the heart-stopping moment she proposed to homeschool Jessie. I didn't know what to say. She worked full-time in real estate, took care of her mother in her home, had a busy life with her own family, and was spending a large portion of time with us already. I was overwhelmed. She had given us so much. How could I possibly allow her to give us so much more?

As I sat in prayerful discernment, more questions rose, pointing to the direction of the answer that had already been given. How could this experienced homeschool teacher, who still had all the homeschool curriculum from her boys' days in school, be my neighbor? How could this licensed nurse helping me care for Jessie at her worst, already know all of her health history and her cognitive challenges? Why would this dear friend offer such an essential answer to the ongoing question of what is next unless God had stirred her heart?

With the resounding YES reverberating through my soul, Jessie officially began her new chapter in formal education, paving a new road toward her graduation. For months, Anne would walk across the street every morning to escort Jessie back to her home to sit at her kitchen table for school. I would watch out the window as the two would walk together, Anne talking with her the entire way. Her day would begin with prayer and Jessie would then read the Bible. Her curriculum alternated between reading, writing, comprehension, arithmetic, antonyms, synonyms, money, and listening skills. She even brought homework home.

I marveled at God's provision and how He orchestrated something so desperately needed and made it so simple and available that I couldn't say no. I remembered the words of Joni Eareckson Tada, who also recovered from a brutal, life-altering injury: "Great faith isn't the ability to believe long and far into the misty future, it's simply taking God at His Word and taking the next step." We had taken the next step, and God had provided homeschooling for Jessie.

With homeschooling in place and woven around her scheduled therapies, her weekdays were full. Weekends became our family time to further "break down the barriers of her brain injury" by focusing on practicing social skills and family fun.

Play and Personality

Home | Oklahoma City, OK
September 2010

One Saturday, we chose Putt-Putt miniature golf as our family outing. Although it wasn't the family fun experience I'd hoped it would be, it proved to be far more—an awakening and beneficial rehab-filled afternoon I would never forget. Bill and I watched Jessie struggle on each hole, navigating the uneven surfaces while coordinating the movement of the putter. The simple act of hitting the ball challenged her balance and concentration, which was compounded even further by the visual challenges of complete blindness in her left eye and no peripheral vision in her right. Her efforts were nothing short of heroic.

The hidden emotion of frustration would try to emerge when she couldn't hit the ball or get the ball in the hole, yet her beautiful smile would always return to celebrate when she or others found any sort of success. I began to see her initiation of "trying" peeking up and out of her brain-injured posture, along with her cheering mantra of

"Good luck" each time someone would step up to take a turn—all revealing glimpses of a personality beginning to peek through. She radiated her kind, loving spirit living within her own broken flesh, as she wanted everyone to win. Watching her hibernating emotions trying to reappear evoked such emotions within me, guiding me to not protect her so much from feeling frustration or moments of failure.

Putt-Putt golf changed for me on that day. I learned to see it as much more than a simple, fun game of miniature golf. It proved to be a gentle training ground to practice the challenges of mobility and coordination along with the experiencing and expressing of different emotions while surrounded by the safety and love of family.

Birthday Revelations

Home | Oklahoma City, OK
October 2010

"Biscuit Bob" (a.k.a. Bill Boone) had prepared a special breakfast on Jessie's birthday. His signature sourdough biscuits had just made their steaming, fragrant appearance on the counter when she surprised us with the unexpected statement, "Today I am seventeen years old, and I am not driving."

"I know," was all I could muster as I studied her face to see where this was going. She had never mentioned any interest in driving since her accident.

"When I wake up on my eighteenth birthday, Mom, I want you to start teaching me to drive."

"Okay, I will," I said, never wanting to limit any of the possibilities of her future.

Bill and I looked at each other in silent wonderment, astonished at her recognition of something she wanted to do and her ability to voice a long-term goal, yet also remained steeped in the painful reality of her profound lack of awareness of her deficiencies in visual and information processing along with her movement challenges.

Artist aprons and blank canvases on easels were tenderly arranged in Bill's "man shed," resembling an art studio right out of a cowboy movie, chuckwagon and all. Paints and brushes intermingled with colorful cupcakes and balloons awaited Jessie to help capture the celebration of her life.

Celebrating her birthday felt completely different, as it was now a life celebration of all that had been given back.

Her precious life. God, this day could have been so different. She is always one seizure away from having her life taken again. Anything could happen to her at any time.

So how does one celebrate the life of someone so very fragile yet so precious?

I knew first it would be inviting her dearest circle of friends. These young women missed their friend. They had kept moving forward in their lives even as their hearts held a deep sadness for the one who had left them. Their visits and calls were hard for all of us, meeting the brutal reality that she couldn't reciprocate in her old Jessie ways. I would try to comfort and help them by interceding in their conversations with her while my own heart was shattering at the cruelty of the circumstances. It was so hard to see her beautiful friends "fully living" and Jessie struggling to have a simple conversation. We all missed the "Jessie Boone" chatter and personality.

I wanted this celebration to be for all the girls and an opportunity to find healing and fun through exploring their inner landscapes in hopes they might discover deep truths within.

Part 3: Reseeding the Forest

My dot-n-law, Erin, a beautiful, passionate, creative creature, is incredibly talented in the arts. I had asked if she would be willing to step in as the artist in residence and share her big personality and gifts, guiding the flow of each painter's expressions to create a masterpiece in hopes of revealing their inner creativity. Her gracious yes allowed me to be fully present to Jessie, as I wanted to encourage her to rediscover something within herself, in hopes of revealing more of her aliveness.

Erin set an intentional tone with her reading of Karl Paulnack's quote to all the guests, "Art is part of survival; art is part of the human spirit, an unquenchable expression of who we are. Art is one of the ways in which we say, 'I am alive, and God has given my life meaning.'"

Each canvas touched slowly unfolded a different story of life. Colors, strokes, and imaginations outlined their human spirits, highlighting the different dimensions of depth and style of each girl. What a humbling, gratifying moment to honor the theme of being alive as the floor beneath the feet of these celebrated friends became its own canvas, capturing the drippings and splatters in remembrance for the day we celebrated LIFE!

Cupcakes added to the colorful sweetness of the afternoon as we listened to each girl give voice to their unique creation, sharing a glimpse of their own personal inner canvas. Being given this moment in time to celebrate life with Jessie and each of these girls propelled my heart deep into the gratitude for the gift of friendships showing up in the hard and awful with kindness and love no matter how different and difficult life circumstances may be.

Bedtime prayers held my heart a little differently that evening as Jessie's voice sweetly whispered, with our help, each of her beloved friends' names who loved her fiercely and came to share in her/our special day.

"A sweet friendship refreshes the soul," (Proverbs 27:9 The Message), and my soul slept well that night in the refreshing waters of her treasured friendships.

Mountains and Stones

Home | Oklahoma City, OK
October 2010

"We are going to do what?" was Bill's response when I told him I thought she was ready for the bigger challenge of an outdoor family hiking trip. I knew it would also be medicine for our sedentary lifestyle that had been an obligatory consequence to us all.

We traveled south for two hours and stayed in the Secret Garden Cottages at the foot of a national forest. Unlocking the front door of the quaint cottage, my eyes immediately found the words written upon the simple plaque, "With God, all things are possible." I looked at Bill as he was helping Jessie up the steps and quietly said, "Look at this. Goodness, we haven't even crossed the threshold and God has already placed His reassurance for us on the wall of this sanctuary."

As one of the cornerstones of faith, deeply embedded into my heart, displayed on a glass yellow cross hanging in our dining room window, it now made the same proclamation of truth as it hung quietly in the background of our temporary refuge, preparing our hearts to face the next mountain to climb.

We got up early the next morning and found the trail marker to guide our family hike. We traveled the different terrains in the unfamiliar land, making our way up the side of the mountain. Finally reaching the top, we found a place to rest while taking in the breathtaking view of the overlook, beholding the expansiveness of her accomplishment.

It wasn't easy. She required much help along the way. She had to do it one step at a time. Sometimes she paused to rest. Sometimes she needed a steady hand, or a drink of water. Sometimes she needed encouragement to push on. But she did it. We did it. Silence held us all as we sat with her on the edge of the rock, my heart trembling at this monumental moment of being on the top of the mountain with her.

My son broke the long silence with the most poignant words echoing into the vast, far-reaching view before us, "She climbed *yet* another mountain."

I pondered his words, remembering all the yets within her journey. *YET.* What a powerful juncture of grace. The moment where God steps in and completely turns the circumstances upside-down. The moment where God sends the helpers. The moment where God pauses and waits. The moment where no matter what happens, God is present and co-journeys the horrificness with us. The moment where God takes the worst and turns it into good. The moment where God says, "NO MORE." The moment where God holds the shattered heart so close it can't be destroyed.

"Yet" is the crucial moment where God will do the impossible.

As we traveled through the tiny town that hosted and witnessed this great feat, my eyes suddenly locked onto this huge, orange-stained piece of baked clay sitting in a yard full of miscellaneous clay creations.

"PULL OVER NOW!" I insisted with a much louder voice than I intended.

It's perfect.

"What are we doing, Lisa?" my sweet husband asked as he reluctantly surrendered to my spontaneous command.

I hopped out of the car to get a closer look.

It really is perfect.

"Can you just tell me what's happening here? Why are you buying this oversized pumpkin looking chiminea?"

"Just help me load it into the back of the pickup, and I will tell you," I answered.

"Tell me now, or I'm not helping. This makes no sense to me." My husband's insistence grew to frustration and forced me to explain myself.

"I want this to be our Ebenezer Stone to mark this moment of her first mountain climb. Every fall we can place it on our front porch and put a candle in it as a reminder of how much God has helped us get to this point of her recovery," I quietly shared, my tears marking the tenderness of this moment.

After his comforting embrace of understanding my impulsive and strange purchase, he quietly helped me lift our new "stone" into the back and proceeded to firmly tie it down.

As Bill drove us home, my eyes were closed, and I was remembering the "carving pumpkin parties" Jessie would have with her friends. They would shriek and be "grossed out" by the slimy forced removal of the seeds and flesh. It was hard and messy work, but eventually it would be time to carve and Jessie would always carve a big smiley face in hers. Their favorite moment was taking their pumpkins outside on the front porch after dark and putting a candle into the hollowed out core. They would sit outside for hours watching the light dance and radiate from their treasured images they had carved.

The light always radiates out into the darkness.

Part 3: Reseeding the Forest

My thoughts drifted to Jessie and all that had been forcefully removed from her life. And yet she still carries a big smile on her face with a beautiful light radiating and dancing through such darkness. All of the darkness in the world will never stop the light from getting through.

Rocky Remnants of Recovery
Home | Oklahoma City, OK
October – November 2010

Her vocabulary and speech slowly rerooted with the endless repetition of phrases we would say again and again. Her laugh would spontaneously appear as an old friend, bringing both Bill and me to laughter in the midst of the hard. Her fatigue, even though crippling and requiring extended naps throughout her day, would transform upon her awakening, gifting us with the sweetest smile and the gracious willingness to get up and engage in more therapy.

Battling sufficient intake of oral nutrition continued, as mealtime for her could easily extend into two hours. The extended time it would take for her to chew and swallow one bite was so limiting and would bring her to utter exhaustion, leading to insufficient caloric intake, causing her body and mind to demand another extended nap.

Cognition therapy continued full throttle as problem solving, thought processing, and intensive memory work were all woven into every moment she was awake.

Christmas Musings and Magic
Home | Oklahoma City, OK
December 2010

The Christmas season held sweet moments of recovery. She had always loved singing Christmas carols with such outbursts of volume and emotion, and our long drives to her outpatient therapy appointments would give us extended radio time to have "music therapy." I smiled as I recalled that the year before, she was struggling to mouth the words as I loudly serenaded her, hoping to find connections within her dulled, disconnected mind. This year, she was sweetly serenading me with songs, many I couldn't even remember all the words to.

One quiet evening as the three of us snuggled on the sofa under blankets watching the twinkling lights, I whispered into the darkness, asking her if she had a Christmas wish this year.

Her pregnant pause to answer was familiar, and I waited and wondered if she would be able to find words or thoughts to express her future hopes. Waiting and wondering had become our core posture of life, a perfect reflection of what the Advent season invites with the focused hope of what is to come.

"Mom, I want to see Christmas through God's eyes this year."

Oh, child, those prayerful words did not just come out of your sweet mouth!

Tears glistened as my heart pondered her prayerful wish. Her simple, profound witness of her heart moved me to recognize a profound witness of my own.

I AM seeing Christmas through God's eyes when I look at you, Jessie—a vision of resurrection, pure love and light, and the rebirth of a beautiful child. What a gift you are to all who need Hope in this darkened world. You are like the twinkling lights of our tree, sweet gentle movements of light piercing the darkness of tragedy and grief.

Our annual Christmas tradition of Jessie putting out the nativity scene was never broken. The first Christmas after her accident, Bill held her body as I guided her hands in the unwrapping and placement of each holy figurine, retelling her the story of "The First Christmas," while she was propped up with pillows.

This year she was able to maneuver and unwrap the entire nativity scene, setting each piece into the wooden stable without my help. Sharing my grateful excitement about her masterful accomplishment, I then invited her to use the scene she had just created to tell me the story of "The First Christmas."

"Well, Mom, here are the boys with the sheep, and the royalty men with the camel. Here is baby Jesus and this is baby Jesus's mom and dad."

I smiled at her struggling and broken presentation and simply asked, "What are baby Jesus's mom and dad's names?" She looked at me with that blank stare that was a frequent visitor to her memory recall. Eventually, I quietly mouthed, "Mary."

She said, "Oh, I got it—Mary."

"Yes Jessie, Mary and … ?" I waited for the spontaneous answer that would appear from time to time.

She looked at me with her confused expression and said, "Mary and Robert?"

I burst out laughing, "NOOOOOO, not Robert! Jessie, it's Mary and Joseph!

The relief on her face was priceless, as if she had found the missing treasure, "Yes, Mom! That's right! It is Mary and Joseph!"

I reached out and gave her one of those huge hugs of joy to celebrate her moment of discovering yet another truth that had been hidden by her injury, simultaneously reaching up and hugging God for the gift of such a special moment with her.

The Golden Rain Trees

Taking her to my annual work Christmas office party was another moment of new revelations. It was the first time my coworkers had seen her since her accident. Dirty Santa was well underway when Jessie's number was called. She refused to "steal" anyone's gift and chose her own gift. When she opened up the tinsel-covered box and found a beautiful angel inside, she announced no one would "steal" the angel from her.

"Mom, if someone comes up to me and says I want to take your angel, I am gonna say, 'Jesus says, you must not steal.'"

Laughter filled the room at her declaration.

Her "literal" standing on the truth was evident as I studied her flint-faced decision during the rest of the game. Watching her interact and be vested in something she wanted was simply a joy.

As we headed to the car, angel in her hand, she so proudly reported, "No one stole my angel."

As I watched her tightly clutch the newly acquired victory, I couldn't help but marvel at her and this newly emerged attitude, nodding my head in agreement, as I humbly prayed under my breath, *And thank You, God, that no one stole mine.*

Later that evening, I was sitting on the floor wrapping one of her gifts to place under the tree when my heart was enveloped with the fullness of gratitude, knowing that just being able to wrap a gift for her was a huge gift of grace as the gift of life is so precious. To have another Christmas with her and witness her continued healing is a gift I will never take for granted.

On Christmas Eve, I posed the question to Jessie if she would like to help me write a Carepage update. Her smile was all the answer I needed. We nestled close together in front of the computer screen, and I began by asking her the question, "What would you like to say to all the beautiful souls that are praying for you?"

Her answers were simple and full of Christmas love. I guided her as her fingers found their way on the keyboard and tapped out one letter at a time. The heart and her name was all her. I knew deep within my heart it wouldn't be long before she would be able to write her very own Carepage.

> ## Carepages
>
> **Post A Message**
>
> Thank you for praying for me. Merry Christmas! I pray you have a good Christmas! God is always with you. My brothers will be here with me on Christmas Day. It means a lot to me. Also other family will be here, which means a lot to me. Being with my family is good and makes me feel loved. <3 Jessie

Change is always on the horizon, and this new year was already ushering in another huge change to our home. The State of Oklahoma had been providing us with part-time in-home nursing care since her discharge from the hospital in July 2009. As of December 31, 2010, we received notice these services would end as she had progressed to the point of no longer meeting their criteria for subsidizing in-home care.

Progressed to the point of not needing nursing care! What an end of the year statement!

On New Year's Eve, we celebrated all the gains we had witnessed, prayed for all the struggles that remained, and hoped as we stepped into 2011, she would continue to improve and recover more of her communication abilities, memory recall, and processing challenges.

Two Years of Good News
Home | Oklahoma City, OK
March 16, 2011

Driving to an early morning hospice call to visit a patient, I was listening to KLOVE radio as they began sharing a miraculous survival story of a family in Japan. It promptly ushered in the remembrance of our own ongoing miracle survival story. When they announced their verse of the day was John 3:16, I was swept away to the remembrance of this being her second year anniversary. Within moments, the hallowed song "Mighty to Save" made its entrance into this scene of emotion. This very song had quietly risen from my deep groans of grief to sing over Jessie on this very night two years ago. My voice of praise and thanksgiving began to rise high above the volume of the radio as I belted out in joy, "Savior, You can move this mountain, Our God is mighty to save, mighty to save."

Spontaneous prayer lifted out of my heart, above the rhythm and words of the musical grace filling my car and soul: "Good morning, Jesus! Thank You for being the FIRST to remind me of this meaningful day within this timeframe of our lives. Thank You for Your intimate thoughtfulness that You would gift me with 'THIS' song at 'THIS' perfect moment. Thank You that You are mighty to save and that You moved the huge mountain that was placed before us. Thank You that You never forget Your children. Thank You for carving John 3:16 (NIV) on the lives of your people, 'For God so loved the world, He gave His only begotten Son that whosoever believes in Him shall not perish but have everlasting life.'"

And I know those ancient, redemptive words remain carved in a tree that still stands on a Colorado mountain alongside a cross and Jessie Boone's name bearing witness to His mightiness to save.

KLOVE radio had given a challenge to all listeners to share this verse with one person today. I smiled with a knowing that the intention of that challenge would be accepted today as an offering back to God for the beautiful gifts He had already bestowed upon me, and it wasn't even 6:00 a.m. I didn't know who or where, but I did know I would be watching for the opportunity to share this very special scripture.

Later in the day, Jessie and I were over at a friend's house having a lunch date, and there "happened" to be a handyman who was working in her home. My friend "unexpectedly" invited him to join us. Joining us at the table, he asked a "spontaneous" question that opened up a door to talk about how special this day (3/16) was to our family. When he asked what made this day special, I stepped through the threshold of his wonder with a passionate joy to briefly share some of our story. When he asked, "What does John 3:16 say?" Jessie's resurrected voice began to recite the ancient words of eternal life that had been engraved upon her tender heart and soul.

Witnessing Jessie reciting this verse to the unexpected lunch guest after it had been so deeply embedded within our own story of survival, and remembering the earlier radio challenge, magnified His presence and power in helping to orchestrate the sharing of the Good News of the Gospel in the most unique and unusual ways.

*"'For My thoughts are not your thoughts,
neither are your ways My ways,' declares
the Lord. 'As the heavens are higher than the
earth, so are My ways higher than your ways
and My thoughts than your thoughts.'"*

~Isaiah 55:8-9 (NIV)~

Two Years of Milestones

Home | Oklahoma City, OK
March 16, 2011

After two long years of intensive physical rehabilitation, she had officially graduated from PT, meeting all her physical goals! What a moment in time to stop and give thanks. It was unthinkable to remember the first day of OP therapy when the PT did her baseline evaluations, making short-term and long-term goals that seemed impossible to comprehend or attain. And now she was officially independent physically.

OT and ST continued three days every week, focused on specific goals within cognition, memory, recall, thought processing, problem solving, and intensive work to speak more slowly and clearly.

Homeschooling remained consistent five days every week with some slow signs of memory improvement and increasing abilities to complete assignments.

One of our big family therapy-focused accomplishments was the completion of a small lagoon pool in our backyard, designed to add more exercise with the hope to gain more cognitive recovery and increase social interactions and play. The heated salt water underneath the sunny skies held all the ingredients for healing medicine for her body, mind, and soul. Watching her as she swam across the pool on top and then under the water aided in the healing of mine also.

In the name of pet therapy, two beautiful kittens joined our family after we lost our beloved "Henry," in the hopes of providing irresistible invitations of initiation. In less than ten minutes of her meeting them, she had named them Emma and JoJo. I couldn't have chosen better if I'd tried.

These adorable fluffs of fur helped to bring forth so MUCH MORE LIFE, encouraging and drawing more out of her recessed self. Her added responsibilities included helping me with feeding, cleaning out the litter box, and enjoying all the cuddles she could stand. Pet therapy holds so many different aspects of inviting connection, companionship, and even cognitive initiation with follow-through.

I never hesitated and often aggressively sought new ways to challenge and exercise her frontal lobe injury deficits. I always believed the more I could offer and help her have interactive experiences, the more she would be able to recover over time.

Girls' Trip

Home | Oklahoma City, OK
March 2011

Jessie and I were invited on a new adventure to fly with my mom on a girls' trip to visit my aunt. She lives on a sprawling ranch with cows, horses, geese, kitties, and lots of dogs. Even though there were numerous travel challenges, I couldn't resist the opportunities for stimulation and new experiences she would encounter, especially hoping to find ways to reconnect her to her deep love for animals.

Before her accident, she had volunteered her summers at Tiger Safari, feeding and caring for a great variety of exotic wildlife. She loved spending her time outdoors with all the unusual species of this unique outdoor sanctuary. And this trip promised to be deliciously filled with animals.

Besides the immersion in all the animal life of the ranch, we took her on a tour of the Wildlife Safari Preserve. Relishing in the warm temperatures of Arizona, she gazed upon the many creatures held within the preserve as we traveled slowly through each habitat by tram. I wondered if she remembered her days at Tiger Safari and her devotion to the care of her special friends, and quietly reminisced in the precious memory of the time she brought the orphaned baby kangaroo home in a pouch, relishing in the role of being its momma.

The spaciousness of the ranch, the unhurried family time, the sweet attention of her aunt and Nanny, and the six Yorkies that bathed her daily in kisses and wiggles all poured special ingredients of healing deep within the recesses of her body and mind, and mine too. I believed every moment mattered in her recovery.

As we traveled back that Ash Wednesday, I knew I wouldn't arrive home in time to attend the service held within our church. Waking early that morning, I felt deep yearning to reconnect with the ashes of remembrance of how fragile life is, and to ceremoniously recommit my heart to God in gratitude for the abundant life that had been returned.

An overhead announcement in the Arizona airport unexpectedly answered the cry of my heart.

"Ash Wednesday service in the airport chapel, terminal four, level three, at 2:30 p.m."

Part 3: Reseeding the Forest

It was 2:20 pm. I looked at Mom and said, "Our plane doesn't leave for another hour. I am going to try and make that service if you can stay here with Jessie."

Her concerned and disapproving look didn't deter me. I found a security officer and asked him for the shortest path to the chapel.

"Come with me. I am also going and can show you the way."

The speedy pilgrimage across the airport took less than five minutes. Arriving at the tiny chapel overflowing with the diverse body of Christ, I felt at home.

The priest opened with a scripture and beautiful words surrounding the meaning of the ashes. During his story of the volcano's lava and ashes, he wondered if we knew that pumice comes from lava and if we knew of the abrasive properties it held. His challenge to his listeners was using this time of Lent to allow things to be abrasive, viewing them as helping to remove the residuals of life that had been holding us back from the healing our hearts needed.

As I walked out of the chapel, my head and heart were marked with the crossroads of the burnt death of the palm branches mingled with the holy anointing oil of life. My heart felt the burning of my own crossroads asking the question, What residuals of life need to be removed for my healing to come forth? So much dirt and dust of the pain remained interwoven in the folds and crevices of my traumatized life.

Where in the world do I start, God?

The security guard who had been appointed to me for that moment in time approached. His presence quickly reoriented my mind to our impending departure. His quiet, faithful presence was comforting as he guided me to the departing gate, and I wondered if he too had heard a question from his crossroads. My question of "Where do I start?" continued to linger long after arriving home.

An Unexpected Loss

Home | Oklahoma City, OK
May 2011

Unexpectedly, the reality of the fragility of life hit once again as we were getting ready for bed one evening. I had taken Toasty for her bedtime bathroom break, leashing her on a yard stake as I had done for the last several years. When I went outside to get her, she was gone. Her leash was ripped in two. Bill and I grabbed flashlights and frantically called and searched for her. Tragically, we came across her remains strewn in the backyard. It looked like an owl or hawk had grabbed her.

Jessie's faithful, furry friend had refused to leave her side after she had gotten home from the hospital. Toasty's presence had provided the sweet companionship of a friend when she was no longer surrounded by her human friends. Her gentle, warm body seemed to have a greater interactive purpose as she would pet and attempt to pick her up. I witnessed the calming effects Toasty would have upon her frequent agitation and confusion episodes. Her presence had also been a great source of comfort for me, assuring Jessie never felt alone.

Our family was devastated as we grieved the loss of our daughter's best friend. We didn't know how we were going to tell Jessie that her Toasty was gone.

Her response was as gentle as her soul, "It's okay, Momma." She patted my hand with the simple assurance, "Toasty is with Jesus and she is having fun."

Her "no tears" sharply contrasted my uncontrolled sobs in the middle of the night, with her simple, truth-filled words bathing me in the sweet comfort of Jesus. The pain of my deep grief seemed to find a spicket of release through the tragic loss of our beloved fur baby so close within the walls of our family.

Her Own Miracle Run

Home | Oklahoma City, OK
May 2011

With her continued pace of physical training, Bill and I agreed she was ready for her first race. The upcoming annual "Jim Thorpe Courage Run" sponsored by her rehab hospital was widely supported by the community. The bib she wore was no longer needed to catch food she drooled, but to announce her stunning presence in the one-mile fun run. She ran amidst her therapists, doctors, peers, and other supporters. Her slow, assisted stride was guided and surrounded by the team of heroes who had seen her when no one else could, inspiring wonder and amazement. It was such a mesmerizing contrast to the months spent inside the therapy gym with these same people commanding responses of movement.

My steps were accompanied with deep inhales of the sky, expanding my soul with the enormousness of God. It could have looked like pride to the passerby, but it was so much bigger. It was a humble mantle of gratitude taking its rightful place on this sacred rite of passage as the vibrations of miracles hummed in each pounding step on the pavement of her future.

Puppy Therapy

Home | Oklahoma City, OK
June 2011

Father's Day seemed to be the perfect time for a road trip out of town to reveal a secret only Jessie and I had been keeping. The week before, I had whispered to her the surprise for her dad, continuing to repeat it several times a day, hoping this secret-telling exercise would spark some excitement inside her heart and escape into her standing blank facial look. She used to love secrets and would never be able to keep one! Truthfully, I was hoping she would blab, but she didn't.

Driving out in the country gave us an unexpected sense of freedom, the feeling of leaving everything behind and heading toward something new and different. The scenery and the scarcity of traffic created wide open spaces within the framework of our tightly scheduled lives.

As we wove our way around Gracemont, Oklahoma, I eventually found our destination and pulled into the gravel driveway. Bill saw the large white lettered sign hanging on the metal gate entrance and looked at me with his crooked smile.

"No, you didn't!"

"Come on. Let's go look!" I opened up the car door on Jessie's side and helped her out and said, "Are you ready to give Dad his surprise?"

She smiled, "Yes, I am."

There were six of them—white balls of wiggly fur with black-buttoned noses. We sat on the ground in the midst of the swarming puppyness, wondering which one would be ours. Jessie was intently trying to pet the moving targets as Bill was looking into each puppy's eyes, hoping to find the "one" with the special trait he wanted it to have.

This puppy search was happening for two reasons. First, because we missed Toasty and her loving presence of comfort in our home. Second, one afternoon, a large white Labrador had found his way to our driveway and decided to sit for a while.

Bill had called me outside, "You gotta come see this dog! My gosh, he looks like royalty. I would love to have a dog like that, but he has to cross his paws just like this dog does."

We had never seen this dog before and yet he seemed strangely comfortable in our driveway. For a moment, I

Part 3: Reseeding the Forest

had hoped he had found his new home in the midst of our Toasty grief, but quickly discovered he belonged to one of our neighbors less than a mile down the road.

Driving home with our newest family member, the name game commenced.

Bill, "his new master," ultimately spoke his name into being, holding him up for all to hear as he proclaimed, "And you, young pup, shall be called Moses." My heart leapt at this unusual Ebenezer Stone marking this moment of hope that Moses would be the one to continue to help lead Jessie through the promised land of healing.

Little did we know what a speech therapy adjunct he would become!

"Moses, get down. Moses, quit chewing. Moses, stop chasing the kittens. Moses, don't pee in the house. Moses, don't do that. Moses, stop it," as each of her words became clearer and louder.

Initiation, inflection, and insistence all being practiced by Jessie within the days of raising our puppy. She was now talking to Moses more than any one of us.

As Moses grew, Jessie grew. One of my most favorite moments to behold was the afternoon in the backyard when Bill was playfully kicking a yellow ball to Jessie and Moses. Jessie suddenly took over and began kicking the ball to Moses. He would  chase the ball and hit it with his nose and she would call out, "Moses, Moses, come get the ball." She would kick it again and Moses would again run to the ball and hit it with his nose. Watching this girl in playful play with her puppy while balancing and kicking seemed a simple thing, yet it was another monumental moment of continued recovery to behold.

Leash training ensured a more in-depth therapy of coordinated walking while she tried to make verbal corrections. Jessie struggled, and so did the puppy as I watched them both work on overcoming the challenges of walking with a leash.

Our once chaotic, unpredictable, painful, very difficult journey had slowly evolved into a steady, constant moving forth. We found ourselves in a new normal of becoming. We laughed, we celebrated, we breathed, we danced, we sang, we shared, we cried, we anticipated, we hoped, we listened, and we continued to celebrate each and every moment we had together.

What beautiful gifts we beheld of this little girl who once was in a grave unknown, now being unwrapped of her cloth strips, one by one, as she answered Jesus' words, "Talitha Koum, little girl, I say arise." She had stepped out of her grave, one hand in Jesus's and the other open, reaching out to what God would give her next.

Lagging Liver
Home | Oklahoma City, OK
July 2011

A routine checkup with her endocrinologist resulted in an urgent referral to a hepatologist, as her liver enzymes revealed a concerning upward trend into a critical zone. This unfortunate finding led to her being scheduled for a liver biopsy with a follow-up MRI for further investigation in search for answers.

The results ruled out his concerns of cirrhosis of the liver, and he concluded her critical liver lab values were the probable result of scar tissue from her original injury of the common bile duct during her emergency cholecystectomy in Grand Junction. This scar tissue had caused a constricture, which prevented her bile duct from draining properly. This unfortunate residual effect would require quarterly visits and lab monitoring in hopes that it wouldn't progress to the long-term consequences of liver damage with possible liver failure. Bill and I kept our concerns shielded with a quiet hope for an easy resolution as we moved forward with frequent checkups with her specialist. Underneath the surface remained a continuous simmering stress of not knowing how or when this would be resolved.

Sloughing Hardware
Home | Oklahoma City, OK
August 2011

Another concerning reveal was in the discovery of one of the twenty tiny screws holding her skull pieces together erupting out of her scalp. One could visually see the head of the screw peeking out. The first one to appear led to an urgent visit to her bone mender doctor. Unimpressed by what he saw, he simply took a small Phillips screwdriver and within a minute had it completely "backed out." He smiled and handed Jessie the screw, saying, "Okay, little missy, we are done here. This is how your skull tells us this is no longer needed."

Shocked, I glanced at Bill as I questioned his speedy resolution, "What? Is that all there is to that? It's already out?"

"That's all there is to that," he confirmed.

"Is that something I should do at home if this happens again?"

"Absolutely, you can if you are comfortable. I would cleanse the area well and remove the screw with a small screwdriver. It is almost out by the time you can see the head."

I drove home, shaking my head in disbelief of what had just transpired.

How could that not have been a bigger ordeal than it was? That was just too easy! I'm so thankful for easy, and it didn't cause her any additional pain or unnecessary surgery.

Daily checks of her scalp for these wanted yet unwanted appearances became a part of her personal care. It wasn't long before one of the metal plates that had held her pieced skull together made an angry announcement it was no longer needed. The sharp edge had worked its way through her scalp causing a reddened sore area. After another consultation, he scheduled her for a short outpatient surgery with a light sedation. His gentleness and compassion demonstrated great concern for her cognition and strived to preserve it at all cost. We took her home only after a few hours, grateful for the little bumps in the road that always seemed to have another hidden agenda to keep moving us forward as we witnessed her letting go of what was no longer needed.

Curating the Birthday List

Home | Oklahoma City, OK
October 2011

"What do you want for your birthday?" was a question we posed to her during the week leading up to her eighteenth birthday celebration. I was wondering if teaching her to drive would reappear in any of her answers. But it never did. Her response to any questions seemed to always include silence. Even with the generous spaces of time waiting for her to find her answer, it wouldn't come. She was simply unable to locate the information needed for her response. What we did discover was, if she was given cues or "hints," she could sometimes bridge her absent or disconnected thoughts and find an answer.

Part 3: Reseeding the Forest

The enormity of the suggestions through our guided conversations were met with her usual response of, "I don't know," or, "I don't want anything," resembling a brutal, full-length mirror of what was missing. Each day, we would continue to put forth great effort and intention in helping her to unearth her hidden words, wants, and desires.

Her "discovered and yet generated" birthday list was finally finished—a steak dinner, a sleepover/pool party with friends, a good book, a trip to the animal sanctuary, a fun game, a homemade cinnamon roll, a ride on Dusty (her therapy horse), lots of cupcakes so she could share with her friends, and a shopping trip with Mom. We made the extraordinary effort to ensure she would recognize and experience each and every one of them in the continued hope and determination of helping her to reconnect lost pathways to herself.

Wrapped with Love

Home | Oklahoma City, OK
December 2011

Christmas season was upon us once again and left me reeling with all of the extra lists that wanted control over the already bursting-at-the-seams recovery and care schedule. Every extra was done in a tandem spirit of rehab as she continued to require verbal step-by-step directions with decorating, hanging ornaments on the tree, baking, and wrapping gifts, all in the hopes she would one day gain more initiated independence. Even with the recovery distance she had already traveled, the struggles continued with her processing speeds, her lack of executive functions, and her visual disabilities, making each task extremely challenging.

This year, opening one of her "imperfectly" wrapped gifts wrecked me, as I had intimately witnessed the incredulous feat for her to "simply" wrap a gift. It isn't what one finds within the box crookedly covered in snowmen and Christmas trees and adorned with an unevenly placed ribbon or bow. The real gift comes from it being given with such love—the kind of love that will push beyond her abilities despite facing the overwhelming challenges to never give up until the wrapping is finished. Witnessing any and all of her failures and accomplishments as she battled for her ground of independence were some of our most cherished gifts wrapped up in the grace of this sacred season of "Love Made Flesh."

Ready to Show and Tell a Miracle

Home | Oklahoma City, OK
December 2011

In preparation to speak at a monthly women's gathering about Jessie's journey, I began to entertain the idea of creating a video to show the stunning progress of her recovery.

The fierce resistance to taking pictures or recording videos of her early in her recovery was real, even to the extreme of demanding my son immediately delete the pictures he took of her during those first days in the neuro ICU. My grieving, crushed heart couldn't bear any thought of anyone wanting to permanently catalog my beautiful daughter's grossly devastated physical and neurological condition, nor could I ever imagine ever wanting to revisit any of those gruesome moments of complete destruction.

The first video taken of Jessie was recorded without my awareness by our private duty nurse. I was on my hands and knees beside Jessie, physically lifting her limp body up with her hanging head into a crawling position, attempting to simulate crawling.

"Want to see the video I just took of Jess learning to crawl?' she asked too eagerly.

What? I saw her excitement as she was showing me her new Flip video camera.

Hesitation to respond harshly helped me to discern how my stone resistance had lessened, evidenced by my uncertain willingness to watch the video. Even though it didn't feel good, there was a noticeable shift in my attitude to no longer demand the deletion of its existence. Each photo or video taken of her after that moment of breakthrough (not by me) seemed to part the waters a little more as she slowly progressed across the terrain of recovery.

Her terrain continued to be challenged in outpatient therapy for her memory, thought processing, and planning as her speech pathologist used interactive life skills, including a checkbook with a budget and afternoon outings to the mall for some supervised therapy in the form of shopping experiences.

The outline of my talk spoke to the story that was waiting to be told. Her story of how she was resurrecting—how her independence in her activities of daily living was a slow grow, but with the use of many verbal cues, could be accomplished. The story of the miraculous ability to sleep throughout the night in the absence of headaches and how daily medications were preventing those life-threatening seizures. To reveal the truth of her need for close supervision when out in the community, as she could easily lose her way with her visual, memory, and spatial perception challenges. To show that she was still progressing in her homeschooling, focused on math and English with the possibility of one day obtaining a GED

The Golden Rain Trees

and enrolling in some kind of program for job training. I was ready to show her strong, upright body running independently on the road in front of our home.

I had so much to tell! So much to show! So much I wanted more than words ... I now wanted a video.

CHAPTER 13

The Frozen Trees

Grief and Determination

"Tree carnage" was one of the many terms being used as vegetation and power lines were collapsing beneath the weight of the accreting ice. Lightning-infested sleet and freezing rain storms were hitting central Oklahoma, making it the first-ever ice storm disaster in the month of October. Trees don't have the ability to anticipate the coming winter, except by registering shortening days and falling temperatures. So when this disruptive and dangerous ice storm came, the trees were caught in the crosshairs. Burdened, crushed, collapsing, and crashing down to the earth below.

And with no electricity, the snapping of a branch or crashing of a tree was amplified, its defeat reverberating through my bones, leaving me feeling so ravaged and helpless in the war zone of devastating ice.

After years of planting and attending to the sacred forest just feet away from my bedroom window, I gasped as their canopies of grace were forced to surrender and bow to the icy ground of reality—the harshness of Mother Nature. Each passing moment was a witness to the heavy load taking more life than it—and I—could bear. Snap, crash, snap, snap, crash! I could feel the storm of grief rising up within me as if daring me to just try and do something. The immensity of the frozen holocaust seemed unapproachable and hopeless.

Then, another large crash jarred me into a familiar feeling. Up and out of me erupted the words, "No more. NO MORE!"

Preparing for battle, I donned my armor-coveralls, boots, gloves, and hat. I found my weapons—a rake and broom in the garage. It didn't take long before I was in full battle, hacking away at the ice, willing it by force to release my loved ones from its death grip. The slow rising of limb after limb intensified my fury. Through screams and groans, my refusal to allow the preciousness of life to be destroyed (again) by some freak accident seemed to fuel my mission. After four hours, I collapsed on the ground bone-weary, screams replaced with sniveling as my numb body shivered from the penetrating, frigid air.

Rising slowly, I opened my eyes and saw the forest lifting their eyes to meet mine. In that moment, I knew my offering of fierce love had made a difference.

Hope in an Unexpected Storm

Integris Hospital | Oklahoma City, OK
February 2012

Jessie's persistently elevated liver enzymes escalated to another referral, this time to a hepatobiliary surgeon. The latest imaging revealed the injured bile duct from her cholecystectomy was severely constricted and unable to drain correctly. As bile backs up into the liver, it causes more inflammation, resulting in liver damage over a period of time.

This extensively experienced liver transplant surgeon explained to Bill and me that it was surgically impossible to correct her bile duct due to the size and location of the stricture.

"There isn't anything to reattach it to," sounded futile and hopeless for the survival of her liver. His only plan of action was daily medication to "thin" the bile, trying to help facilitate drainage with monitoring of her liver enzymes and a liver biopsy every three months to monitor any progression of liver damage.

Her first scheduled liver biopsy resulted in intense abdominal pain and vomiting for forty-eight hours. Even with numerous phone calls to the emergency room, reporting the pain and vomiting, we were told to just treat the symptoms. After she spiked a temperature of 102 degrees with her sunken yellow eyes pleading for help, we made an urgent trip to the emergency room. They found critically high levels of bilirubin and positive blood cultures for bacteria. Within a matter of hours, she'd hit yet another tree of devastation.

This time I was by her side, witnessing the emergency sepsis protocol initiated to save her life. The battle ensued with intubation and a ventilator, central lines ushered in vasopressors and fluid boluses to help maintain her blood pressure, along with fierce antibiotics to fight the septicemia. We watched her newly given life slipping away without regard to the preciousness of the recovery that we had battled so fiercely to gain.

Her organs responded catastrophically as dictated to us, "Her kidneys have shut down, her heart has weakened to less than 10 percent ejection fraction, and she isn't able to maintain a blood pressure. Critical condition." The ICU intensivist continued to disclose, "A complication occurred when the needle pierced the engorged bile duct, leaking toxic bacteria into her bloodstream, causing septic shock. We need surgical consent now to thread a catheter through the obstructed bile duct to drain her engorged liver or she won't survive."

Those words felt like a terribly fast-moving freight train headed for my heart.

She won't survive.

This was all too familiar.

My head knew what was happening, but my heart was looking for the escape.

"Can you do that?" I asked, looking into the eyes of Dr. Lee, the interventional radiologist standing before us.

His response, "We better hope I can."

Hope is what we do.

Hope "blossoms" had deeply infused their fragrance throughout our world of fractured life. Hope was where we lived, showing up 458 times in the Carepages, making everything possible. Hope flowed throughout my body. Hope was our way of life. Every day, we breathed in hope and breathed out fear or worry. Hope was everywhere. Hope for cure, hope for comfort, hope for healing, hope for reconciliation, hope for release, hope for whatever someone was desperately needing. And Hope came down, became flesh, so we might never be without it. Hope made flesh walks beside me every day.

> *"Hope is more than just a word—it's a state of being. It is a firm belief that even if you don't know how, even if you don't know when, God will come through and better days are ahead. Life sends rain. Hope dances in the puddles until the sun comes out again."*
>
> ~Holley Gerth~

Dr. Lee found us in the chapel with our heads bowed in deep intention. His simple words of victory, "We did it," released our hearts just as he had released her poison. He ushered us into radiology, spending extra time educating us on the placement of the biliary drain until her bile duct could be repaired. The external biliary drain did what the common bile duct was no longer able to do—allow bile to flow out of the liver, rerouting to a bag outside her body. Little did we know this emergency temporary drain, combined with the engorgement of the bile duct, would hold a tiny miracle hidden, not yet seen by the human eye. No one but God knew this "tiny" perfect thing would open up the door of impossibility, ushering in a future miracle for the world to witness.

Her surgeon tells us it's unrepairable, but You already know that, God. You also know her heart is failing, and her kidneys have shut down, with the inability to maintain her blood pressure. Here we are again, looking You full in Your face, waiting for Your response to this assault on her precious body once again.

This is what hope looks like. All had been done that could be done, so now we waited upon the only One who could make a way when there seemed to be no way. Breathing the prayer that had been imprinted on my heart three years earlier, "Be At Peace," proved to still hold me steady and helped me to find peace in the midst of the devastating storm bearing down upon us.

A Welcome Watershed

Integris Hospital | Oklahoma City, OK
February 2012

Reading *Jesus Calling* devotional that morning at her bedside called my heart to attention: "Keep your antennae out to pick up even the faintest glimmer of My Presence." It wasn't long before I caught sight of the glimmer appearing in her foley catheter tubing. "Bill, look!" There it was, one glistening drop of hope. Slowly it grew into more drops of clear yellow urine.

Part 3: Reseeding the Forest

My spontaneous newly-written song of prayer joined the movement, "Let the urine flow, let the urine flow." My tears intermingled with this welcomed flowing evidence of life that was returning as her body began to slowly awaken after the brutal storm the day before. God had barrelled through the squall storm with a loud "No" once again to bring her forth out of the almost watery grave to re-establish her roots in the soil of this world.

But it was not without suffering a mighty fallout. In the midst of resuscitation, several liters of fluid were forced into her petite body evidenced by her weight gain of twenty-two pounds overnight bringing great misery and discomfort. With her history of diabetes insipidus, a hormone imbalance from her brain injury making her body unable to regulate fluids correctly, IV medications were being given to help restore her balance. Unfortunately, she received much more than she should have, resulting in an immediate halt in her urine production. After thirty-six hours of waiting for the medication to wear off, still no urine. Her endocrinologist was hopeful the dam would break any moment as he remained concerned about her elevated sodium levels that caused an increased risk of brain swelling and seizures.

During the weekend, the floodgates slowly opened as her ICU intensivist rolled the black clouds away with the words, "Her heart and kidneys are beginning to show signs of functioning with a definite return of her spontaneously breathing." We stood at full attention as we watched her slowly being unwrapped of the suffocating bindings of septic shock. Her weight dropped nine pounds in a day through the massive watershed evidenced by the massive flow of the very waters that had saved her life just a few days earlier.

Lab values began to settle into a normal range as her blood pressure found its footing again within her body, pulsating her heart function to full force with a miracle smaller than a coffee stirrer inside her assaulted liver emptying all the pent-up poison that had ambushed her precious life.

Within twenty-four hours, she had been extubated and we witnessed her foggy re-entry. When her neurologist rounded at the bedside, he emphasized the importance of reestablishing the frameworks of her daily routines as soon as possible, as her fragile brain would take a much longer time to clear, steady, and realign. The underlying deep hope was that another brain injury hadn't occurred.

Getting her up for the first time in the chair invited more than upward mobility.

"Do you know where you are, Jess?"

"Yes, in this building with all these angels around," she responded as she looked upward and waved her fingers.

My heart trembled with the words, "Angels? Who are you waving at?"

Her raspy hoarse voice declared, "Jesus, and He has wings on too."

The nurse and I immediately looked at each other and then the monitors to check her vital signs, both of us knowing what this could be forecasting. Her vitals were stable, but my knees weren't, as they bent to the sacredness of this threshold of heaven she was ushering to my feet.

I was reminded once again how we are never alone. In the thinness of that moment, for some unknown reason, a comforting grace was given. We were given a glimpse of that powerful promise through the eyes of a child who had just briefly touched the hem of heaven again.

That evening as I was giving Jessie Boone a shower, I was immersed in reflection on what had just happened.

As the warm water flowed over her weary skin, cleansing and massaging her sore muscle fibers, there was a warm flowing over me, cleansing and massaging my sore heart, bringing comfort and rest to us both.

I was reminded how He hears and knows everything, so present in every moment, working to lay low the mountains of difficulties and smooth those tough places.

Bill asked Jessie that evening if she wanted to say her bedtime prayers. Her tired voice immediately raised our hearts, "God, thank You for today. Thank You for everything that happened. Thank You for all the kindness and love shown to us today. Thank You for my family who are so loving and kind." And she drifted off to sleep.

How beautiful is the Christ that indwells, even when we are completely out of it and gravely ill. And how beautiful that He would grace us with a moment where He revealed Himself so perfectly within the body of a child. We laid our heads and hearts down that night with a great peace and rest, knowing He has the WHOLE world in His hands, including Jessie Boone.

Roller Coaster of Recovery

Integris Hospital | Oklahoma City, OK
March 2012

For the next eleven days, we found ourselves on a roller coaster of recovery with many moments of Jessie's gut-wrenching pain and vomiting from the oversized stent forcing dilation deep within her abdomen, to exhilarating relief that her body was draining the life-threatening poisons, to the steady downward decline of her recovery, to the sheer terror of the night she was receiving a blood transfusion for critical anemia when Bill and I helped her out of bed to walk to the bathroom.

Cautiously maneuvering her weak body with the two IV pumps and tubings along with the oversized IV poles, suddenly she passed out, getting tangled up in the lines and pole, hitting the cold hard floor before we could catch her. Screaming for help as I hit the emergency button, we picked her lifeless body up off the floor and placed her on the bed. As I was checking her for breathing and a pulse, nurses came running in her room to offer assistance. By Grace and Mercy and those angels surrounding her, she wasn't hurt. But I was. It took days for that huge fear wave of unexpected trauma to recede into a quieter place of thanksgiving.

Positive blood cultures for bacteria revealed the underlying reason for her rapid downward plunge. Watching her being forced to drink 1000 cc's of contrast solution in between the waves of abdominal pain and nausea, I could feel my anger rising up with each swallow she forged. She remained so obedient and kind, no matter what was being asked of her or what she was suffering.

After an unimpressive CT scan ruled out an abdominal abscess, a request for an infectious disease consult was made to further evaluate her deteriorating symptoms. Setting my face like flint to God in response to this downward plunge, I fervently sought His deliverance from this hospital hell.

Within this furnace of emotions, a timely plate of freshly-baked chocolate chip cookies appeared at our door with a note of promise:

> "The Lord God is with you. He is MIGHTY TO SAVE. He will take great delight in you. He will quiet you with His love." Zephaniah 3:17 (NIV).

Part 3: Reseeding the Forest

Those comforting cookies helped to lessen the flames that were raging and quiet the convulsions of my heart with the memory of an earlier day when another heaping plate of warm chocolate chip cookies with a gallon of milk were placed on the coffee table in the midst of our family. We had just returned home from the hospital after the unexpected death of Bill's dad. Within the generosity of a caring neighbor, our hearts found quietness by settling into the comfort of cookies and milk as we shared stories of the life we had loved so much.

Around 3 a.m., Jessie wasn't sleeping.
"Mom."
"What, baby?"
"I have some thoughts I want to share with you," she clearly stated.

Thinking it was going to be about the severe abdominal pain and nausea, I was surprised when she said, "Mom, when you worship, others worship with you. When you read scriptures, other people listen to you read scriptures. God chose you to be a minister, and when you minister, it makes Him happy. And He chose you to be my mom."

"He sure did, darlin', He chose me to be your mom," I whispered in her ear as I tucked her blanket a little closer to her face. I looked at her with such curiosity, wondering what was the deeper meaning of her professing heart.

I took out my journal and wrote exactly what she had spoken in hopes of keeping her sacred words forever. I mean, who says those words in the middle of the night in the midst of such a battle with pain and nausea?

When I worship, others worship. When I read the scriptures, other people listen to me read scriptures. God chose me to be a minister, and when I minister, it makes

Him happy. He chose me to be your mom. Being your mom ... goodness ... what a privilege to be your mom.

In the dark still of the night, I treasured up all these things and pondered them in my heart. I was deeply quieted by His love yet still left wondering what it meant.

In the midst of suffering, there is a God, speaking, loving, holding, and revealing Himself always, even through the belovedness of a sick child.

Oh, what love comes through the suffering of another.

Reprieves like that would quietly appear within the extremes, bringing heart-stopping moments of rest and providing infused strength in many different forms.

For example, during this time, my prayer sisters came to the chapel of the hospital instead of the usual meeting place within the church, enabling me to physically join this powerful circle of prayer and love, and fueling my faith and strength to forge forward. Another evening, Jessie's small group of six came to her hospital room to gather around her bed to have their weekly bible study, bringing ice cream and handwritten get well cards, helping to reorient our hearts to the love and strength that continually surrounds us even though many times, we were unable to see or hear it.

One morning, as I helped Jessie to stand, I gave her a big hug and promised, "Jessie Boone, we are getting better and better."

"Yes, we are, Momma, with God and patience," she whispered. "We are getting better and better."

Out of the mouth of babes. With God and patience, Lisa. Did you hear her?

As I walked alongside her in the hallway during one of her PT sessions, she became very lightheaded and dizzy.

"Jessie, are you okay? Are you going to be able to make it back to the room?"

She smiled with that sweetness and answered, "Yes, Momma, I'm gonna make it 'cause God is right here and He is helping me."

Oh, child, what sweet honey drips from your lips.

During one of her rests later in the day, I received a text. With her eyes closed, Jessie asked, "Who is texting you?"

"One of my friends," I answered, amused at her listening when I thought she was asleep.

"What does she want?" she asked, keeping her eyes still closed. My heart danced at her awareness.

"She wants to know how she can be helpful."

Jessie opened her eyes and turned to look at me.

"Tell her she may pray."

She is speaking the mantra of our hearts.

As I texted what Jessie had dictated, I smiled at her knowing request.

My friend's response, "That is so sweet, Jessie, and I am praying, praying, praying, and praying."

One afternoon, a couple of her special friends from Coffee Creek Riding Stables came by for a visit. She had just awoken after a deep sleep, recovering from an earlier episode of intense pain and nausea.

Jessie's greeting was gentle as they lovingly brought her a freshly-baked loaf of bread wrapped in a cloth. Cradling the warm bundle brought my heart such comfort, not only physically but spiritually, transfiguring my seeing to holding the Bread of Life wrapped in swaddling clothes. I was reminded of how Christ uses the example of ordinary bread to teach us how He feeds and sustains his people. These beautiful women brought forth their offering of love with the hopes of bringing healing and restoration to one of their "sisters in need," opening a gush of gratitude from deep within my heart.

Thankfulness for her being able to rest after a rough twenty-four hours. That He continues to reveal His presence with us through His children. For a biliary stent that is in place and working. For this heart in our daughter being so beautiful, loving, and faith-filled. For neighbors who were managing our home and pets once again. For each and every word and breath being uttered from the lips of others to our loving God. For the provision being given by His Great Right Hand.

The evidence that God was so close to Jessie's suffering was revealed so clearly in how He held her, comforted her, taught her, led her, healed her, saved her, loved her, created her, and continued to reveal His truths to her in each moment of her day. Her daily posture of walking and talking with God was astonishing to witness and helped reorient me to His presence and strength helping us each step of the way.

Late Sunday night, the Infectious Disease doctor finally made his appearance. It was odd a doctor would be so late in rounding on a clinically confirmed blood infection, but I was thankful for his presence. After a close review of her case, he diagnosed her with VRE and changed her IV antibiotic for this new resistant organism. Within six hours of administration of the new antibiotic, her clinical picture was transformed.

During the night, the storms began to calm. She began to quieten her complaints of abdominal pain and nausea. It was that night I received an unexpected text from a friend who was driving the streets around the hospital so she could stay awake to pray for Jessie. I believe this sacrificial act of love helped in her recovery, echoing the night Jesus was in the garden of Gethsemane and asked his disciples to stay awake and pray, but they kept falling asleep. I mused at the thought of them needing to be like Joy; maybe all they needed was a car to drive around to help keep them awake while praying.

Early the next morning, Jessie arose with the sun, and both were smiling light and life. She ate breakfast, was assisted with a shower, and walked the halls with her dad and me before noon. Her central line was removed and replaced with a PICC line. During her PT session, she climbed an entire flight of stairs. Later, we went outside in a wheelchair to get some vitamin D and fresh air. She even enjoyed a small vanilla milkshake, compliments of her doting sister-in-law.

Another page had turned.

All Things Being Made New
Home | Oklahoma City, OK
March 2012

After an in-depth coordination between her doctors and the home health agency, we were finally prepared to take her home. After three long weeks of battling for her life, home was such a welcomed contrast. Her IV antibiotics continued through her PICC line for the next ten days with her biliary drain requiring flushing and emptying twice a day.

On the eve of her third anniversary, we celebrated as a family the gift of home, the gift of love, and the gift of her life in the quietness of deep gratitude. Rest and recovery became the priorities for the next several days.

We were notified soon after that something remained amiss with one of her blood markers with no explanation as to why. Her extremely elevated calcium levels resulted in another urgent referral, this time to her endocrinologist. I was hesitant for her to see another doctor about any issue until she had some lengthy recovery time but quickly became more concerned about what harm the high calcium levels could cause her already weakened, fragile body.

With a consultation and an ultrasound, she was diagnosed with a parathyroid tumor in her neck, unrelated to her brain injury or liver issues. Our next urgent consultation was with a general surgeon, which involved a lengthy conversation about her complicated medical history with the risks and benefits of another surgery to be done as soon as possible.

The non-malignant tumor was quickly removed with no complications. During the postoperative conference with the surgeon, we received an unexpected, astonishing gift. During his explanation of the surgery, he revealed that he had carefully removed her jagged circular trach scar from her neck, only leaving a small line in the fold of her neck.

"As it heals, it will hardly be noticeable," he shared.

How did he know that by his extraordinary effort to remove some of the obvious fallout from her past trauma, he was removing some of mine also? How did he know something so insignificant, compared to all she had and was still enduring, was so incredibly refreshing to this momma's heart? How did he know he would bring fresh wind and fresh fire to my fatigued battling heart? How did he know?

Really, God? What a special surprise! A gift I hadn't even thought to ask about. But You already knew. You continue to make ALL THINGS NEW!

My heart had been refueled and rekindled for the next right step.

Prom Joy
Home | Oklahoma City, OK
May 2012

Her small group from church began to dream of the possibility of giving Jessie the experience of a "once in a lifetime" prom since she was unable to attend hers. They had grown up together at retreats and Wednesday night small groups. Many were with her on the ski trip and had prayed fervently for her life. Their knitted hearts were hoping to honor her life by giving her back one of the memories she was never able to have. Somehow the celebration they had specifically designed for the end of the school year became a greater magnification of praising God for her life by creating memorable moments of joy for her.

The moments toward her recovery were paradoxical. I glimpsed brief moments of joy and moments of great grief, trying to navigate finding a dress with her inability to choose one, along with her protruding stomach complete with a biliary drain. Choosing the color for a mani-pedi was even a struggle as I remembered her strong opinions were usually in opposition of what I would choose, but we faithfully forged through "the hard" to arrive at the special moment.

Arriving at the "decorated for prom" church, she was quickly surrounded by young, divine souls in elegant prom dresses all swaying gracefully to the rhythms of her stutters and slowness. Her smiles were real as she readily yet clumsily nestled into those she hadn't been with for years.

Stepping back was easier than I expected as Bill and I watched her friends spontaneously shepherd her while taking photos, eventually guiding her into the waiting limousine destined for their special dining spot. Fears of seizures or incontinence were quickly dispersed as she was immersed in a sea of laughter, selfies, and love.

Oh, Jessie, I can't imagine any better medicine for you than this.

"A sweet friendship refreshes the soul."

~ Proverbs 27:9 ~

Repairing the Tiny Tree Within

Home | Oklahoma City, OK
June 2012

Deep within the body is a life-giving tree emerging from the duodenum. Branches lifting high to connect the liver, gallbladder, and duodenum as a ductal system, transporting essential bitter gall to digest fats and eliminate worn out red blood cells and toxins from the body. When Jessie's biliary tree was cut, her life-digesting sap became a life-threatening toxic spill.

Three times a day, I knelt at the toilet emptying a simple drainage bag connected to her life-sustaining tube. Reflecting the Liturgy of Hours, this ritual was marked with prayer, sanctifying each day with gratitude for the feat of rerouting a continuous greenish-brown river around the dam of death.

Four months of four biliary drain replacements and four balloon dilations took its toll on her petite-framed body with increasing complications of pain and vomiting. We didn't know how much longer she could bear the intrusiveness of the biliary drain and were concerned about her upcoming appointment with her hepatobiliary surgeon. We knew surgical repair wasn't an option for her.

Part 3: Reseeding the Forest

Her surgeon met us with these words, "I have some good news and some bad news."

I glanced at Bill and in unison, we made the same request, "We want the bad news first," bracing ourselves for what we already knew.

"The attempts to dilate her bile duct were unsuccessful, meaning surgery is unavoidable."

"But you said the duct was unrepairable and any attempt to repair it would increase the risk of further injury, leading to liver failure and a transplant."

"Yes, I did, which leads me to the good news."

Good news? Father, You're the only Good News I know of at this moment.

He continued, "The event of septicemia with septic shock caused such great pressure within her engorged liver and vessels that it increased the size and length of her obstructed bile duct." He reached into his white coat pocket retrieving an ink pen. "Her bile duct was the size of this tip before, and now it is the size of the pen circumference itself. I can fix this!"

My eyes stared in disbelief at the tubiform hope uplifted before me.

"You can fix her?"

I felt Bill's arms encircling me as my knees weakened, uncertain of this unexpected offering from her near-death experience being laid on the altar of restoration.

OH GOD, is this true? Help me in my disbelief!

"I can fix her," he affirmed, powerfully professing this miracle being laid before us. "The imaging I now have provides a perfect visual of where to resect the stricture with reanastomosis. With her biliary tube placement as a guide, I can easily find that 'tiny' little bile duct within the scar tissue of her little abdomen."

The reverberation of "I can fix her" was deafening within my spirit. Unable to fully embrace the magnitude, it hit me like fierce rapids bursting forth from the dam that held them captive.

I had no idea this could ever be a possibility, and now God had made it possible. The miracles of God, so tiny, so unseen, right under the surface of hard, waiting to become magnified mountains of hope and possibilities. This ushered me into the morning words I had read earlier in *Streams in the Desert*, "Dare to trust Him! Dare to follow Him! Then discover that the forces that blocked your progress and threatened your life become at His commands the very materials He uses to build your street of freedom."

The forces that blocked your progress and threatened your life become, at His commands, the very material He uses to build your street of freedom. Freedom! She now has a chance to live in freedom without that biliary stent. She now has the chance to live! Oh God, I have no words!

Profound gratitude held me firmly upright in my preparation for this next battle with God impressing upon my heart, "This battle will be different from the March madness, as you won't be fighting for her life. Though you will undergo great challenges, the gift of a healthy liver will be given, closing this particular life-threatening chapter forever, stepping into the next!"

> *"Everything should be done in a fitting and orderly way ... God is not a God of chaos (disorder) but of peace (order)."*
> ~I Corinthians 14:33, 40 NIV~

The last two weeks with Jessie were very carefully orchestrated as we prepared for her "freedom" surgery. Everything was fitting and orderly. Step by step, all the preparations were completed and she was ready. We were all ready.

Beauty in Chaos
Integris Hospital | Oklahoma City, OK
June 2012

As she lay surrendered to anesthesia in hopes of new life, I vigiled across the hallway in awe and wonder. Praise music flowed into my earbuds as intentions of thanksgiving flowed from my heart, giving thanks for her brilliant transplant surgeons, Dr. Duffy and Dr. Kholi, and their hands guided by God fixing Jessie's bile duct, for the Nazih Zuhdi Transplant Institute providing exceptional health care, and for eight more weeks of a biliary tube before being permanently removed.

"Her liver is beautiful," beamed Dr. Duffy. "The surgery couldn't have gone better. She did perfect with minimal blood loss. I was able to clearly see and repair her bile duct. When I removed the strictured area, her bile flowed freely." His spoken words echoed a rhythmic poem fulfilling the plan written for her long ago.

Her liver is beautiful, God! Her liver is beautiful! Thank You for this unimaginable miracle of new life. Your living Word being fulfilled, "And we know that in all things God causes ALL things to work together for good to those who love Him, to those who are called according to His purpose." (Romans 8:28)

Then chaos hit. Pain, blood pressure issues, diabetes insipidus reappeared, and vomiting—all of it disordered. Harsh waves hit hard, but we were prepared. We knew the Master of the waves. We stepped forward fearlessly, not becoming reactionary to the chaos but choosing to stay ordered and focused on how the perfect shelter for storms had been provided.

The Frozen Trees

Her entire crew were masters in storm management. Her endocrinologist managed the electrolyte imbalances, her Infectious Disease doctor was on high alert for possible sepsis, and her liver surgeons at the helm prepared for squalls, watching every developing cloud. The exceptional nursing staff of 701 provided her with compassionate companioning care in the midst of all. We kept our eyes lifted and took each step with gratitude for it all.

Sacred moments of communion would mystically appear. During Jessie's PICC line insertion, a nurse was having difficulty finding and keeping a vein located under ultrasound. I knew what was happening but refused to "pause at the difficulty or survey the damage." He had already given us His directions to "lift our eyes to the hills." Jessie and I started quietly singing "How Great is Our God" as she continued her intense search for the one vein that could hold the medicinal tubing of healing and hope. Then just like in heaven, she spontaneously joined in, all three of us singing at the top of our voices. Within moments, she returned to the ultrasound, cleansed and prepped, injected a local, and placed the PICC line with ease, stabilizing it with the adhesive strands of faith. Removing her mask and gloves, the nurse raised her hands and proclaimed, "Only by the grace of God did we get that in!"

Yes, only by the grace of God.

Such a sweet moment of holy seeing beyond the waves to the outstretched hand of God Himself.

The moments of these days were fully embraced as the very gift of life was being delivered in front of our eyes. Moments of extreme pain and then a simple position change would bring a smile of relief. Moments of extreme fatigue would be answered with her sleeping so soundly that nothing would awaken her. Moments of taking her first steps around the nurse's station. Moments of listening to her tell a nurse what she needed. Moments of telling her brother about a dream. Moments of her first bite of Jello or her first taste of apple juice, bringing a huge smile to her sweet face. Moments of telling her she can't have anything to drink. Moments of her asking me to hold her hand when she was getting a belly injection so she could "hurt" me too! Moments of freezing in the arctic of the ICU to moments of drinking hot soup. Moments of watching *The Lion King* and listening to her share how she doesn't like the part where Simba was fighting Scar. Moments of watching her eyes light up when receiving a text, to moments of watching her eyes close when she just couldn't keep them open anymore. To the moment of removing the dressing and seeing her abdominal incision for the first time, to the moment of perfect peace when the IV pumps were turned off. Moments of rounding doctors, compassionate and caring, working long, difficult hours to give patients the important attention they need. Moments of hearing the words, "It is time for her to be discharged home." So many moments. All these moments within moments of other moments adding up to this newly given gift of life. Each of these moments, full of the richness and fullness of God's enduring love for His creation.

God is in the Wound

Home | Oklahoma City, OK
June 2012

Going home to a quiet sanctuary of privacy was deep soul medicine for us all. Within two days, the receding storm decided to reorganize with a sudden onset of intractable abdominal pain. Within hours, her incision gushed forth copious amounts of purulent drainage, forcing us back to the shelter of the hospital.

Dr. Duffy had already prepared us for the strong possibility of a postoperative wound infection because of the location of the surgery. His calm, ordered voice helped to reassure and anchor our hearts as we stood helpless, witnessing this aggressive onslaught.

He gently removed each staple that was holding her dehisced incision together, allowing the river of infection to flow out of her body. After irrigating the inside of her abdomen, he carefully packed her open wound with considerable amounts of moist saline gauze.

My thoughts began to jump forward to the obvious hospitalization that was next to come, envisioning lavaging the open wound with weeks of IV antibiotics and the awful side effects that would be on the horizon of the powerful antibiotics she had already experienced.

I felt the ground shifting beneath my feet, my heart moving toward immersion in all of the expected chaos, when Dr. Duffy matter-of-factly said, "You are a nurse. You think you can do this at home?"

WHAT? Home?

Immediately reorienting and grounding to the present moment, I breathed a sigh of relief and without hesitation said, "Yes, of course I can."

He patted Jessie's arm and asked, "Would you like to go home with Mom and Dad?"

She was lying on the gurney with her eyes closed and quietly answered, "Yes, I would."

"Okay then, I'm going to let you go home and see how you do over the next couple of days. I will write a prescription for an oral antibiotic for five days. Mom is going to have to change your dressing and pack your tummy twice a day until it is completely healed. I want you to come back and see me in two days. We will decide then if you have to go back into the hospital."

I loved the way he spoke to her as if she had all her own decision-making power.

Immediate relief came to my heart from not being hospitalized, yet was followed with the chaos still looming at the thought of packing her wound twice a day, faced with the risk of septicemia (we had already played that game, and it was horrific) haunting in the background. The results of the cultures taken of the drainage would take at least two days, so we could only hope the oral antibiotic was sensitive to the organism causing such havoc.

After two days of the gut-wrenching, pulling out purulent drainage-soaked wound packing, repacking her abdomen with saline soaked 4x4s, and hearing my sweet girl's negotiations, "Gentle, Momma. Gentle, Momma. GENTLE, MOMMA!!" I was cringing against my own physically ill symptoms during these rituals of necessary torture.

We returned to Dr. Duffy's office and received the good news that it wasn't a MRSA infection. Instead the culprit was the gram-negative bacteria which originated from the biliary tree area. He was confident the current oral antibiotic would be effective. The wound showed slight improvement, and our next right step was returning home to continue with our current plan of care.

One of the questions I voiced was when it would be safe to shower with her extensive wound.

"Oh, she can shower anytime. Just remove all of the wound packing before and let the water flow over her open incision. After her shower, pat the wound dry and repack her abdomen with the moist saline gauze."

Driving home with my pained and dreaded thoughts of showering her without the wound packing reminded me of an earlier conversation with my spiritual mother,

Bobbie, surrounding the brutality of Jessie's wound. She had shared with me a conversation she once had with Sister Benedicta about God being the wound. She left me with the direction to pray with the words, "God is with the wound, God is in the wound, God is the wound."

Anxious to get Jessie showered to remove the residue of the postoperative infectious grime, I gently removed her dressings and then all of the inner packings. She was standing with her head tilted back, her arms outstretched to hold herself up in the shower. As the warm water flowed over her head, her large abdominal wound gaped open across her body and red blood began to ooze out of her wound and freely flow down both of her legs. Unprepared for this horrific visual image of my naked daughter, I kneeled down to steady myself as I was on the brink of an emotional breakdown.

Wrestling with "God is the wound" as I stood face to face with the large gaping hole, I prayed for the grace to understand what I was to receive from those words.

As the water began to blend with her blood, something divine happened. Suddenly my vision was transfigured to a higher dimension as the words "God is with the wound, God is in the wound, God is the wound" were whispered within my spirit. Within that moment, I saw Christ wounded on the cross, now standing in our shower, the water flowing freely, comingling the blood from Jessie and Jesus's wounds. Transformation happened as her wound became sacred, holy—it became Christ's wound—and I had been given the sacred privilege of tending His wound.

Packing and changing her dressings were no longer dreaded, nor did it cause me gut-wrenching pain or nausea. Instead, my soul assumed a humble position of servitude, serving Him so intimately, ever so gently and lovingly, cleaning, packing, and dressing His wounds. God had answered my prayer of understanding "God is the wound" and transformed this painful task into His sacred service of caring for the Crucified Christ. "Self" was gone and serving Him became my sole focus.

During one of her wound check visits, Dr. Duffy said, "Jessie Boone, you are a good healer."

She smiled so sweetly, "Thank you, Dr. Duffy."

Her spirit of kindness and cooperation infused any room she found herself in regardless of what she was being asked to endure.

It is Finished
Integris Hospital | Oklahoma City, OK
August 2012

The last biliary tube had reached its maximum length of stay within her healing body, raising red flags of redness and pus pockets around the insertion site. A cholangiogram was ordered to determine if the bile duct was healed and functioning. If healed, the biliary tube would be removed permanently. If not, a new biliary tube would be placed for another four weeks.

My spirit was believing the bile duct was healed and singing in unison with her precious body screaming, "Get this tube out of my body!"

And God was whispering in my heart, "It is finished."

And Jessie was saying, "I want this tail off my belly!"

All were in agreement with the same hope—no more tube!

"IT IS FINISHED," continued to be my breath prayer waiting for her scheduled procedure. Before leaving for the hospital, I took a few moments to sit before God, listening and seeking. The verse I took with me was from Exodus. God came to Moses in a burning bush to let him know he was chosen to deliver His people out of Egypt.

When Moses asked how he was going to do this, God said, "I will be with you."

How are we going to do this, God?
"I will be with you."

I held those five words like a worn security blanket. What more could I ask for but the very presence of God!

Jess was barely able to walk into the hospital. Bill was a few steps ahead, retrieving the much needed wheelchair. The worsening infection around the tube made it extremely painful. Yet each step of this journey, we were reminded of "God with us." The kind and patient admission clerk, the familiar face of Jessica from OP surgery, and a clock reading 11:11 as she was being wheeled into Interventional Radiology (IR). A nurse working in IR took a few minutes to share with us how God had used Jessie's story to save her sister-in-law's life! (What a story!) The gentleness of the nurse who hung IV antibiotics and the kind compassion oozing out of the recovery nurse.

Then there was the highlight of our day! I will never unsee the unscripted scene when Jessie broke out singing the praise doxology after the nurse announced her belly tube was out, and there would be no more!

And just as special was the moment when Jessie whispered to her kind male transporter, "You are the preciousness of God."

His sweet smile was enough to know her love had reached out and touched his heart.

This profound abundant peace flowed over us all as I kept hearing those resounding words in the present, lived in this moment, "I AM WITH YOU."

Yes, You are with us, God. How can we ever thank You sufficiently?

The interventional radiologist Dr. Lee had a huge grin on his face as he came out of the OR to her bedside. I immediately ran to hug his neck.

"Wow! In all my twenty years of medicine, I have to say I have only seen one surgical repair of a bile duct better than Jessie's! Her bile duct is big and open and healed! Her bile duct is SUPERB! Dr. Duffy did a superb job! And today is my birthday, and I couldn't have asked for a better birthday present!"

"Happy birthday, Dr. Lee! Thank you for your present! We love it!"

To see his face and hear his GOOD NEWS was priceless. He was truly happy for our family. He knew what this really meant for Jessie's future.

It is finished, God! You told me that a few days ago, didn't You? You also said it over 2000 years ago, didn't You? Which means we never have to be without Your presence. You are with us always, even 'til the end of the age. Thank You for my daughter's life. May I never fail to give back to You what You have given to us—everything.

CHAPTER 14

The Desert Willow

Celebration

Her work anniversary celebration called for ice cream. Jessie Boone loves ice cream! We were driving to a new ice cream place called The Super Scoop. The founders had a vision to create a workplace inclusive to people with all abilities. Scoopers, with special needs, are hired into an environment that fosters teamwork and innovation while serving super ice cream that's made in-house. What a perfect place to celebrate her work success, to support more flesh-covered light, and enjoy one of her favorite treats.

Stepping up on the porch, my eyes were delighted by the tree entwined around one of the posts, "Well, hello there." I marveled as the canopy sprawled out like a green tulle ball gown, glistening and swaying showy pink flowers to the songs of the wind. "I don't believe we have ever met! What do they call you?" I spoke out loud my fascination with this unusual tree.

Over ice cream, Jess and I researched this new love interest of mine and found its name, Chilopsis linearis or the Desert Willow. We learned some of its attributes included fast growth, ease of care, and tolerance to heat and drought. It was invaluable as a habitat for hummingbirds, bumblebees, and butterflies. The open canopy and thin leaves created a dappled shade so other partial shade loving plants would thrive underneath.

Part 3: Reseeding the Forest

"Hey Jess, what would you think about going to the garden center after eating our ice cream and seeing if they have a Desert Willow? You could buy it with your own money, and I would help you plant it. This could be a way we celebrate your work anniversary by marking it with a tree planting in our backyard?"

She smiled with a big nod as her mouth was full of one of her most favorite things—vanilla ice cream.

The Carepage Vow

Home | Oklahoma City, OK
October 2012

As a statement of faith early in her journey, I vowed to never stop writing the Carepages until Jessie wrote her first one. And on this day, with very little assistance from me, she did.

Carepages

Post A Message

Hello everyone, this is my first post and I have some really good news. My liver is completely healed. Our friend Becky came and stayed at our house. We had a lot of fun hanging out, shopping, and playing games.

We are flying to Colorado soon to hang out with our friends, Scott and Gina. October 11th is a special day. It's my birthday and I will be turning nineteen. Mark it on your calendars. Thank you for praying for me. Wait until next week for more news.

Four Years into Recovery
Home | Oklahoma City, OK
March 16, 2013

Our anniversaries are these unique moments filled with remembrances and celebrations sculpted gently by the experiences of our hearts. This remembrance can be likened to our Ebenezer Stones along the way, acknowledging how God helped us through the joyful and the painful events within our lives.

Four years earlier, we remembered being plunged into the deepest dark night of profound loss, wandering in the foreign land of a severe traumatic brain injury, being cared for by angels in the wilderness, and fiercely battling with God's help for recovery. On this day, we celebrated with gratitude for every tiny little brain cell that had been able to recover any type of function big and small.

Her checkup with Dr. Duffy was perfect. Her liver enzymes and blood work revealed a long-awaited chapter end with a fully functional bile duct. He was hesitant to say, "We are finished," and still required quarterly lab studies with an exam.

We helped her (in all arenas of her life) to gain more independent thinking and process planning through any avenue we could find as she remained tightly connected to her weekly therapy sessions.

Memory continued to be a huge challenge. We likened it to a bridge being out. When she couldn't remember something, many times a simple clue could help be the bridge she could cross to find the hidden information.

Her progress in outpatient therapy had moved to the point of being able to drop her off at the front door, requiring her to find the check-in desk, sign herself in, and wait in the waiting room until the therapist called her name. (And of course, the desk ladies knew her well and kept a close watch on her for us.)

Physically, she was strong and healthy, and we were helping to train her to run the 5K in the upcoming Jim Thorpe Courage Run while maneuvering around her lightheadedness and dizziness that would appear without warning.

Her school studies had progressed to using a calculator and formulas in geometry. Her brain was beautiful and working in so many ways, except where it wasn't. And that chasm was deep.

Her extreme challenges with memory, conversational skills, processing, planning, executing, and initiating continued to reveal her deeply damaged right frontal lobe and her diffuse axonal injuries which also prohibited her from attending the normal GED classes that I had been researching in hopes for the one day she would be functioning highly enough to attend.

A Lost Dream Reignited

Home | Oklahoma City, OK
June – July 2013

Helpers always show up in a timing that is unexplainable, offering the tools and heart for the next right step. Unexpectedly, I received a call from a mom of one of Jessie's dearest friends. Sally was a schoolteacher, friend, and fierce prayer warrior. Her question was unanticipated and startling. I didn't know how to respond. I didn't know if it was possible. I just didn't know if I could. So I buried her question like a seed within me waiting for an answer to germinate. I asked God for help, to give me wisdom and discernment to know how to answer this unimaginable offering, while waiting in the midst of my visitors, Fear and Doubt.

Waiting had become a forced way of life for me, lengthening time frames into gardens of hope and expectations. I knew waiting would provide space and time to allow for something more than I could have ever imagined or hoped for. Waiting invited me to an open posture of prayer, preparing myself to be ready to receive what was coming next.

Isaiah 40:31 (King James Version) spoke directly to my waiting, "But they who wait upon the Lord shall renew their strength; they shall mount up with wings like eagles; they shall run and not be weary; they shall walk and not faint." I just wanted to be able to walk and not faint if I said yes to her offering of help.

I called her a few short days later asking if we could continue the conversation around her question. After sharing my truthful concerns and realistic fears of Jessie's volunteering to be her "assistant" in the three-year-old room of Mother's Day Out over the summer for two days a week, I took a deep breath and hesitantly said, "I don't know how this is going to work, but let's try it."

Very few people knew the magnitude of her brain injury with the severe deficits that presented in her daily activities, especially in communication and socialization. My fear stemmed from that reality and how it would impact her classroom—if Jessie would be of any help or would instead be an added responsibility to my friend. Also added to the unknowns of, would she wet herself, get lost, or even perhaps have a seizure? Would she be able to be of any help at all? Could she even do this?

What I did know was my friend loved Jessie like a daughter. She was a wonderful school teacher, spending her summer break in church providing a nurturing and safe learning environment for three-year-olds. I couldn't imagine a more perfect place for Jessie to take her next step toward recovery.

As the program was coming to a close at the end of summer, Sally walked Jessie out to the car and told me how she had lost contact with one of her college friends and had recently reconnected, having dinner with her the previous night. She learned she had become the Director of the GED program at Francis Tuttle Vo Tech. She shared Jessie's story with her and how I had been searching for a GED program.

She handed me her business card and said, "Susan said to give her a call and she can help you with a GED tutor and program for Jessie. That is what she does."

The asphalt parking lot held my feet firm as my head and heart were trying to catch up to the tangible proof of grace unexpectedly placed in my hand. I didn't know how to respond as I had made many unsuccessful calls in search of a GED program that could help her. But this time, it wasn't about fear or doubt visiting. I was overwhelmed and humbled.

You did this, God. You gave us another next right step.

My head shaking in disbelief, my heart pounding in my ears, I hugged my friend in an effort to share how deeply appreciative I was for her presence in our lives and all she had given us.

My daughter had just been nurtured and gently mentored by a loving teacher/friend who had unknowingly prepared her and myself for the next steps to come. When the timing was right, a simple reconnection and conversation took place, enabling the answer to be ready and placed directly in my hand. Only God.

GED Grit and Grace
Francis Tuttle Vo Tech | Oklahoma City, OK
July 2013

After an in-depth promising phone conversation with Susan, I had set out with a joy and confidence toward our meeting to get started on Jessie's journey toward a GED. However, walking onto the campus of Francis Tuttle Vo Tech, holding Jessie's hand, I unexpectedly met ambiguity. Uncertainty-colored anxiety slapped me in the face as I watched the able-bodied and minded students getting out of their cars and going to class with backpacks and phones in hand.

What was I thinking? How could this possibly be a good idea? Grief and reality were drumming on my heart again. Fighting back tears and the urge to turn around, I kept my eyes down, putting one foot in front of the other. *Breathe, Lisa, breathe. You know that you know this is the next right step. Stop comparing and looking at the obvious.* Breathing in, *Jesus.* Breathing out, *Calm my anxious heart.*

Finding Susan's office was our first victory. Meeting her was our second. It didn't take long behind closed doors to find a sanctuary of safety, confirming we were in the right place. Her professional office and appearance were quickly overshadowed with her compassion and deep interest in helping Jessie get her GED. Her clearly outlined path was evidence of her experience and intent for success.

Susan looked at Jessie and said, "Here is your locker number with a combination. You can put your things in there and meet me in the computer room. We are going to have you take a pretest right now. Mom, can you come back in a couple of hours? We should be through by then."

Part 3: Reseeding the Forest

What? I didn't know what to say. I didn't know what to do.

I don't know if she can even find a locker or do a combination. I don't know if she can do a pretest on the computer. I don't know if I can leave her alone. GOD, I DON'T KNOW WHAT TO DO HERE!

Susan could see I was struggling so she reached out, touched my arm, and assuredly said, "Trust me, I have her. She will be okay. I will text you if we need anything."

But you don't understand. She needs so much help. The pain was physical, the releasing not willing, and the angst rising.

The door opened as I was trying to convince myself to move, and Susan said, "Lisa, I want you to meet Fonda, my assistant. She will also be here to help Jessie."

Fonda reached out her hand for mine saying, "Hi, Lisa, you don't know me, but I know you and Jessie. I have prayed for her recovery since her accident. My next door neighbor, Helen, works with you at hospice and she shares Jessie's Carepage updates with me. I have been waiting to meet you both."

You know Helen! You have been praying for Jessie? You have read her Carepages? You have been waiting. Waiting to meet us? Oh God, how do You do that? How do You know what I need for each of these hard yet necessary steps?

"Oh, Fonda, it is so good to meet you." I reached out to hug her, trying to settle myself into these revelations. "Yes, Helen has been such a huge support to us. Thank you for your prayers and for being here now for this next part of her journey."

I took a deep breath and walked out that door with my head up, my pain lightened, feeling the highlighted

The Desert Willow

presence of God, knowing these two ladies had been appointed for such a time as this.

Tutoring classes soon began in the lab on campus. Each day, she struggled from one concept to another. Reviewing her daily worksheets provided a constant reminder of what her brain injury took from her, but the tutor was relentless with encouragement and support. She pushed her, believing in the more. Day after day, she would say, "Good job, Jessie. You worked so hard. I will see you tomorrow and we will do some more."

One day, as I was waiting for her session to end, the tutor motioned me into the study room. She wanted me to observe Jessie independently using a calculator with formulas in the geometry section figuring the cubic volume of cylinders. It was inconceivable to me how her brain could work out these problems yet still have such profound challenges of conversation, initiating, processing, and memory. It was a profound moment for my continued wrestling of "How is she going to be able to do all that is expected of her?"

After completing all four study sections, including the practice testing, she was ready for her GED test. My heart was pounding with anxiety when I left her in the testing room, and I found a quiet corner in the student union where I sat in prayer as she officially sat in the room of recall. With reading support so time limits of testing could be met, she successfully passed, certifying academic knowledge equivalent for a high school diploma.

She eagerly donned the purple gown and cap that had been a part of photo sessions of those who had gone before her with a 2013 tassel, posing for the cherished and esteemed picture of completion we shall call "Graduation." What seemed impossible for months was now made possible with God and His timely guidance to the chosen "ones" who availed the substantial help to bring this cherished rite of passage to fruition.

Spreading Her Wings
Home | Oklahoma City, OK
July 2013

Her occupational therapist surprised me with some information about a program called Project Search. She wondered if this might be a place Jessie could have some focused job training with coaches since she had just completed her GED.

Quick research revealed this application approved program was designed for students with significant disabilities to assist them with a plan to transition from school to employment through innovative workforce and career development. To benefit the individual, community, and workplace by offering on-site job skills training and support, with career exploration in a variety of entry-level positions, internships, interviewing and assessment practice, and job placement.

Upon learning Integris Baptist hospital was one of the host sites for the training opportunities, I reached out for an application, remembering how my employer had supported our family in unimaginable ways during Jessie's catastrophic events. I wondered if this could be a way to give back, for Jessie to come full circle, to receive job training with possible employment in the very place that helped save her life.

When I discovered one of the requirements was one year of vo-tech or college attendance, I had no idea how that would even be possible. Scanning the class catalog of the vo-tech, I found it all too advanced. I had even scheduled a private meeting with an instructor of the child care classes to discuss any additional help for her, and we both agreed this wouldn't work at this point of her recovery. I couldn't find the way forward to Project Search.

Conversations were ongoing with OT and ST about our future steps as our time with OP therapy was nearing an end. I knew as we were embarking upon these new opportunities, therapy would also shift into these new areas of focus. Upon a recommendation from Jessie's OT, I called the program director of Project Search to talk about my dilemma of not finding a program Jessie would be able to participate in. It was only then I was given information about two offerings, Culinary Arts and Groundskeeping, at Francis Tuttle Vo-Tech specifically designed for students with disabilities.

Saying goodbye to the last four years, "her way of life," took great courage and caused many different emotions. Reflecting back on the "ALLNESS" of what was given by our therapy community overwhelmed my being, knowing each person we encountered added their own bricks and mortar to the rebuilding of her life, solidifying an attachment that could never be severed. How does one communicate the deep gratitude for the hours upon hours of experienced rehabilitation offerings that help to bring your child back to life?

As I looked forward to the future of the "ALLNESS" yet to come, I knew the only way to do this was to release our old rehab routines to the season that was coming, as I have so intimately witnessed over and over again in the seasons of creation. I knew this end was truly her beginning ... again.

Within a few weeks, she was enrolled in the Culinary Arts program, her monogrammed uniforms ordered. My gratitude proved faithful with the familiar immediate

U-turn to a steady uncertainty. Daily questions would frequently appear and haunt me with the scratching tones of, "With her vision issues, slow processing, and severe difficulty in communication, how will she be able to get through the curriculum? How will she be able to do interactive kitchen training? How in the world will she take care of her personal needs, which always requires some assistance? How can I just leave her in a classroom, with multiple special needs students on a large campus, knowing she is unable to navigate unfamiliar places? How is this going to work?"

I had absolutely no idea the answer to any of these questions but continued to move forward, taking the next right step laid before us with the hopes of continuing the trudge forward toward the more. I didn't know what else to do.

The dress code requirement was a full chef attire including a chef's hat, a cravat, pants, shoes, and a hand towel. She was required to come to class in full uniform, or she would be sent home. All of it was overwhelming to my rational mind and her petite frame as she struggled to simply attempt to navigate through the double doors to find her classroom. Struggling to leave her alone on the first day brought escalating anxiety with one main concern—her being able to find the bathroom and navigate her garb in time to not have an accident. I remember sitting in the parking lot for the three hours of her class, refusing to leave in protest of my own battle of demanding gains of recovery and independence.

Soon she was attending five days a week, three hours a day, learning the basics of cooking from two special instructors in the midst of several special students. I was amazed at her endurance every day. Eventually I found my way of surrender and could leave the parking lot to run a few errands close by or take a long walk on the jogging path around campus.

"Goodbye, Jessie," said the tall, lanky red-headed young man in full chef's attire as I greeted Jessie at the door to pick her up. I looked up to behold his huge smile and smiled back.

"Hello, I am Jessie's mom, Lisa. And who are you?"

"My name is Peter, and Jessie is my friend."

I melted.

Jessie is my friend.

His speech was exceedingly slow and yet perfect in its annunciation. My heart was tendered toward his gentle voice. Her friends from school, church, and gymnastics were no longer present in her life. They had graduated and moved on with life in college, work, and in other relationships. Her inability to have social interactions had been deeply painful to witness as her friends would attempt to connect with her with little response. *Jessie is my friend.* Those words kept playing over in my spirit, bathing those bruised heart places with the simplicity of his declaration.

"Jessie, tell Peter goodbye and that you will see him tomorrow," I encouraged her.

"Bye-bye," she quietly responded.

She slept all the way home as my thoughts drifted back to the very first day I struggled to leave her alone at the small church with my dear friend, Sally. I slowly began to awaken to the realization that each struggle of release was a necessary preparation for the next bigger step. This next step into attending a vo-tech seemed to resemble an imperfect staircase of ascending recovery with unexpected doorways at each level, including this extra special gift of making an unexpected friend.

One afternoon while waiting in the parking lot for Jessie, the director of her culinary program, Bruce, came to my car window. He introduced himself and shared how he had been wanting to meet Jessie's mom. We exchanged greetings, and he proceeded to tell me how wonderful Jessie was doing in the program. He was an encouraging soul with a similar story of being helped through his own life struggles, inspiring his life passion of being someone to help others succeed.

His car window visits happened frequently over the next two semesters as he wanted to share special stories about Jessie. They ranged from how kind she was to her fellow students, to her surprising math skills, to her telling funny stories that would make him laugh. His stories were treasures to my heart, giving me brief glimpses of her school day as parents weren't allowed to come into the classrooms and Jessie was unable to remember any details. One day, in his most serious voice, he posed the question of whether I knew how special she really was. I smiled as this gentle warmth traveled to my toes.

"Yes, I really do know how special she is, and I am thankful you know too."

During one of our "car talks," he brought up the Project Search program without knowing this was our end goal for her attending culinary classes. He began to "educate" me on how he thought Jessie would benefit from this type of job training. I smiled at the synchronicity and the shared common goal of getting Jessie into Project Search. He was thrilled and encouraged us to promptly fill out the application and get it turned in before the deadline, which was rapidly approaching, as they could only accept four students from Francis Tuttle. I was so thankful for his prompt, as I had no idea there was a deadline for submitting an application.

After submitting the in-depth application, we waited, knowing there would be a private interview process with the staff of Project Search, which would include a hospital representative with a selected few of the Francis Tuttle staff. We practiced interview questions with her for days, focusing on her ability to answer questions and to remember to speak slowly and clearly. We worked on helping her identify a dream or a goal that she would be able to communicate. She continued to have great lapses of poor memory recall when attempting to respond to any question. My heart was extremely pained as I couldn't imagine her being interviewed by six people when she struggled to barely communicate with me. I just couldn't see how she was going to be able to answer any of their questions.

Her dad and I sat outside the conference room as our girl stepped through the door to the interview by herself. I caught a glimpse of Bruce sitting inside smiling at her, and my heart released some tension, as I knew he was her ally in this arena of expectation. We knew it was a long shot, but we believed this was her next right step to our long term goals for her. We just kept moving forward, trusting God would help her.

On our drive home, Bill attempted a gentle interrogation about the interview, but she couldn't remember anything. I was so proud of her for taking on a challenge like this, regardless of the outcome. We knew it was miraculous she was even there and had just completed two semesters of culinary school.

A few days later, my phone rang and it was Bruce.

"Hey there, I just wanted to let you know she wasn't accepted into Project Search. I am so disappointed in the selection process, as I believe that Jessie Boone is a perfect example of why Project Search was created." He encouraged us to try again next year.

I took a few steps back to catch my breath. I wasn't surprised due to her inability to communicate but was deeply disappointed as well. It hurt and it wasn't the answer I had hoped to hear. It didn't take long for me to choose to release that disappointment, turning right into summer activities. But toward the back of my heart, full of gratitude for what we had been given back in Jessie's recovery, was a small splinter quietly festering with the question, "What's next?"

Late summer, we were vacationing on the beach in Pensacola with our kids. Checking my phone late one evening, I saw a voicemail from Bruce, emphasizing with great urgency to please call him back. The next morning, I reached out, "Hello, Bruce, this is Lisa Boone. We got your message. Is everything okay?"

His voice exploded through the phone, "Lisa, you are not going to believe this but one of the students dropped out of the program, leaving an opening in Project Search. I wanted to ask you, is it still possible for Jessie to join us?"

Catching my breath, I waved Bill to come closer and switched to speaker phone so he could witness what I was hearing as Bruce triumphantly continued, "Oh, and the other big news is, I have accepted the director position over Project Search and will be leaving my current position to begin working at Integris Baptist."

What!? I was stunned. *How is this even possible?* Her biggest cheerleader was now stepping over the sidelines to be cheering her on in an even bigger arena of challenge and accomplishment.

"Bruce, congratulations! That is such wonderful news. How exciting for you and Project Search! And yes, Jessie Boone will definitely join you on this next adventure! I can't believe this is happening! *Thank YOU, GOD!* When does it start?"

"Next Monday," he said. "Will that work?"

I swallowed my shock and grabbed the edge of the counter to steady myself, my brain racing with anxious excitement at the moment when the heavens opened, reaching down close to earth to personally usher my disabled daughter right through the doors that had previously been locked.

"Of course it will work," I answered with an eagerness to receive the offering we had been reaching for, noticing the familiar pounding of my heart in anticipation when God was bringing forth the impossible once again.

Faith Over Fear
Home | Oklahoma City, OK
August 2015

On her first day of Project Search, Jessie and I stood side by side at the entrance of the ten-story building attached to the campus of Integris Baptist Hospital. As I paused to look up to the very top, I took a deep breath as these words spontaneously flowed over my heart, "I lift my eyes up to the mountains, and where does my help come from? My help comes from the Lord, Maker of heaven and earth." This was a song of ascent from Psalm 121, a song I had led worship with, a song I would pray in my private prayer time, and now a song lifting us to the next level of "more".

Part 3: Reseeding the Forest

Once again, questions were pounding in my chest, increasing the volume of my fear.

How is she going to find her way to the bathroom? How many thousands of people come and go on this hospital campus? Will she be safe? Will she get lost? I don't know if she can do this. I don't know if I can do this. God, You put her here. Help me be able to leave her here.

As we stepped off the ninth floor, I was speaking the directions out loud as I continued the ritual of attempting to create pathways of memories to help her find her way.

"Project Search is located just off the elevators to the right as we pass Employee Health. Here are the bathrooms on the right. Jessie, you have your phone. If you ever get lost or need help, you can call Bruce and he will help you. You can call me, and I can get you help. Do you understand?"

She smiled so sweetly as she responded, "Yes, I do."

But I knew her challenges so well. It would take much more than an understanding of what I had just said for her to find her way through this labyrinth of her future. It would take a village to guide her safely within the walls of this huge medical complex.

God, here I am again. How in the world do I leave her in such a place? My stomach is sick and my knees are weakened by the thought. I know the drill. I remember every time I have left her, You have had someone to catch her and help her. I know Bruce is here, but this is a huge hospital and I'm not sure how safe hospitals are with all the types of people that come and go. She is so vulnerable and unassuming with no sense of direction or awareness of where she is.

We stepped up to the door opening the next chapter of life toward her future. The outside keypad needed a code to gain entrance into the Project Search classroom.

"Jessie, do you remember the code we talked about earlier to get in?"

"No, I do not," she answered, standing immobile in her initiation and thoughts.

"Get your phone out and look at your notes. I wrote it in there so you would always be able to find it."

After a few minutes and with my help, she found the code and put it into the keypad. The door opened, welcoming in its latest student.

As we went inside, I called out to the empty room, "Hello, anyone here?"

"Back here," a baritone voice returned.

Out came a tall, gray-haired, gray-bearded smiling man to greet us.

"Well, hello, you must be Jessie Boone. I am George," he said, reaching out to shake her hand, "and you must be Mom," reaching out to me next. "I have heard a lot about you, Miss Jessie. Come here. I want to show you something."

We followed him back into his office, and he handed Jessie a framed picture of the soccer team he coached.

"Do you know who that fellow is?" He pointed to one of the blonde players kneeling in the front row. Jessie examined the picture closely.

I asked, "Is that Dillon?" as I recognized one of her best friends who had been skiing with her when the accident happened.

He said, "It certainly is. I have been coaching Dillon in soccer for years. He called me that day from the ski resort to tell me about his good friend who had a skiing accident and asked me and my wife to pray for a girl named Jessie Boone. Jessie, we have been praying for you since day one, and now here you are. How about that for answered prayer?"

She smiled, "Thank you for praying for me."
How about that for answered prayer?

I stood in reverent silence, knowing the answer to my prayer stood right in front of me in the form of this modern day Santa Claus ready to pour forth gifts of his specialty.

Traveling the nine floors back down was no longer a cry for how I was going to leave her, but a gentle release with each floor passed to whom I was leaving her with.

Over the next nine months, five days a week, three hours a day, she rotated through four different areas of the hospital—medical education, women's health, volunteer services, and employee health—working with different individuals helping her to overcome challenges and develop job skills in an effort to prepare her for future employment. Her most successful rotation seemed to be medical education. She was able to successfully scan records and index them into a computer database, reviewing them for accuracy.

I don't know how she did all she did, but I do know Who helped her, along with many appointed helpers along the way, family, friends, church families, therapists, nurses, doctors, teachers, coaches, institutions, hospitals, and businesses, all helped to bring this completion to reality, pouring love and hope into our family and especially our daughter.

The Possibility of Not Yets

Home | Oklahoma City, OK
August 2015

One evening after an intense hailstorm, Jessie and I were taking our dogs for their evening walk in the neighborhood. I was drawn to several trees that had piles of shredded leaves underneath them. Never having seen this before, I stood gazing at the ravaged leaves, wondering about this unusual phenomenon.

I began to feel God's interpretation speaking to me, "Life always brings us storms. Some are so devastating, like Jessie's." I thought of all her shredded abilities just lying on the ground. Then He gently shifted my gaze up to the green canopy still holding. "Lisa, look at the tree and not what the tree has lost. Look at what remains and what is still yet to come. Focus upon what you have and not what you have lost. Embrace all the NOT YETs, be thankful for all that is left, and look forward in hope for all that is to come."

Her job coaches were supportive, encouraging, and believed in the "NOT YET," pushing forward to places that could become her next level. I remembered the others, also so perfectly placed to help us, believing I could not have done the releasing without them.

Graduation Grace

Home | Oklahoma City, OK
May 2016

Bill and I were seated in the large sanctuary at Crossings Community church in a sea of people awaiting Pomp and Circumstance. I was reeling with emotions at the thought of Jessie walking across the stage. One of my intense heart griefs had been not seeing her experience her high school graduation with her friends. And even though it looked different than what I had always imagined for her, my girl was going to walk across a stage in a cap and gown and get a certificate for completion of Project Search.

Only God!

"Are these seats taken?" a familiar voice came from behind me. I looked up to see our friends, Steve and Ivy,

Part 3: Reseeding the Forest

pointing at the empty seats next to us. Ivy had prayerfully journeyed the last seven years with us in the midst of her own great grief and tragedies. Even though we hadn't sent out any invitations to her graduation ceremony, here she was announcing she wouldn't miss this for anything. She wanted to watch "her girl" walk across that stage. I had no idea how powerful her love was until that moment, as my emotions could no longer be contained within my well-developed compartment.

Jessie stood tall as she marched in with a massive moving sea of other students in royal blue caps and gowns, finding her seat beside her friends. It was surreal to hear the booming voice of the president as he called out her name, "Jessica Taylor Boone." She proudly walked across that sacred stage, reaching out to receive the scroll that held the magnitude of this miraculous moment. All I could see was her magnificent smile beaming brightly.

"WITH GOD, ALL THINGS ARE POSSIBLE" were the words written on the special graduation card given to Jessie by Ivy. Underneath those words of truth was an unusual picture of a graduate standing tall with angel wings on her back. I had never seen a graduate with angel wings and now I had seen two. What a picture to behold and ponder in my heart—the one on the card and the one that I had just witnessed walking across the stage. I knew God Himself had orchestrated this very moment.

Someone once shared with me about how the number seven reveals completeness, divine perfection, something finished. She finished it. She completed it. She is divine perfection. Seven years after that one tragic moment in time that changed everything, she had finished something my heart couldn't have ever imagined possible but had always deeply hoped for.

Standing in the crowded room of the graduates and families during the reception of cookies and punch extended the unique opportunity to have conversations with the classmates of Jessie and their parents, and then the unexpected happened. I discovered these girls had developed a special bond with each other that had grown into a small circle of friendship within this program where they had spent the last year learning and growing to become better prepared for their future employment. With Jessie's memory and communication challenges, she struggled to share what her experiences were within her day, much less details of any of her classmates. I had never heard anything about these girls and even on this day, she still couldn't remember their names.

A New Fragrance of Friendship

Home | Oklahoma City, OK
May 2016

Receiving her first invitation to the birthday party of one of her classmates was a confirming continuation of the special gift of her friendships. Seeing those girls gathered together, laughing and celebrating life within their circle, was such a life-giving offering for my heart.

I will never forget the moment when I picked up Jessie from the party, and the mom of one of the girls shared her deep appreciation of her new friends.

"This is the first time she has had friends at her birthday party. It has always been just our family. I am just so thankful these girls have found each other."

My heart joined hers in intense gratitude, celebrating this new facet of life for our girls.

Their friendships provided social time together with movie nights, game nights, swimming parties, bowling,

Part 3: Reseeding the Forest

or just hanging out to eat some pizza. They gathered to celebrate birthdays, carve pumpkins for Halloween, make Gingerbread houses for Christmas, and have New Year's Eve parties.

One afternoon as the girls were hanging out on our back porch, I made a gentle attempt to intervene with Jessie as she was talking nonstop to one of her friends.

Her friend matter-of-factly told me, "Oh, no worries, I get her."

I simply smiled and retreated back into the house.

You truly do get her, don't you, precious girl. Wow! I just can't believe the gifts that come from the other gifts that come from the other gifts. One strand of unlimited gifts within the hard, holding the tension with love and fun.

I couldn't believe the magnitude of these friendships and how God had made a way for her to have friends again.

Each girl has been incredibly fragranced with love and kindness and given the unique understanding of each other's needs. Sometimes I wonder if friendship is one of the most needed keys in having a more fulfilled and completed life as we find belonging and our life happenings are witnessed and shared with others.

CHAPTER 15

The Aspen Tree

Connection

Perfect alignment of the two newly-painted canvases assured the tree stood straight, becoming the finishing touch on Jessie's newly-remodeled bedroom. Her sister-in-law, Erin, had been "family" commissioned to paint a masterpiece to christen her twenty-fifth birthday.

When she agreed to this special appointment, she asked if there was something specific I wanted her to paint. I smiled and shook my head. "I don't. Just paint your heart for Jessie."

"Colors? Can you give me some ideas?" she probed.

"I really just want something from you on her wall."

I sat on Jessie's bed studying this creation from the heart, my mind traveling back through images of "the aspen tree trunk" she hit while skiing, the yellow leaves of hope of the daffodils, the yellow blanket of comfort, the yellow ribbons of faith calling her home from Colorado, the yellow gowns of praise, and the yellow leaves of her new life—all a part of this beautiful thread woven into the mystery of God's story of resurrection.

I was stunned with the expansiveness of the story told within the simplicity of the gray-trunked aspen tree with the uncomplicated, almost childlike, yellow leaves, and the appearance of a sacred dove making its presence known as the weaver and author of the stories. The dove bathed in the soft blue hue whispered the tender story of the bleeding woman in the bible who was healed when she reached out and touched the blue hem of Christ's robe.

Was that the same color? I wondered.

The yellow leaves awakened my heart to the hope of one day witnessing the spectacular show of shimmering yellow leaves of aspens as the slightest breeze makes it look like thousands of yellow fluttering butterflies echoing the quaking sounds of praise through the mountains. One day, I will sit in the midst of such a triumphal symphony, feasting with my eyes, and ears, and heart, remembering how those thousands of yellow butterflies took flight within the thousands of Carepage responses with the breeze of the Holy Spirit echoing the quaking praise and prayers through our lives.

The quaking aspen tree is one of the most beautiful of all tree species and shares an interconnected root system. Above ground, they grow as individual trees. Below ground, they are given life by one interconnected set of roots. They are one living organism within one living community. This powerful metaphor spoke directly to how intricately woven together our lives are within our community. We experienced this in such magnitude by physically witnessing the deep, interconnected root system within Jessie's Carepages.

Our community rushed spiritual and physical nutrients to "us" like the grove of aspens rushes nutrients to the damaged and suffering tree, teaching us the essential need to stay connected to everyone so we can be ready and willing to rush nutrients of love and compassion to others when they are damaged or suffering.

Community Celebrations

Home | Oklahoma City, OK
August 2016

Jessie's Mat Trotters gymnastic family had remained connected and supportive during her years of recovery. From traveling to Grand Junction to see Jessie after her accident, to sending get well posters drawn by the gymnasts, to having fundraisers, to coordinating blood drives in her name, all with the intention of sending love and great hope to us from the gym family of her childhood. Their powerful support reached back into our past affections, resurrecting memories of the community of support we had been immersed in for years, bringing a familiar surrounding comfort to us heartbroken parents of a benched gymnast. But they never benched her.

Jeff and Trish, her coaches, contacted us with an irresistible invitation, "We would be so honored if your family would join us for this year's award banquet for our gymnasts." Jeff went on to tell a beautiful story of how they had established the "Jessie Boone Courage Award" to recognize and celebrate her exceptional courage, steadfast resilience, and enduring spirit of hope and perseverance. He was hoping we could be there so they could honor Jessie with this award. He continued by sharing how at the end of each season, this award would be given to the gymnast who demonstrated qualities and characteristics that honored the impact that Jessie had made on countless others.

Her plaque was presented to her as she stood between her two coaches, with Jeff speaking of their philosophy at their gym, "Courage is the collective strength of heart, mind, and soul, but the character plays the key role! In Your Honor, Jessie Boone! Established in 2016."

We were genuinely moved at yet another profound proclamation of dedication and commitment they exemplified toward their gymnasts. They modeled what they expected from their gymnasts in every aspect of their lives. We always knew Jessie was receiving far more than gymnastic lessons each time we witnessed their coaching but could never have imagined the breadth and width of their love and support.

Jeff had asked if I would share a few words about Jessie's journey at the banquet. I was honored to stand before these heroes and share the impact they have had on our lives and others. Grips, Rips, and Kips titled the sharing of my heart, as I wove the challenging things gymnasts contend with into a warm, familiar, funny, truthful, and hope-filled message, honoring Jessie, our coaches, and gymnasts. I only hoped they felt our love and gratitude as much as we had felt their never-ending support of cheering Jessie on from the stands of their gym hearts we loved so deeply.

Employment Endeavors
Home | Oklahoma City, OK
August 2016

Daunting was the word that came to mind as Bill and I conferenced around the subject of employment during Project Search. Her job coach had secured and prepared her for an interview, even helped her complete a resume for a full-time position in the medical education department, where she had just finished a ten-week rotation working on her skills in computer and data entry.

I still was unable to wrap my head around her being interviewed, as her ability to communicate remained severely limited, being unable to answer most questions due to her memory deficits and her processing speed. Conversations remained almost non-existent as she was unable to form or find responses. It was like she couldn't "keep up with the words." How could she possibly keep up with the work? It seemed absurd to allow her to go through such a defenseless, exposed examination. But there was more weighing on my heart as this interview approached.

How do I begin to embrace the idea of accepting assisted employment when she has been given so much more than we could have ever hoped for?

Rehabilitation and job coaching are specific to the recovery of a person. Employment for Jessie seemed to cross this hidden line by asking or allowing someone else to make sacrifices in order for her to be employable.

I began to struggle with how to receive this next level of growth and healing for her, knowing this would impact other people working hard and being asked to go beyond their own job descriptions to provide assistance so she could do hers.

There must be a special place in heaven for those who create and make work spaces for others requiring a different way to be productive and who need additional structure and time to complete their work. They must have exorbitant patience to slow their lives in order to provide a slower space to help the special one be successful in the areas they can be. This way of humanizing a person is a powerful reflection of the empathy and compassion abiding deep within these human soul lights making themselves the special one.

She was offered a position in the medical education department of Integris Hospital, but I had serious concerns. Her profound fatigue and poor eyesight with her continued navigation of brain injury issues were incongruent with a full-time schedule. Concerns of compromising her overall health by work demands of a full-time job guided me in unsuccessful attempts to negotiate a part-time position which resulted in the ultimate decision to decline the offer.

Voc Rehab was another resource enlisted to help look at potential part-time employment opportunities, providing safer and better aligned opportunities for success as she continued to work toward overcoming the significant challenges of her injuries.

We explored many different options with Jessie but continued to be unsuccessful in finding the "perfect fit" for both her needs and our goals for her.

One day I received a phone call asking to speak to Jessie Boone. I recognized the voice but didn't know the reason for the phone call. I placed the phone on speaker and called Jessie to the phone, "Jessie, this call is for you."

Jessie took the phone and answered, "Hello."

"Jessie, this is Ivy Snider. Do you have a few minutes to talk with me?" she asked.

"Yes, I do," Jessie replied sweetly.

"Jessie, I have a home health company that provides health care support to people in their homes. I have been looking for a part-time office assistant to help with some data entry and scanning, and I was wondering if you might be interested in applying?"

Jessie looked at me and I nodded my head, softly whispering, "Say yes."

Jessie said, "Yes, I would."

"Okay, Jessie, that is great. What I will need for you to do is come by the office and get an application to fill out and return it back to me. Will that work?"

As I nodded my head again, Jessie said, "Yes, that will work."

After she completed the application, Ivy scheduled an interview with her. For the first time, my heart didn't lurch into the ritual of fear and anxiety about her challenges with communication. My heart knew she would be safe and treated with the greatest respect and dignity regardless of her abilities. My fierce momma bear protection wasn't needed in this small office space that held kind and compassionate people who would assume the role of protector and teacher, friend and mentor.

I drove Jessie to her interview and pulled up to the office. Jessie got out of the car and walked into the building, and I sat in the car in perfect peace marveling at the place of employment that was chosen for her.

When Jessie returned, I asked, "Well, how did your interview go?" I waited for her to gather her response.

"It went okay. She said she needed to check my references and get back with me."

My heart was immediately infused with a strange warmness that felt good and right by the thought of Jessie being treated like a "regular" interviewee. I had never known that feeling until that moment, helping me to realize how powerful human medicine can be when one who is different is treated the same as others.

Within the week, she was offered not only a part-time position as an office assistant with job duties of data entry with Excel spreadsheets, scanning, and shredding, but something even greater. She was offered dignity, expectations, opportunities, responsibilities, growth, communication, relationships, independence away from home, problem solving, all while being immersed in an incredibly empathetic yet highly expectant office staff that reaches out and reaches under to guide and support her in her day-to-day work flows and flaws.

Part 3: Reseeding the Forest

The collaborative support she has received from her coworkers and boss have helped her continue to be given amazing learning opportunities in the unique work environment that was placed before her, carrying the inspiring message, "We don't focus on what people can't do, we focus on what they can do in this workplace."

One day, Ivy stood at the window of my car as I was waiting to pick Jess up, excited to share a story about Jessie and the successes she had that day.

I smiled gratuitously, remarking, "Isn't that just incredible? Do you remember when you had to put a note on the front of her computer reminding her to not go to websites that weren't related to work?"

Ivy matter-of-factly said, "No, actually I don't. I just see what she is doing today."

Her words jarred me into the awareness that I was standing in the presence of "a powerful advocate for all" who was choosing to create and nurture a place where the workforce is stronger when all are included. I was awakened again to the realization of standing on holy ground.

> *"When we begin to cross the threshold, we are confronted with the greatness of our unknowing. We are called to recognize that we do not know what the future brings ...*
> *A threshold is a liminal place, the place of not knowing how things will turn out. I believe it is the place of possibility. We must learn to live in the liminal place, where the old is released but the new hasn't come into being."*
>
> ~*The Soul of the Pilgrim,*
> Christine Valters Paintner~

In the many thresholds we have been forced to face, we have crossed each one with great fear and unknowing. What God has revealed over and over again, is that He is with us, leading us by a cloud by day and a pillar of fire by night. Just as the Israelites came to the sea, and it seemed to be the end, God suddenly parted the mighty waters, making a way for His people to cross the threshold, safely protecting them from the enemies close behind and leading them into a new way of life.

Recognition
Home | Oklahoma City, OK
May 2017

When we were unexpectedly notified that Jessie had won the "Supported Worker of the Year" award given by the Oklahoma chapter of APSE, Association of People Supporting Employment First, we were deeply grateful for this remarkable recognition of her continued efforts to push forward through the many struggles she has to face every day.

Curious about how she was nominated and what this meant, I did some research and discovered that APSE is the only national organization focused exclusively on Employment First to facilitate full inclusion of people with disabilities in the workplace and the community.

Who are these saints of people that keep reaching in to help elevate and recognize those who don't have a voice themselves?

As we sat at the banquet table with Jessie, her job coach, and some supporting friends, I marveled at this organization that would choose to recognize and honor our daughter for overcoming overwhelming odds to maintain employment. But quickly, I became acutely aware of what was missing in that extraordinary moment. My thoughts went immediately to her employer who was willing to employ Jessie knowing she would need extra support and accommodations. She should be standing next to her getting an award for "Outstanding Supporter of the Worker of the Year" award to recognize and celebrate the immeasurable extra effort put forth ensuring she could be successfully employed with such dignity and care.

PART 4

Emerging Saplings

—

5 Years of Growth, Grief, and Grace

CHAPTER 16

The Great Oak

Legacy

When Maya Angelou wrote the timeless poem, "When Great Trees Fall," she compared the loss of "great souls" to the fall of "great trees," the impact of which is felt in *every* direction. When she passed in 2014, David J. Bauman wrote an article titled, "When Great Trees Fall, Remembering Maya Angelou," and I paused on his words, "But the longer I live, the more it sinks in that not only is death an inevitable part of life, but knowing and acknowledging the impermanence of our existence is what makes each moment of our lives so precious."

Impermanence of our existence ... each moment of our lives ... so precious ...

In my home stands a black shelf holding an altar of remembrance overflowing with favorite pictures of my daddy.

My goodness, my daddy. My heart still trembles at the mention of his name.

Overlooking his pictures is one of my most cherished comforts, a canvas painted by my talented and creative daughter-in-law, Erin, after his death. This Ebenezer Stone honors a towering ancient oak tree firmly rooted and growing within the open fields of rolling green pastures with a powerful presence of strength, protection, and life. Within the massive branches of this extraordinary portrait, she subtly painted an excerpt of Maya's words, "And when great souls die, after a period, peace blooms, slowly and always irregularly. Spaces fill with a kind of soothing electric vibration. Our senses, restored, never to be the same, whisper to us. They existed. They existed. We can be. Be and be better. For they existed."

He existed. He existed. And I can be. Be and be better. For he existed.

Rivers of Love in Grief
Mom and Dad's Place | Stidham, OK
November 2017

Dad's cancer had returned with a vengeance. Battling fiercely for two years, with his voice steady, he made the "announcement" he was tired and didn't want to do "this" anymore, telling us he and Jesus had a talk and it was all good. "I am ready to go."

With no opportunity for further discussion, he disappeared into his bedroom, closing the door behind him.

I glanced at Mom who was silent, not moving from her chair, eyes fixed on the closed door. What had just been witnessed was drumming the familiar sounds within my ears from years of hospice nursing—the announcement of what was coming.

Daddy, will you even be here in the morning?

Early the next morning, he woke up having difficulty breathing, engulfed in excruciating pain. Within minutes of arriving in the ER, he "suddenly" died. When asked about resuscitation, with great courage and strength mingled with the grace of God, Mom simply asked, "Is he gone?"

"Yes."

"Let him go."

The Great Oak

She knew his wishes. She knew he no longer wanted to live this way. That wasn't life for Lee Henry. He was ready to move on to his next adventure. "Our great tree had fallen."

Comfort arrives as a cavalry when grief hits hard.

All of our immediate family circled around Mom like wagons getting ready to endure a fierce attack but instead became "a good ol' fashion wake," as my son, Justin, put it.

Toasting Dad with a little too much of his favorite Evan Williams 1783 until "it was finished," shooting his hallowed guns, and going through his ammo like they went through his whiskey. Whooping and hollering, maybe even knocking a security light out, and popping his whips with sounds of lightning underneath the full moon. Telling tales of being popped by the very whip or being taught a hard lesson by Papa, pulling out photo albums to the pages revealing the magnitude of his well-lived life, and crying while laughing as songs were belted out, Lee Henry style. Raiding his closet and wearing his scarves, timeless and treasured (don't touch my cowboy hats), and recording these moments with priceless selfies and group photos, with his favorite cowboy movies providing the background noise. Eating the sacred leftovers of his last meal, the Thanksgiving feast, all of it honoring and remembering all the extra that Daddy put in each of our lives, holding our hurting hearts close to his. Witnessing the loud and intentional heart offerings that evening on the farm echoed Dad's way of life to others, bringing each of our hearts the intense comfort desperately needed.

The next morning, we slowly gathered around their table after the late night gala of grief and remembrance. The familiar smell of the sourdough biscuits coming out of the oven, lovingly made by "Biscuit Bob," warmed the

Part 4: Emerging Saplings

empty seat at the end of the table as the grief and sadness permeated our family home with a sober empty quietness.

Oh, God, what do we do now?

Time stood still as grief held us all captive, unable to move into the next moment. Unexpectedly at that very moment, more cavalry arrived.

It was the familiar popping sound of the back screen door that jolted us to attention. Suddenly appearing was one of his oldest, dearest friends, Craig Conlee. He had driven eight hours to be with our family on the first morning without him. He was dressed in his full cowboy regalia, looking stately like "Gus" from *Lonesome Dove*. Cowboy hat, chaps, and spurs were singing in unison as he moseyed in.

Of course, my dad was the Woodrow F. Call in their friendship, resembling the two former Texas Rangers who had lived many adventures together including chuckwagons, cattle drives, cookouts, sourdough biscuits in Dutch ovens over open fires, business dealings, and plenty of shooting the bull around the campfires of their lives.

At his side was his Lorie darlin, "Carol," looking like a Texas rose fragranced in all her lace and beauty. Both carrying a love feast in their arms full of freshly smoked brisket with all the fixin's and a new bottle of 1783, honoring my dad in such an extraordinary way.

It took my breath away.

Love does that. It takes your breath away, just when you don't know how you're going to take your next breath. Tears of comfort and gratitude flowed, replacing the sober emptiness of the morning with powerful memories of love, giving us the ability to take yet another step.

The Great Oak

The river of love continued flowing by all who followed afterwards, bringing generous offerings of presence, tears, sympathy, stories, and food, helping to carry our family through the hard of loss, creating movements of grace within the paralyzing moments of grief. This orchestration of grace only God could have created and gifted in such a way to guide our family with such comfort. My precious and beloved mom revealed the power of the presence of others when she said, "My heart is so full of peace. I had no idea it would be this way," as one of Daddy's truths echoed once again in my heart, "God sends 'love' to help us through times like this."

His epic life celebration was a historic time full of sharing and experiencing many of the different aspects of the leavened life of Lee Henry. We gathered on the other side of the pond where the chuckwagons and cowboys live. Music and song was flowing out of the Waterfall amphitheater from the musical sides of his family, his poetry spoken by a granddaughter, full military honors with Taps including his enlisted grandson who currently served in the same branch, pictures and paraphernalia from dad's well-lived life in the Dry Bean Saloon, a dance in the Cast Iron Kettle Pavilion with Laredo (his grandson's band) performing live, a visit to Boot Hill cemetery where one can experience a full-sized chuck box built with love by a couple of his boys to specifically hold the remnants of dad in the white buffalo urn.

Everyone was invited to leave a permanent note of remembrance written inside the walls of the chuckbox with a black sharpie, echoing love and gratitude for all he had given and meant.

The question had been asked by Pastor Jay during Dad's service, "How do you celebrate Lee Henry and the enormity of his life?" He shared his experience of simply being invited to the family Chuckwagon breakfast earlier in the day. He confessed he knew nothing about the sourdough starter used for the cowboy biscuit making. He spoke of the special family crock in the chuckbox that held the ancient sourdough starter said to be over 100 years old, daring to question if it was legend or truth. He told of the cowboy biscuit maker taking a large helping of the starter from the batch that went before and pouring it into the well of flour in order to make the biscuits, and how Lee's life was like that sourdough starter.

"Every part of him is in every part of us. To see Lee is to see all of his family and the community of friends that he invested his life in. That sourdough starter is Lee Henry. He leavened the very lives of others—the very ones now leavening our lives with comfort and hope."

Eight years after her accident that changed our lives forever, another unwanted hard season of loss found its way to my family's heart. Once again, the community of love showed up, helping to navigate and carry us through the tossing waves of grief, surrounding us with their presence, prayers, and provision, reminding us that none of us are ever meant to journey this life alone. It was through the presence of others and their unique gifts of love cushioning our shattered hearts, helping to hold the pieces together like a Band-Aid, that healing could come.

My bedroom dresser holds a powerful visual icon, a heart sculpture speaking this truth, created by my dear friend, Bob Willis, who is an author, grief specialist, and sculptor. Laid over the deep chasm left behind from the unspeakable loss is a large Band-Aid holding the clay heart together. You can also find healed scars over other parts of the heart that will always remember the loss but now speak to the hope of the healing to come. Etched in the base is the promise of Psalms 147:3, "He heals the brokenhearted, He binds up their wounds."

I believe God is always inviting His people to become a part of His Band-Aid in the unique ways we can show up in the midst of others' overwhelming loss and grief.

CHAPTER 17

The Serenity Tree

Amidst the Chaos

Heart-racing anxiety took up residence within my body and spirit with the Covid chaos coming from all directions. The turbulence unearthed deep reminders from Jessie's accident to find God's presence in the earthshaking, unpredictable, and shattering moments of the unknown in our lives.

One day, I came across a heart-stirring painting posted on my friend Kristi Self's art page. She had just finished the canvas filled with soft hues of blues, greens, and turquoise. The trees were standing in perfect stillness with their light lavender canopies open receiving a soft pouring of gentle, golden yellow grace from above. The meandering river of glassy, light blue calm surrounded them in perfect peace. The simple, brown path was a quiet invitation to come and sit beneath the sacred peace trees for a time such as this.

A powerful call reached into my unsteady center as I studied her intimate work of art and heard the words of Mark 4:39 (KJV), "And he arose, and rebuked the wind, and said unto the sea, 'Peace be still.' And the wind ceased and there was a great calm."

When I reached out to her about the painting, my first question was, "Is this painting available?"

She replied, "Well, yes it is!"

My second question was, "What did you name this beautiful piece of goodness?"

"I named it, 'Serenity Amidst the Chaos.'"

Of course you did. What a perfect name for this creation of peace.

It wasn't very long before the whispering canvas was in my home and pouring its gentle grace of serenity, surrounding and calming the chaos within the walls of my heart and soul.

Changes in Community
Home | Oklahoma City, OK
January 2020

Without warning, we found our church life becoming a remodeling project. After years of worshipping, serving, and being nurtured within the sacred walls of our church home, the earthquakes of Covid with other questions within our denominational disciplines began to crumble the walls around us, driving us to find God's direction for our lives outside of the walls of the chaos within the building.

Even though the grounds shook deep disturbances within our hearts, the firm foundation of God held. This drastic disorientation of change unearthed us from our worship community, yet it seemed to be following the rhythm of the other changes in our lives, only driving us to cling harder to the Rock we had built our house upon. Wandering and searching within the constraints of Covid's limited face-to-face contact opened up new experiences for my heart.

Covid Catastrophes
Home | Oklahoma City, OK
March – December 2020

All was steady and stable in the world of Jessie Boone with a balance of work, home life, church, and social activities until it wasn't.

The emergence of Covid was unexpected and brutalized the entire world without warning. Our household, like so many others, was thrown into becoming an emergency response team as I dealt with the ever-escalating, ever-changing health care requirements surrounding my career as a hospice nurse within a major health care system, an elderly mother-in-law with advanced dementia, and a daughter who was always in need of assistance.

My normal night work of being on call for patients with end-of-life care escalated to insurmountable heights of stress with "full requirements of PPE (personal protective equipment) with K95 masks" without the controlled safe environment of a hospital. The act of donning equipment for safety reasons outside my car in the midst of weather and darkness while unable to see where I was walking or unable to be aware of my surroundings, the consistent attempts to maintain these lifesaving precautions during procedures, and answering the on call phone or finding patient information on my work computer was nearing the impossible mark.

It took on a whole new level as I would enter into the sanctuary of a home looking like someone out of a science fiction thriller. This gear thwarted any attempts to provide the compassionate end-of-life care families and patients deserve, as many could not understand the voice enclosed within the vacuum chamber covering my face.

Working at night with the increased amount of Covid-positive patients being sent home to die so they could be with family was excruciatingly painful to witness. These unimaginable tragedies along with the adverse effects of the pandemic upon the people forever changed me and the trajectory of my career.

The difficulties of speaking, hearing, seeing, and providing compassionate touch were also interwoven with my realistic fears of being exposed to the virus and taking it home to my vulnerable daughter, my husband, or his elderly mother who now lived in our home.

We had recently decided to move her in when I was told by her assisted living facility that I wasn't allowed to open her door even a tiny crevice to say hello and try to calm her anxiety-filled dementia with my presence and voice. The care burden within our home was profoundly intensified, but the alternative was not an option for our family.

It was not long before Jessie's employer notified us that the staff would be working remotely, charging us to set up a home office in our living room fully equipped with her computer and desk. Processes and procedures were quickly outlined and learned, so I could be her "resource" person, monitoring and helping her with the accuracy of tasks inputting data for denied insurance claims in Excel and other responsibilities in her job.

She adjusted well to her new work surroundings and enjoyed working in her comfy clothes and being "supervised" by her mom. She also gained other opportunities for work when her grandma needed someone to watch TV with or eat lunch with. Her kind, gentle presence helped keep us all in a more gracious attitude.

One of our winter rehab activities included a paint by number canvas of a rose in hopes of stimulating creative flows within Jessie's hands and heart. With her visual perception challenges and processing, it took several weeks and some help from Mom and Dad, but she finished it. Its beauty was stunning as was her own accomplishment. She named it "Jessie's Rose."

Intentionally living moment by moment had become our way of surviving and functioning through tragedy and suffering. Daily breath prayers and taking non-negotiable daily walks with Jessie and our dogs, with the sun and creation speaking their wisdom to God present within all, helped to keep my heart more leveled. I bent my knees in the gardens around our home, finding the beauty and life within the dirt and weeds threatening to overtake their world. Online barre sessions enabled me to continue to forge physical health, key for accountability and the encouragement that comes with such powerful, healthy friends. Weekly Zoom meetings with my prayer circles held my heart steady with the powerful medicine of witnessing each other's hearts. My morning and evening prayer time centered my heart on the one true north, using meditation, journaling, signposts, and stones from my past journeys to guide me through this different type of unknown.

Zero turn mowing, combined with famous Oklahoma winds, became its own outdoor therapy. It helped to blow the unwanted clippings of grass and anxiety to the side of my path, empowering a sense of freedom given by God to not fear or be overwhelmed but to trust Him and stay within the moment, knowing morning always comes after the dark night. All such powerful medicine was key in helping maintain my spiritual, emotional, and mental well-being.

The next several months were alarming, a stressful chaotic blur of uncharted change and continuous care, with the world around us shutting down with Covid fears in the hopes of everyone coming out on the other side of this history-changing global pandemic. Many people didn't, including some very special friends of mine. The devastating losses were heart-wrenching and difficult to understand.

The mandatory isolation was unprecedented for our elderly population. Much of the workforce was halted to a neutral gear, putting many families in a financial crisis and at risk of losing their place of habitation. Other parts of the workforce were forced into overdrive with the extreme burdens of assisting in human survival. The gathering places of worship locked the doors to protect the people who would have continued gathering in the very place one would run when the earth gave way and the mountains were crumbling into the sea.

Technology became the survival of connection and communication. Everything was changing. Everything except God Himself, as He does not change. (Malachi 3:6)

My heart recalled how technology had helped us survive the worst catastrophe of our lives when we were hundreds of miles away from our home and community. Through the simple gift of a website, Carepages, we found a lifeline connection to the world while we were isolated within the walls of a tragically injured daughter for months. Eleven years later, technology was once again playing another important role in survival.

CHAPTER 18

The Breathing Trees

Moving Past Fear

June 2021

The sudden abnormal blood marker appearing in her lab work disrupted me like a boulder hitting a still body of water. Biannual lab draws for her blood tests had been uneventful, as her liver enzymes had long settled into the normal range. Her fully-functioning liver had been the ultimate miracle, ushering her into a "more normal" life. Each lab report would bring forth "remembrance" of the season of sepsis and liver failure with deep gratitude to God for delivering her from death and making a way for her bile duct to be repaired.

This unusual marker now glaring at us in red could be associated with cancer, and Jessie's history of exorbitant radiation placed her at an increased risk. The confusion and concern led to a consult with her PCP (primary care physician), followed by another consultation with a hematologist oncologist within weeks. The story loop of "what if" was met with breath prayers and meditations of my heart as the walls of our newly found expansiveness were threatening to close with these incessant waves of fear and panic that kept crashing in, keeping me from finding the safe shoreline within.

During one of my morning meditations, which was really a pleading to God to not let it be cancer, my eyes fell upon a bracelet gifted by a precious friend. It laid prominently on my desk with the imprinted words, "Simply do something different."

Hmmmmmm. Something different? And what would that be?

It wasn't long before I alerted Bill to the something different and Jessie and I were checking into a downtown hotel overlooking Scissortail Park.

"Here is your key, you are on the 11th floor in room 1138."

God, the 11th floor! Really!?

I could feel the shift—the giant waves receding as remembrance appeared as an old friend. Stepping off the elevator, I paused in a deep posture of gratitude for His spoken presence to me with His continued promise "I AM WITH YOU" each step. My heart stilled, leaving the waves and story loop in a far-off place. As I found the keycard, my spirit pieced together the added familiarity of 1138—my dad's birthday month and year.

Oh my gosh, Daddy! You're here too?

I gently tiptoed across the threshold to an untrodden sanctuary of *different*, drinking in a view of a sky full of new expansiveness.

After we got settled, it was time to explore. Jessie and I walked throughout the park area breathing in the fresh air, enjoying the horticultural gardens with water fountains drawing attention to the lake and wildlife. Walking across the Skydance Bridge and experiencing the scissor-tailed flycatcher sculpture soaring two hundred feet in the air was a life-lifting experience.

Stepping off the bridge, I glimpsed a shiny dime on the pathway. As I reached down to pick it up, the penny was

The Breathing Trees

waiting just a few feet away. Warmth traveled through my veins as I gazed at the "11" cents, hearing the words, "I AM WITH YOU."

Discovering the annual downtown Arts Festival was another beautiful synchronicity of God's invitation to do something different. We found our way through colored crowds of life, enjoying the weather and beauty displayed in the different arrays and smells of extraordinary talent and creativity.

We watched a sunkissed artist wrapped in a sleeveless blue dress and perched on a stool. She was rhythmically teasing oil on a canvas, using a paint brush as though she were conducting an orchestra of delightful creativity. Her warm greeting invited us closer. Her paint-covered hand was as welcoming as her gentle smile and kind eyes. She appeared as a painting herself.

"Tell me about this one," I invited as I pointed to the two black trees "side by side" with movement and life coming up from the roots. Their treetops burst with whimsical colors, as they held watch over the teetering home on the sloping shoreline.

"I call it 'A Breath of Fresh Air.' Do you like it?" she inquired with her curious, lighthearted tone.

A Breath of Fresh Air.

I felt the fluttering movement within.

"Oh my, what beauty you have captured and certainly speaks to my heart. I would love for my husband to see it. He works downtown and will meet us later."

"Great, I look forward to meeting him." She smiled again as she turned back to her wet canvas waiting for more.

Meeting up with Bill launched a new adventure. When he told me about cruising through the art booths during

Part 4: Emerging Saplings

his lunch and finding his new favorite painting, I smiled, sharing a similar story of my own new favorite painting.

With his crooked smile, he said, "You show me yours, and I will show you mine."

Shaking my head in amusement, and pulling his warm hand into mine, the search was on.

Adventure shifted to amazement when we both found ourselves standing in the same booth.

"Really? Same artist?" His tone was incredulous.

"Are you kidding me? For real?" I asked suspiciously. It took us a moment to believe each other.

"Okay, which painting?" we challenged each other.

Our playful banter had attracted the artist's attention and she joined us as we both reached for the same painting, delighting in each other's heart.

This grace-filled story of being on an appointed adventure deepened into a sweet flow of soul-bearing conversation with the artist around the possible serious health concerns of Jessie and God's beautiful way of inviting us to get a breath of fresh air and rediscover another way of traveling through alarming unanswered questions.

In the midst of the waves of people and noise, the artist's heart paused and with her words, parted the heavens and lifted our beloved girl into His divine healing Light. This hallowed moment calmed our seas as this beautiful painting, now anchored on our wall became another "Ebenezer Stone" on our journey of faith.

After two weeks of waiting and more in-depth blood studies, we were given the ultimate gift from our hematologist, "I can confidently say I can find no evidence in her blood work that would indicate cancer," who remained unsure of the reason for the strange marker found within her blood.

Our teetering home on the sloping shoreline had just been firmly anchored once again as we gave thanks for every breath of fresh air given to our beloved Jessie.

Healing Circles and Direction
Home | Oklahoma City, OK
August 2021

Weary and worn from the unexpected battles in healthcare, the endless energy expended upon the reality of the burdens and challenges of her brain injury with the continuous search for "more," the overseeing of Momma Boone's dementia care, the loss of our church community, and the night work of hospice left my heart resembling a dense, tangled mass of a rootbound tree. My thoughts returned to the wisdom of the tree doctor in my front yard years earlier: "This big guy has never been pruned. He is trapped within his own life."

Trapped within my own life.

Gratitude and grace had carried me each day faithfully, but my heart needed a deep pruning in hopes a spaciousness could be created, helping to give freedom and movement a new direction so it could begin to dance within my bound-up soul.

An invitation unexpectedly appeared via email to join a circle of women through the Yellow Butterfly Foundation. This invitation gave flesh to what it means to lean into the sacred and essential, committing to walk the path together while keeping the Fire burning within ourselves and fanning the flames of others. Through this lived intentional connection, one is able to experience deep transformation in healing wounds while experiencing great abiding love, with the wounds becoming medicine for ourselves, our families, and others within our communities.

Embraced within this new community of healing, an awareness of my deeply hidden unresolved grief slowly began to rise to the surface. Through online retreats, weekly zoom meetings of witnessing others' stories, and eventually meeting in person after Covid, I began to settle into the safety within the sacred space of the circle.

God had been stirring up an overdue remodel of my own heart. Through gentle love and soft guidance, He led me on a path of various retreats directed by wisdom and love, with the intention of providing sacred spaces of belonging, caring, witnessing, questions, and listening. These sacred spaces helped to invite the unattended brokenness to unexpectedly break through the hard shell that had been holding it while it was in search of the releasing care and healing it was desperately needing.

CHAPTER 19

The Still Standing Trees

Perseverance

It was a beautiful weekend to be outside, and I knew that some of my artist friends were displaying their creative pieces of beauty and grace at the Edmond Arts Festival. Wandering through the painted messages of life and love was irresistible, so off I went.

Breathing freely with the newly given space enabled me to move with ease in and out of the displays until I discovered my artist friend from Colorado. Reuniting with her spirit after three months was surprising but timely as she inquired how Jessie was doing. With a different lens, I began to speak with hope about our newly discovered dire circumstances and the gift of Faith that was given to me a few days earlier. She quietly put her paintbrush down and took my hand, as I had hoped she would do. Her supplicated words were for this momma's heart as she prayed specifically over Jessie and the brutal unknown we were facing, believing she would come through this battle to find a full life again. Her reassuring comfort and hope steadied my heart onward.

One of her paintings was shimmering a bit in the sunlight. I stepped in closer and reached out to touch the frame.

"Tell me about this beauty," I invited, studying the contours of cloud-covered mountains standing behind the wisdom and experience of the failing structure of the barn. Her colors danced the beauty right into the old. The trees seemed to lean into the weakened sides providing hope for more time as the meandering stream trickled the stories of the past.

Her smile seemed to appreciate the invitation as she began telling the story of being commissioned to paint an old barn in Colorado. After some history, her story shifted to a more personal place, "I value those things that are falling apart. I have seen how many times it may look hopeless, but I believe putting energy and love into fixing it back up will help to find its life of beauty again. This painting has been hanging in a gallery for two or three years and just recently expressed it was time to travel with me in search of its forever home."

Intensely enchanted by her devotion to her creations, I wondered out loud, "What did you name this one?"

She answered with the words that spoke to the deepest desire of my heart in that moment, "Still Standing."

Oh my goodness. Still Standing!!??? God, yes!

And all I could think was, *You can't make this up.*

Walking in Faith

Home | Oklahoma City, OK
September 2021

Just a few days earlier during our evening walk with Jessie, I had discerned something was amiss. Her inability to voice a complaint or a problem was a residual remnant of the disordered processing which affected her ability to communicate when something was wrong, but I could usually detect discomfort by seeing it on her face first. When she was able to successfully voice a headache or her tummy discomfort, I would respond quickly, knowing she could have been uncomfortable for an unpredictable amount of time.

"Jessie, are you okay?" I asked, noticing her beginning to limp.

"I'm okay," she answered, as she kept walking but was noticeably slowing down.

"What's wrong? Are you hurting?"

She stopped on the road.

"My back hurts," she answered, bending over as if to catch her breath.

My heart stuttered. Jessie never stops walking unless I stop and she never physically demonstrates pain except with a confused look on her face.

"Can you walk home, Jess?" I asked, knowing with encouragement, she usually would.

"No, Mom. It hurts too bad."

I knew something was seriously wrong. Suspecting a kidney infection, she was seen by her PCP the next day. Her exam and lab work were within normal limits with the exception of a slight elevation of white blood cells. The migrating pain from her lower back to her groin and down her legs along with her challenges of the accuracy of her reporting left diagnosing difficult. My thoughts moved from a strained muscle to a pelvic infection, even possibly bone cancer as her pain intensified.

Sent home to observe over the weekend, we ended up taking an urgent trip to the emergency room which brought to light the unexpected alarming diagnosis of blood clots in bilateral legs, with complete obstruction of four primary veins. Anticoagulants and compression stockings were prescribed with direction to follow up with a cardiovascular surgeon as soon as possible.

Slapped with shock, we left the emergency room silent. The stinging reality intensified with burning tears on the

Part 4: Emerging Saplings

way home as I began to review my mind's card catalog of all of the possible outcomes. Flipping each page, I saw amputation, pulmonary embolism, clot burden, chronic pain and immobility, and possibly death due to the severity of the thrombosis. Moving to the risk factors, I found only one, hormone therapy, which she took as a result of her brain injury. Closing my eyes, I leaned my head back on the headrest.

How did we get here again, God? Her life is so fragile, I know, but this? Where did this come from? Her mobility? Really? After all the years of fighting to get it back? And not just one blood clot? Veins completely occluded?

Once again, we were facing an unknown severity I had never experienced before.

Sleep was a stranger that night as I wrestled with this intrusive threat of maliciousness. By morning, I had devised a simple strategy—to seek God's protection of her life and limbs while making a same-day appointment with a cardiovascular surgeon.

The surgeon was young and friendly, introducing himself first to Jessie. Witnessing this moment of a doctor seeing her first and speaking to her like another person relaxed my "mom mode." Comfort and respect appeared spontaneously as I settled back into the chair.

After a brief history and exam, he gave us two options of treatment, "You can do nothing except anticoagulants, or there is a more invasive treatment called the INARI procedure." He went on to explain, "This new procedure focuses on the critical vessels of venous thrombosis and removes clots to minimize clot burden. There is a small mesh basket that is threaded through her veins and is opened like an umbrella, gathering clots as it's pulled back through the occluded veins. I like to call it a clot retriever."

"Does this actually work?" I asked, incredulous, having never heard of this, even as a nurse caretaking the most vulnerable population.

"They have done this type of procedure for years with pulmonary embolisms but this is a new procedure for venous thrombosis and the hopes are it will change outcomes."

"How many have you done and have you had success? Complications?" My nurse voice kicked in.

"Around a dozen, and all were successful." He went on to explain the complications, including increased vascular injury, cardiac injury, clinical deterioration, bleeding, and death.

"If she were your daughter, what would you do?" The mom voice returned and pressed him, seeking an experienced truth.

"I don't know what I would do."

His honesty burned in my heart, making me pause and take note.

"How much time do we have before the success rate starts to decrease?"

"You need to schedule this within a week if you choose to do it," he said gently, rising from his stool.

"Thank you for your time and help. We will need some time to gather more information and prayerfully discern our next step. We will let you know within a few days."

Research and second and third opinions, with fervent prayer, quickly revealed this procedure was the only path we could take with the obvious confirmation of the severe discomfort and immobility she was enduring. Surgery was scheduled for the following week.

Familiar friends began to reappear uninvited during our days of waiting. Fear would come announcing the end of the road for her mobility and possibly her life. Anxiety was impatient and wouldn't even wait her turn. She forced her way in, shoving Fear over to the side, assuring she had my full attention. No amount of attending or ignoring would make them leave.

My evening walks without Jessie only emphasized the impending threat being made to her mobility along with the absence of her telling me sweet, silly stories, leaving me drowning in the projected grief of "what if."

Choosing Faith
Home | Oklahoma City, OK
September 2021

My dance of "Stay in the Moment" was in full swing as I struggled to navigate the normal life in between. One of the "normal" errands was taking our dogs to the vet for their yearly visit. Driving down one of the back roads seemed to create more space for breathing. Moses's head was hanging out the back window as he enjoyed one of his favorite pastimes. Worship music was louder than the unwanted friends' voices and Jessie was reclined in the passenger seat with her eyes closed. All seemed right for the moment.

Suddenly appearing on the side of the road was a white sign with the words, "Faith Over Fear." My heart stopped in tandem with the car as those words leaped over my mountain. Within seconds, I had made a U-turn in order to capture the message that had erupted my bondage.

As I was maneuvering my phone to take a picture, a gray-haired, farmer-looking man appeared out of nowhere, "Can I help you?" His expression conveyed his intent to help.

My words quickly tumbled off my lips as I began confessing this powerful experience I had just had with

God, knowing I must look strangely out of place or in desperate need of help.

"I just wanted to get a picture of that sign." I pointed to the right of where he was standing.

He reached down and pulled the sign right out of the dirt into which it had been rooted.

"Here, I think we can do better than that. You take this with you as the sign you need to help you through whatever it is you are having to face."

Time paused with his offering.

My heart was pounding with the power of faith as he turned toward my car. The chaos of the dogs and the excitement of fear being threatened created a struggle, but the faith message won as it settled into the floorboard of my car.

"Are you sure?" I asked, searching for something in hopes my uncertainty could be quieted.

His smile was deep and sure, "I am sure."

My trembling words were falling from the window of my car, "How can I thank you, sir?"

"When your battle is over, pass it on to the next one who needs it. Faith is to always be shared with others." His hand lifted to the sky and then he was gone.

When I pulled away from the ditch I had been parked in, the unwanted friends were left behind in the dirt with no room left in the car. As I looked in the rearview mirror, they had already dissipated into the dust of nothingness from whence they came.

The sign of faith was deeply seated on the hearth of our home speaking out and over the impending days, grounding my soul once again into the bedrock of my strength and salvation.

Part 4: Emerging Saplings

Beyond Imagination
Integris Hospital | Oklahoma City, OK
September 2021

With the newly hung masterpiece etched with the hope for her to "still be standing" at the end of the day, we entered the hospital early with wisdom and experience, leaning into her weakened condition with hope for more time as we remembered the stories of the power of God in our past moments, having "faith over fear," asking for the ultimate gift—that she still be standing on both of her feet.

The answer was given within a few hours. Bill and I were sitting in the private consultation area waiting for the surgeon to appear.

His smile greeted our expectant hearts, "There was so much more clot burden than I could have imagined. She had clots in her groin, pelvis, reaching all the way to her heart. It is so good we did this. We removed as much clot as possible." Reaching into his blue scrub pocket, he pulled out his phone. "Just look at this," he said, revealing a picture of several inches of dark blood clots that had just been retrieved from her precious vessels of life.

"How did she do?" I asked, holding back the cascading emotions of anxiety, relief, and gratitude.

"She did beautifully and is in recovery now. She has full circulation in both of her legs and should be in her room within the next hour."

Both of her legs ... Full circulation ... Oh, God ... Thank You ...

How does one truly thank a person who just handed your daughter's quality of life back to you? The one who spends time and energy, sacrificing much of his life fixing up the things that are falling apart in order to bring back the beauty to her life? I reached up and hugged him tightly, hoping the force of gratitude would somehow seep into the pores of his body, filling any empty or broken places he might have within, helping him to know the powerful differences he is making in the lives of others.

The night battles of hypotension, intravenous fluids, and monitoring quieted as the morning light appeared. I knew the battle was over when her eyes found me through the rails of the hospital bed and she whispered, "Momma, I don't hurt anymore."

In an ugly cry moment, I rejoiced, "Oh, sweet Jess, that makes my heart so happy. Breakfast is almost here. Are you hungry?"

"Yes, I am."

Helping her out of bed into the chair confirmed the triumph. Her graceful steps were taken without any pain or limping. Besides pressure bandages around both knees, both of her legs were pink and warm, with bounding pedal pulses.

When breakfast arrived, we wondered together what was hidden under the dome of the unknown. She smiled with her chatty voice, "I hope it's waffles!"

"Oooooo, I hope so too!"

Lifting the silver dome fulfilled her simple hope. Her very favorite breakfast, a feast of waffles with syrup and milk waiting to be consumed in celebration of the sweet victory of "Still Standing."

Reclaiming Intimacy
Pensacola Beach, FL
September 2022

Her care was all-consuming and had become the way of life for us. Our pledge to each other for her recovery remained, "as long as it takes," and our intimacy had been redefined as partners in a battle for her life and recovery.

Part 4: Emerging Saplings

Every movement within our lives outside of our full-time jobs was focused on her rehabilitation. Wherever we went, she went, as we would take every life circumstance as a rehab opportunity to help her regain more.

In December, we received an unexpected, irresistible invitation. Justin and Erin informed us their friends had canceled their travel plans with them at the last minute and wanted to know if we would consider going with them on a four-day trip to New York with accommodations. I knew something very special was being offered to us. My answer wasn't "If we can," it was "How we can."

Bill and I had never left Jessie for that amount of time, but the seed Dr. Smith had planted more than ten years earlier—to take some time for ourselves and our marriage—was now a full grown tree, announcing it was time to take a trip alone.

We weren't alone, but we were without her, enjoying the company of our kids whom we hadn't spent much time with since her accident. Our kids personally escorted us and opened our hearts and souls to delight in the holiday sights and sounds of New York at Christmas time with no cares in the world. It was a magical, life-giving, and eye-opening experience preparing us for the more.

Nanny and the quiet, peaceful country life at the farm was the perfect place for Jessie to spend time with family and to experience a few free days away from her parents.

Something shifted deep within me during that trip, revealing it was okay for us to occasionally release her into the care of others. She was medically stable and seemed ready to enjoy other adventures in life apart from me.

Knowing my sixtieth birthday was coming up in September, with our thirtieth anniversary the next day, we booked a condo on one of Florida's Emerald Coast beaches in Pensacola for a week, hoping all our kids and grandkids would join us for a celebration and some much-needed family time.

When Jessie suddenly made the independent decision that she didn't want to go to the beach but would rather spend that week with Nanny, I was taken aback. With her brain injury, initiation and decision-making weren't usually present within her communication, and she certainly had never announced she didn't want to go with us. She always wanted to go with us. This new development bewildered me as I began to grasp the realization she perhaps was trying to announce her desire for independence once again after losing it fourteen years earlier. My heart was warmed as my soul searched for the deeper meaning.

Within a few days of learning that our Oklahoma kids wouldn't be able to come due to a previous engagement, we decided to embrace this unique opportunity being given and stepped into the adventure of a long-awaited week alone together on the beach.

Preparations were exhausting as I navigated the unfamiliar leaving behind and arranging the tasks of dog care and house details for others to do, the packing of her necessities and medications with detailed instructions of her care, and getting her to Mom's. It left me only the final moments to pack for myself and answer the tough question: What does one need for a week on a deserted beach with her soulmate? The only answer coming was, *"It would be easier to stay at home."*

Refusing the easy way was my choice, trusting the more that was to come. Staying in the moment and taking the next right step ushered me to the tarmac portal, buckled in, awaiting takeoff to another chapter to yet be experienced.

Part 4: Emerging Saplings

As the flight attendant's voice came over the intercom, "Welcome to Southwest Flight 1148 to Pensacola, Florida," my eyes closed, my breathing slowed, my earbuds soothed my anxious heart with worship music, and my hand reached for his. Within moments, the landscape of our lives entered into this much needed renovation, updating our past lives with new space and a new focus—a sacred sanctuary of togetherness.

Long walks into the sunrises together on the miles of empty sugar-white sanded beaches would provide open hours of listening to each other along the silky sands of time, whispering changes afoot as the crystal-clear, blue-green waters ebbed and flowed its crashing waves, erasing the lines of the past defining us as caregivers, leaving a blank canvas as an invitation to rewrite our love story.

Mystery
by Lisa Boone

*I am swept up with the memories
of the ocean's waves.*

*The sounds of the crashing against the
soft movable white grains of change.*

*Rhythmic comfort and
intimacy holds my heart.*

*Intermingled in the midst are colors
of change within the horizon.*

Dark yet light, sunrise or sunset?

*The unknowing of what is to come, yet all
contained within the never-ending waves
of grace forever moving and changing
within the landscape of the Creator.*

(written sitting on the beach of our
new lives one early morning)

Beach remnants of vines adorned with white flowers, shells, and feathers for my morning altar became the earthly markings of our 30th anniversary announcement offered on the beach next to the walkway, greeting us each time we stepped onto the beach.

Early in the morning of my sixtieth birthday, as I was finishing an early morning walk on the empty beach, I was captivated by the surprise offering of an old, deflated, sand-covered, happy birthday balloon wedged by the wind in the side plank of our walkway to the beach. Dad's presence overwhelmed me with an instant awareness of his delight to add such uniqueness to my diamond jubilee. I mused at the thought of him convincing the wind to carry it to the exact spot I would be on my birthday morning. This profound expression of love found its place within the morning altar, created the day before reminding me of how close our loved ones are to us even if their earthly presence is no more.

Rediscovering intimacy, reminiscing our earlier years, and remembering the hurricane-like storms we had faced and survived together drove our pillars of love further down into the immovable bedrock deep within the oceanic floor of our marriage.

Breakfast for two adorned the oceanfront deck as we feasted and were serenaded by the white seagulls while beholding the sun's rays dancing with the dolphins on the blue green abyss. Healing powers of soothing peace and quiet awe came with our morning guest of the salty breeze gently penetrating and softening the outer crusts of the rigid unyielding routines of survival, recovery, and caregiving.

Late night dips in the ocean underneath the full moon energy, mesmerized by the beauty of the darkness and the exhilaration of seclusion within each other fueled our recovery and magnified our love.

Sports bars with OU football, beach bars with exotic drinks and unusual appetizers, and private picnics on deserted beaches reignited our laughter and enjoyment of each other as our new afternoon memories reframed our desires to intentionally make time for moments together to experience the "extras" that life can offer if we choose.

Dancing to favorite playlists of romance by candlelight, cooking together in a fully stocked gourmet kitchen, and experiencing the finesses and fragrances of different wines and cheeses recovered our youthfulness, enhancing our senses to see and taste as we serenaded our hearts singing, "You are the reason," and "All of me."

The morning of our anniversary was a remake of our first breakfast together. With fond memories, I would often tell Bill his omelet "extra with tomatoes" was the reason I married him.

Watching him dice the various vegetables, shred the cheddar cheese and crack the eggs, whisking them into the stainless steel skillet as only he can, made my heart settle within the fabric of his essence with such a deep appreciation and love for the gentle attention to detail that transcribes across his life. When he added the sliced cherry tomatoes to the golden yellow scrumptious egg preparation, my entire soul trembled with tears, knowing he is the "extra" to my life. He has always brought the extra to our lives, cementing in the old cracks and fissures that time and extreme conditions had left behind.

I sat perched on the round white leather stool, beholding his uniqueness as he quietly was consumed with his culinary creation.

He consumes me in the same way. His quiet tender gentleness with his extras.

When he held the chair for me, I sat down to our morning celebratory feast of thirty years. With brilliant blue skies, the magnificent ocean, and the empty white-sanded beach as a backdrop, we toasted to each other and to God for this magical moment in our lives redeeming our marriage for the next chapter of our lives.

Imagine our delight upon opening anniversary cards to each other and discovering we had gotten the same card for each other. On the front was the very blue-green ocean before me, with a little boy in blue overalls and a blue ball cap kissing a tippy toeing girl, in a white flowy dress, arms embracing each other with their feet deepening in the sand.

We had embraced and become the living embodiment of those children. When we got home, Bill commissioned a piece of art from my favorite artist, Kristi Self, to surprise me. This "extra" is now hanging in my bedroom as yet another Ebenezer Stone marking this redemptive time on our journey in this life.

CHAPTER 20

The Healing Tree

Expansion

In 2009, our lives changed forever. Today I can honestly say our lives are blessed beyond comprehension. I look at her tree and all that has been left and all that is yet to come. Those beautiful young leaves full of so much life and potential, stripped, shredded, and devastated have now blown away. Her tree canopy is fuller and more fruitful than we could ever have hoped for.

My dear artist friend, Dawn Normali, created a magnificent visual of our daughter's life now. This oil icon hangs above our bed with the name, "The Healing Tree of Light and Healing." This large mystical colorful canopy of the extravaganza of pink and white smears and textures, rooted in the movements of the green ground of life celebrate the resprouting of her life. What moves my heart most deeply about this Healing Tree is not the immense abundance of the blossoms but the unique way it shares its blossoms with the earth. It isn't in a predictable, organized way, but a whimsical, unorganized scattering of love and beauty to others. Much of it falls to the ground unnoticed yet makes the ground a more beautiful place to walk upon.

I see many reflections of Jessie in this painting, as her recovery may not be the predictable, organized way of life so many of us live within each day, but is one of

Part 4: Emerging Saplings

whimsical unorganized moments scattering deep love and beauty everywhere. She embodies and radiates the spirit of this cherished creation of beauty. I hope others will encounter and experience this type of pure love she scatters effortlessly in the spaces she inhabits, bringing Light and Healing to the world upon which we walk.

The Death Lodge
Grand Lake, OK
September 2022

In response to the opening question of this four-day healing retreat, "What do I hope to receive from these days together?" I had written down "the space to continue to explore and enlarge new landscape in relation to life itself, broaden my life borders to step into what God is offering to me in this sacred space of beauty, and unearth places that are in need of healing."

The Native American priest introduced a death lodge as a ritual to help heal our past, say goodbye to our current way of being, and help prepare us for new beginnings. He spoke to the need of confronting one's mortality and building life from there since one isn't able to choose how they die but can choose how they live, move, and have their being."

Song and storytelling filled our spirits, preparing us for the question, "What is the one thing you haven't been able to finish or complete?"

At that moment unexpectedly, fifteen years came rushing in, all trying to speak at once.

I know, I know. But it's just too much. Nobody wants to read hundreds of pages about a brain injury. It's awful. I have tried to write the book more than once and it is just too hard. And besides, it isn't good enough.

Journaling came easy as the answer was just below the surface of my heavy heart that had been held down and out of view, just far enough that I didn't have to see my inability to finish the book.

But I promised God ...

Wandering and wondering up on the hill, I searched for what I could use to represent my death lodge offering.

I began to notice the hundreds of tiny yellow leaves that had been released to the ground so the next season would have the space to emerge.

My heart leaped at the yellow leaves, realizing God's continued weaving of His story of hope, faith, praise and comfort all moving toward new life. For a moment, the gathering of them felt playful and easy, like a child picking up flowers. The beauty and abundance was life-giving, reflecting all the pages of beauty and abundance given within the heartbreak.

With pockets filled and overflowing, I began to wonder what could hold the yellow pages of my story. The answer was waiting a few steps away, in a tree that had surrendered its all, leaving large pieces of rough gray colored bark at its feet. This gray bark perfectly represented the grief that needed to be visited within the yellow pages of my life. These holy gifts of creation had written their own stories of surrender and death now to be used in the sacred search of mine.

Within the walls of the limbs, tied together with rope, I slowly built the book of "too much, not good enough"— the hundreds of pages of pain and suffering, promise and endurance, loss and rebirth, the life that will never be, the life that is now, the unmeasurable love and provision given in the darkest nights of our souls, the years of knowing I was to write a book but just couldn't get it done. All of it laid on the floor of the death chamber, but it didn't feel complete. Something was still missing.

What's missing?

I paused with the question, rising up from the earth floor in search of what was needed to "finish the book." Stepping out of the death lodge, I stumbled over a large heart-shaped stone.

Of course, there you are.

I looked down to see the willing rock placed in my path waiting to be offered. The large stone of my heart was laid on top of the bark-covered book filled with yellow leafy pages, representing the burden of heaviness of all I carried.

A retreatant arriving a day late made her entrance with a book in hand. Holding it up, she was giddy with the unexpected announcement, "Look what I just received! My first published book!"

My heart shook as I tripped over my own shock and disbelief, catching myself with anticipated wonder.

"WHAT? You wrote a book!? I didn't know you were writing a book! And it is already published!?"

I stood holding her printed and published life story, flipping through the pages of her deep pain and healing, wondering about the prevenient timing of this moment.

I am listening.

This perfectly-timed offering was placed within my path the very moment I was releasing my old story to make space for the new story emerging, now knowing my next step would be to ask someone for help.

Witnessing her story that had risen out of the ashes of her life to become a book of hope and healing for others, fueled my heart for the more. She revealed that without the help of a writer coach, she would have never been able to move through all it took to write her book.

"Tell me more about your writer coach," I pressed for details as I heard words of "sacred messenger, using the power of story and writing to help storytellers heal and become the change in the world."

The metronome of her description fell in rhythm with my heartbeat. I knew more was to come.

Uncovering the Right Next Step
Home | Oklahoma City, OK
September 2022

Driving home from the retreat gave me time to reflect upon the powerful messages and moments of unearthing those parts of me that had been held captive in the pain of life, graciously giving a new direction for the next right step.

A writing coach?

After getting home, it didn't take long for my fingers to find Amanda Johnson. I found myself lingering with her thoughts and questions, "Finding healing through writing, Are you finding yourself struggling to write your book? Perhaps there is another reason you are stuck."

Who are you, Amanda, and are you someone I'm supposed to meet?

Her offerings continued to pluck the strings of my seeking, "Therapeutic writing groups, a sacred guide, storytellers, author, manifest messages, everyone heals stories and traverses the messy middle of metamorphosis together with the language of Story, and lots of chocolate?"

CHOCOLATE? You gotta be kidding!

My mouth watered as my heart thirsted.

The string was tied firmly when I found her picture holding a sign, "Your Story Matters," the very words I had painted on a sign years ago, speaking the formational language of my spiritual director's heart.

Part 4: Emerging Saplings

Answering the invitation to connect, I clicked and opened up the next screen to read, "It's so strange, isn't it? How, just like that, a complete stranger can become such a big part of your story. It's actually terrifying, you know? How a single cross with one person you've never met can change everything." Rebecca Peterson, *This Is Us*.

What is happening? That was one of my all-time favorite series!

I had no idea but knew deep within that I was on the right path and ready for the next step.

Portals of Partnership
Home | Oklahoma City, OK
September 2022

I scheduled an online chat with this complete stranger, knowing we were already connected, to seek the next step in this budding relationship. Her response was shockingly prompt with the forward request to review my "manuscript."

With the burdens of my "old manuscript story" newly surrendered in the death lodge, the courage and strength appeared just in time to push the send button for a time such as this.

Our connection time further seeded the possibility of a partnership as we moved into a more formal meeting of details and contracts.

With my friend's impressive recommendations of this coach and my husband's blessing, I was prepared to embark upon a new writing quest to experience the healing power of Story within the safety of this cocoon to fulfill the covenant I had made that dark night many years before and write the story for the one person who is looking for hope in the midst of their own hurtful story.

During a deep dive into her Content Cocoons, I discovered another treasure, strengthening my connection to this healer. On the last page of her website content, there she stood, smiling as she leaned on a "tree trunk" within an open structure built of trunks and limbs. She and this familiar "death lodge" were offering a gentle invitation to come inside and join a community of storytellers and writers—clouds and pillars of fire that would help guide and light the way forward to the promise land of finding healing through writing.

Guidance in the Labyrinth

St. Francis of the Woods Retreat Center
October 2022

Receiving the irresistible birthday gift of a picnic and a walk through the labyrinth at St. Francis of the Woods welcomed a day of retreat and reflection with my deeply loved spiritual companion, Bobbie.

The labyrinth is a slow, meandering circuitous path leading to a center, a point of perfect balance, a "still point," representing heaven, God, and spirit. The path is likened to the path of life, with twists and turns, moments of feeling lost, encounters with others on your path, a moment to pause at the center to ponder and listen to what you might be carrying or seeking to discover.

The labyrinth walk had been scheduled weeks earlier for the day after my unexpected meeting with the writing coach. Bobbie had no idea what had transpired over the last week at the retreat and the decision I was in the midst of discerning.

As we drove out of town, she asked a simple question, "What will you be seeking as you walk?"

The forty-five minute drive carved a storytelling space, opening my heart's answer to her question, "Am I to write this book with this writing coach who lives in Arizona?"

Walking up to the Prairie Labyrinth, my heart began to pound in anticipation. I found this forced hesitation to take the first step, almost as if it knew I was about to embark upon this mighty mission, and I needed to pause and take off my shoes, for the ground about to be stepped upon was holy.

It was within this suspension of time, removed from the rhythms and routines of life, sacred words rose up within me, *"You will have everything you need to do this because I have given it to you. I am Your Co-Author and Co-Journeyer."*

Within each step of the carved out path before me, I encountered many different voices of creation giving clear directions of how I was to navigate this unknown path of writing the book.

Entering into the center of the labyrinth, I suddenly became aware of the enormous large circle surrounded by the tall prairie grass.

This feels like an open death lodge!

As I sat alone within the expansiveness, I pondered the one lone tall piece of prairie grass before me.

What is the one sacred message inside of me waiting to be told?

In the quiet stillness, I sat waiting for the question to find its way to the center of my inner labyrinth. As I rose up off the ground of God, I felt something different being offered.

"Feel your way along the path. You know the path. Just feel. Close your eyes and feel. I need you to feel it all. And after you feel it, move on. Keep moving forward with your arms open."

I walked back with my arms outstretched and open, reaching the prairie grass on both sides. I kept my eyes closed as much as possible experiencing what it felt like to "feel" my way along the path. Toward the end of my journey, I encountered a huge heart shaped hole in the midst of my path filled with the benediction, "*I love you.*" And then the journey was finished.

Sitting on the bench under the shade of an ancient oak, she asked, "Well, did you get your answer?"

As our bodies were being nourished by her generous box lunches, our spirits were also nourished as I recalled the mighty ways in which God had spoken to change my question from, "Am I to write a book?" to "Here is *how* you are to write this book!" giving me clear guidance through His hand of creation, with His blessing given over the new friend He had sent to be my co-journeyer and guide in this new labyrinth of writing a book.

Keeping My Promise
Writer's Retreat | Flagstaff, AZ
November 2022

It was dark, the extra layer around my neck separated the bite of crisp air from the smell of moist pine needles. I was immersed in a cocoon of writers for a seven-day retreat with the hopes for transformational grace to awaken and guide the stories within to the pages. This early morning walk in the midst of unknowing was filled with exploration of questions in hopes of finding messages that would help me to step into the opening of such deep and hidden wounds.

As I witnessed the early morning light peeking in, suddenly something familiar yet different caught my eye. Silence replaced the questions as quickly as my feet

Part 4: Emerging Saplings

shifted off the hewn path of wet grass. A quiet invitation was being offered.

"Come and see," whispered the wind.

The small, white, round stones grew into boulders the closer I came. My heart awakened with anticipation of what was coming as I stood encircled in the very center of these large, living, white stones. I closed my eyes and waited for their message to come as I knew I was right where I was to be at that moment in time.

With a deep breath in, the words finally breathed out, "Expansiveness, expansiveness." I nodded as I opened my eyes to see the mystical circle I was standing in expanding to its fullness as it was illuminated by the morning light, yet I remained safely surrounded by these ancient giants of strength and protection.

It was then I knew great expansion within would be needed in order to help release the hidden stories that wanted to be healed and then shared for the intention of bringing hope and healing to others.

As I walked back to the retreat center, thoughts rushed in, as I remembered the intense stretching pains felt deep within my soul, resulting in the unexpected waves of wailing grief that appeared as I started the process of writing one of the first stories. I remembered the clear instructions given in the labyrinth to "feel" my way along the path, that I know this path, and I know how to journey with Him.

God, I hear You. You want me to feel it ALL. And once again, You have sent me the love-in-flesh help I needed for this time.

This circle of writers were given to accompany me on this journey of discovery and healing, being witnesses and guides on this unknown path each of them were already traveling upon. I knew they would be essential in helping to bring forth the expansive sacred healing space my heart needed in order to write the truest words to her story for the one sacred message waiting to be told, for the ultimate purpose to be carried out: "To share hope with the one person who can't find hope."

With yellow sticky notes, journals, a circle of healing writer support, a laptop, and lots of chocolate, my journey toward healing and writing Jessie's story had begun.

CONCLUSION

From Severed to Sacred

I never could have imagined what would happen within the moment of an exciting spring break ski trip.

The hurricane-like storm hit without warning, leveling our precious landscape in an instant, changing our lives forever. Each storm of life is different. Some come with warnings and others hit when least expected, varied in location and severity with each outcome always different and unknown, uprooting and severing life as we know it.

But what I know is there is ALWAYS HOPE. I believe we are NEVER ALONE. God is always SIDE BY SIDE with us. I believe God rushes to the devastation and SENDS HELP. I believe when we find the GOOD, we can find the sacred in the midst of the severed.

My inner life landscape underwent deep renovations as I was forced into the terrain of staying in the moment, which guided the way when there seemed to be no way to survive, enabling me to walk through the valley of the shadow of death without being completely destroyed with fear and grief. The gratitude muscle of my heart continues to be intensively exercised, helping me to discover the smallest of gifts are the greatest, as there is always something to be thankful for. And through this thankfulness comes light to pierce the darkest night of one's soul, revealing there is more to come.

I hope through these stories you have seen how God will reveal His presence in the landscape devastations by being in the good, no matter how small. I hope you have tasted the profound provision of people's hearts who will run to the disaster to help. I hope you have heard a faith deepening as the unknowns are deafening with the sounds of God close by whispering, "I am always with you." I hope you have smelled the presence of creation as it infuses fragrances of strength and wisdom expanding the moments of life into new possibilities. And I hope that you feel a warmth of comfort knowing others have gone before you and can share deep insights and a great hope of knowing you will get through this one step at a time, just doing the next right thing. *Help will always come.*

Winds of Joy and Grief

Our daily life will never look like the "typical" life of parents with a thirty-year-old daughter. Most all of our moments are filled with an immeasurable joy that she is able to live as fully as she does, yet there still remain occasional moments that pummel our hearts with deep sadness of the life she will never live. Within those shadowed days, her physical and cognitive limits seem overwhelming, insisting I retreat behind closed doors to spend time tending to my soul grief, or old angered grief may resurge at an unexpected trigger that screams the unfairness of suffering, completely ravaging my heart until I can find my refooting in gratefulness for all we have been given.

Suspended upon a nail in Jessie's room is a gifted oiled arrangement of stunning, vibrant, colorful flowers speaking "Beautiful Blessings and Possibilities" each day over her life. Our artist friend, Dawn, captured yet another dimension of hope. We will never stop reaching for any tiny possibility of improvement that may be waiting to be found in hopes that more of her will connect to her life and what surrounds her.

Every morning, I watch for the light under her door to come on. A simple, "Thank You, God," is whispered, knowing the reality of the severity of her brain injury increases her risk for "anything could happen," ushering in a celebration for each day of life with her. When she appears in the kitchen, ready for breakfast, dressed in the outfit we picked out the night before, she faithfully recites a morning scripture that she has read and memorized for the day, ending with her hand over her heart, making a sweet confession, "This touches my heart."

I marvel at her with such awe, wondering how I'm so blessed to live with this form of Love made flesh every day

Conclusion

as I continue to daily witness her miraculous moments of life fueled by the hands of God.

After breakfast, she finishes her morning routine, always waiting on me to "fix" her hair. I remain mesmerized by her freshness of spirit and body and her excitement about going to work as her dad or I drive her to her office.

Picking her up from work at noon I find her eyes weary and her movements a little slower but her cheerful heart continues to shine, sharing about Excel spreadsheets, insurance denials, shredding opportunities, or how one of her coworkers complimented her on her outfit. Her daily excitement over her usual peanut butter and honey lunch date never gets old.

Afternoons at home are simple, usually welcoming a nap, along with her own duties of household chores and challenges with Lumosity, a computer program consisting of games to help challenge and improve her cognition. Daily walks of one or two miles are non-negotiable with time for leisurely reading. But her most favorite time of the day is when she can sit on the sofa and watch "her" game shows of trivia.

Evenings are relaxed with simple meals that she can help prepare, watering gardens, tending to our animals, watching TV and showering before bed. Sunday mornings remain her most favorite time of the week as she eagerly gets ready to go to church. Her single focused worship of God through song and sermon ushers me right into His presence as my heart free falls into pure gratitude for all He has done.

Voices of Hope

Through the generosity of Brainxcite (www.brainxcite.com), a not-for-profit organization for the support of traumatic brain injury survivors in Oklahoma, we were introduced to a fascinating program of hope. Re-ignite (igniting new brain pathways) was developed by Jerad Johnson, an experienced fitness coach and ACE certified behavior change specialist, uniquely focused on using physical fitness to potentiate recovery by improving mind-body wellness in neurological disorders and brain injuries. This one-on-one intentional program is an important part of our continued search for "the more," with the hopes it will open up new pathways, reigniting more recovery and new relationships all in the name of increasing the richness and quality of her special life.

Each day carries voices of hope. Within each day, my eyes scan the landscape for the messages wanting to be discovered and shared for the hope of others.

On a weekend trip to Sante Fe, Bill and I strolled the streets and hiked the countryside of this unfamiliar territory, discovering infinite messages of hope woven within artistic creations of people and God. From "Ghost Sheep" travels to Gib Singleton's exhibits of his deep, meaningful masterpieces, to the delicacies of the Kakawa Chocolate House, to the oldest and rarest cathedrals, to the holy encounters with majestic trees, rivers, and stones within a National Forest, to the abundance of art galleries filled with creative spirits, all spoke the language of hope.

The "Ebenezer Stone" we brought home from this adventure speaks of a miracle on the horizon. Jim Keffer, the modern primitive artist shares, "My past journeys are connected to my future travels." His primitive painted declaration of a "milagro" (Spanish for miracle) on a road sign in the middle of a New Mexico landscape is now perched above the threshold of our front door.

Conclusion

Thresholds are doorways between what was and what is coming, a designated liminal space inviting us to be in the present moment, to breathe deeply, to wait and see what will unfold within us and before us, not knowing what's coming next but believing there is a GOD who does. This is how I believe miracles can be found within each day.

My greatest hope and prayer for you is that you can find those places within your own landscape that speak the language of faith, hope, strength, and comfort to your hurting heart and help you to navigate what seems impossible in the moments of great suffering or tragedy into the territory of knowing there is so much more to come. Just hang on. Stay in the moment. Take the next right step, knowing and believing, "With God, all things are possible."

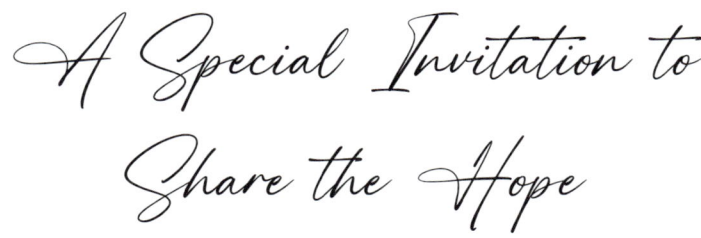

A Special Invitation to Share the Hope

Have you ever thought "I want to help, but I don't know how," or said to someone who has experienced grief or trauma, "Let me know how I can help"? What I learned in the throes of crisis was that I had no idea what I needed. When people asked me, I couldn't find an answer because I was paralyzed in my own feelings of fear and grief and struggling to survive. As you've read, life-saving help just showed up, and I want the same for every other person facing this uncertainty.

Here are some ways to support those in need within your immediate circle and community.

 Download the Companion's Resource Guide and find out exactly how you can support an individual facing the unimaginable unknown right now.

 Write a review of my book on Amazon, so others in need can discover it more easily.

 Make a tax free donation to provide resources and support for families of brain injured individuals.

A Special Invitation to Share the Hope

Purchase a book for a friend or place a bulk order with my publisher at BulkBooks@SavedByStory.house and donate them to the nearest hospital, rehabilitation center, non-profit, or church near you.

Reach out to me for speaking engagements or one-on-one consultations for support, resources, and advocacy.

www.SeveredSacredness.com

About Lisa Boone

Lisa Henry Boone is a Certified Hospice and Palliative Registered Nurse, advocate, spiritual director, writer, and speaker who brings the light of hope into dark places.

After more than three decades of serving in her community as a registered nurse, Lisa found herself on the other side of the hospital bed, uncertain whether her fifteen-year-old daughter would survive a devastating traumatic brain injury. For forty days, she navigated the acute crisis, not as a nurse, spiritual director, or light-bringer but as a grief-stricken mother in the darkest of places praying desperately for God's healing hand to prevail.

Years later, when her daughter had recovered her capacities beyond most doctors' expectations, Lisa set out to keep her promise to write their story and offer hope to others facing the unimaginable in this book, *Severed Sacredness: The Miraculous Journey of Jessie Boone*.

Today, as the founder of Severed Sacred Tree, she writes and speaks about her own journey of learning to find the good within the hard, lean on the powerful Presence that went before and behind and beside her family, and dance in the darkness of tragedy. Seeking to empower those who cross her path and advocate for those who have lost their voice, she uses her twenty-five years of spiritual development and nursing to help others navigate the healthcare system and thrive on the other side of injury, illness, and tragedy.

A faith-filled seeker and spiritual being, her soul is fed by worship, artistic creations, traveling, music, nature,

About Lisa Boone

and the adoration of all living beings—from the trees and the creatures that find shelter in them to the remarkable humans that God places on her path.

Acknowledgments

"I will give thanks to God with all my heart."
~Psalms 111:1~

As I have wondered again and again in written words and in the unspoken crevices of my heart, how does one impart the depth of gratitude to the multitudinous crowds of souls that stood bravely and generously alongside us, becoming streams in our desert, carrying and nourishing our brain-injured, ravished lives? I could have never imagined this journey of devastation. Within these pages, I have taken a deep dive into the fathoms of pain and found safe spaces of healing and release as I have written my heart's song of grief, gratitude, and grace in hopes of bringing hope to others. Great is Thy faithfulness.

Jessie Boone! You, sweet girl, fill our hearts with joy and laughter every day. Thank you for your spirit of great love and kindness, your attitude of never never giving up, and the light you bring forth each day. I love you forever.

My beautiful, faithful, steadfast man, Bill Boone. When we met on that soccer field so many years ago, I knew you were mighty special as I watched you love your boy. Little did I know about your superpowers of loving fiercely and being the "extra" of my life. None of this would have been possible without you by my side. I love you forever.

Our incredible children, Justin and Erin and Joe and Megan, no siblings should ever have to navigate their parents' pain and grief. but you did and still do with such

Acknowledgments

grace. Thank you for all you do to fill our lives with the joyous sounds of your littles growing and expanding our hearts with joy and laughter. I love you forever.

My family has absorbed so much of our pain and yet were able to pour out so much love and support. Mom, Dad (in heaven watching over all our family), Jean, Chuck, Mark and Tracy, Bill and Teri, Herman and Lala, and all the children that go with you, I am so thankful for each of you.

Bobbie Roe. You are my modern day Elijah, my spiritual mentor and mother, my friend. You are the heaven on earth icon for me. You have courageously and gracefully walked this path of suffering with me. Your quiet presence is always with me. Your "Godmothering" of Jessie is breathtaking. She knows your love like her breath. You are knitted eternally in the seams of my heart and spirit.

My innermost prayer warriors, Sherri Price, Penny Hammack, Paula Glass, Jenny Shrauner, Ivy Snider, Kristin Skinner, Becky Smith, Gina Rowsam, Shelley Lamle, Bernice Nithman, Maurie Cole. I shall call you my Warstones, for without your fervent, faithful, kicking and screaming prayers of help and strength, I do not believe we would be standing today. I will never forget every special moment of when you showed up in the hardest parts and stood firm with your faces set in flint, looking boldly at God, asking and sometimes even "kicking at the darkness" for the impossible.

Sister Benedicta (now with eternal eyes watching over us all) and all the Benedictine Sisters of Red Plains Monastery and Mount St. Scholastica. Your sacred spirits of great faith, wisdom, and love changed my heart and my vision forever. "The Resurrection Cloth."

Our Church of the Servant Family and youth group. ALL of you loved us so deeply, prayed without ceasing,

Acknowledgments

joined meal trains, provided unimaginable support in "ALL" the ways and hope for years. Thank you for being the "wings" that carried us for so many years.

Sunlight Ski Resort family. Heroes every day. Thank you for stabilizing and sending her to a Level 1 Trauma Center, and for the visits and the calls and the unlimited prayers of hope for our girl.

Our Carepages family. You were the yeast, the treasure, the bridge, the survival of our circumstances as you daily poured light, love, hope, truth, faith, strength, and joy into the dark night of our souls. How glorious it was to watch the tiny mustard seeds of faith grow into the huge tree of LIFE that watched over us and provided for our impoverished, broken spirits and hearts.

Our Grand Junction family. My tears fall spontaneously in gratitude at the mention of your names. YOU SAVED OUR LIVES. You adopted us and truly were our family in all the ways, so generously sharing your lives, time, provision, homes, cars, prayers, and love. Thank you from the bottom of our souls for being the hands and feet of Christ when we had nothing.

Dr. Charles Breaux. I can't speak your name without my heart leaping. You were appointed to us. You saved her life over and over again. For forty days, you saw her twice a day without fail. You were Jesus with skin on to me. You saved "my" life. You imprinted upon my heart, and I will forever remember your sacrificial giving with your extraordinary medical expertise, all wrapped up in love and compassion. Thank you from the bottom of my heart. (And I will forever want to marry you!)

Dr. Brian Witwer. Your adventurous, free-spirited, wildly-brave and bold presence changed the direction of death on that Friday evening. You went to the edges of the impossible and did it anyway. You saved her life and gave

Acknowledgments

us our daughter back. Our deepest gratitude for all the sacrifices you have made to be the extraordinary trauma neurosurgeon we were privileged to witness while we were under your care.

Doug and Ann Clayton, Diane and Kit Hatfield, and Dave Bowles (saint in heaven now). Your ministry of care went beyond our ability to understand, which is how God shows up when the big hitters are needed. The width, depth, height, and breadth of your attentive presence of kindness and provision bent our hearts low to the ground with gratitude and love. Thank you forever.

Dr. John Duffy, Dr. Vivek Kholi, Dr. Stephen Lee, and all the staff of the Nazih Zuhdi Transplant Institute. Thank you! We will never forget! You saved her life as extraordinary artists, fully present within the realm of healthcare, creating masterpieces of new beginnings, reconstructions of failed bodies, and hope for future life. "Medicine is Art."

To all the caregivers at Integris Hospital, Integris Rehabilitation, and Project Search. You are our heroes. Thank you for every kind word, every moment you "saw" her, every time you touched her life with the interventions of hope for survival and recovery. I am so honored to be employed by such a powerful institution of hope. I shall call each of you Hopegivers!

Dr. Shawn Smith. You met me exactly where I was and heard my heart's groans in the darkest days of our lives. Your presence of compassion and experience didn't hesitate to reach out and give us the opportunities we were praying for. Your navigational expertise through all her storms never stopped believing in her recovery. You never gave up. Thank you for your steadfast loving presence. You will always be our hero.

Acknowledgments

Dr. Timothy Mapstone and Dr. Christian El Amm and OU Children's Hospital. What pioneers of extraordinary experience in the medicine of neurosurgery and plastic surgery immersed in compassion and dedication! Your courage to do what seemed impossible forged us forward in her restoration. We will forever be grateful for all you gave back to our precious girl. You picked up her pieces of devastation and made her "whole" again.

Women of the Yellow Butterfly Foundation. My goodness. What women of strength and beauty exist within this circle. Thank you for the safe sacred space of being which guided me through the muddiness of disorientation, loss, and grief, opening the door of my heart and helping me cross the threshold into the next dimension of healing and writing her story.

Reverend Bude VanDyke, facilitator of "The Death Lodge." Thank you, priest and brother. Your wise guidance through story and song, and being fully present and attentive to the call of healing, forever changed my life and helped me to surrender to the writing of this book. I am eternally grateful for your Native American roots.

BrainXcite Team. Thank you for reaching out and connecting to our family. Your encouragement and offerings of support have provided ways of continued strength and hope on this journey through creating a brain injury community of survivors, providing connections of hope through scholarships to programs like Reignite to continue forging for "more."

Amanda Johnson. Aura. Story Oracle. CHOCOLATE! DEATH LODGE! YOUR STORY MATTERS! All road signs pointed me to you. You were the windy portal I needed to guide me to the next right step. The first moment of the wounds being opened and the sobbing grief escaping, you were there, holding me in all my messiness. Your simple

Acknowledgments

question, "You doing okay?" over and over in the midst of the deep dives kept reorienting me like a life preserver to the surface of light and safety. With your mission of helping messengers reveal and heal their own sacredly-coded stories in safe spaces, write their true stories with intention, and get those "healed messages of hope" into the world through your company Saved By Story, all intersecting in God's perfect timing, you have been my midwife and book doula. God knew I needed help and sent you. You are a springboard into the next. You are an encourager and truthteller. You are a super power that has opened up a whole new world for me to dream and imagine and experience, expanding and growing me, helping me discover the writer within. You are my sacred friend, and I am deeply grateful He chose you.

To the Saved By Story Cocoon-munity—messengers, souls sisters and brothers, mentors and friends—there are no words to express my gratitude for all the adventures, witnessing of story, sharing of struggles and pain, the encouragement and examples you each have been to me. For the hours and hours of the listening spaces within the hearts of you amazing allies, the countless movies consuming our hearts with questions and awakenings, the extended hiking experiences, the morning altars, the feasts of meals and feelings corners, the warmness and richness of the cacao brew, the unlimited Zoom connections creating community writing and support, and gifts of time and love presented with the intentions of reminders of our own "belovedness," I am grateful.

Kristi Self, friend and artist. What a privilege to have your handprints of creativity and heartprints of service and love all over this book. Thank you for your generosity of spirit with the countless hours of painting and generating such beautiful images. "Severed Sacredness",

Acknowledgments

your extraordinary painting for the the cover of the book, is priceless and forever imprinted upon my heart.

To all the creative souls that paint life with beauty, love, hope, and hidden messages of life and the artists who painted masterpieces on my heart with the canvas offerings that will forever sing out, "Never give up!" "Hope has a name!" "Take the next right step!" "Stay in the moment!" Your messages lifted my foot and my heart in the next direction. I am forever awed at how you speak through the tools of your he"art". Thank you for splashing this book with your spirit of love!

To all of the souls who previewed this book, thank you for your wisdom, time, and feedback. This book is even better because of you.

With all my love and gratitude in hopes of pouring it forward,

Lisa Boone